Books are to be returned on or before
the last date below.

LIBREX–

The Conservative Party
and Anglo-German
Relations, 1905–1914

The Conservative Party and Anglo-German Relations, 1905–1914

Frank McDonough

First published in 2007 by
PALGRAVE MACMILLAN
Houndmills, Basingstoke, Hampshire RG21 6XS and
175 Fifth Avenue, New York, N.Y. 10010
Companies and representatives throughout the world.

PALGRAVE MACMILLAN is the global academic imprint of the Palgrave Macmillan division of St. Martin's Press, LLC and of Palgrave Macmillan Ltd. Macmillan® is a registered trademark in the United States, United Kingdom and other countries. Palgrave is a registered trademark in the European Union and other countries.

ISBN-13: 978–0–230–51711–0 hardback
ISBN-10: 0–230–51711–0 hardback

This book is printed on paper suitable for recycling and made from fully managed and sustained forest sources. Logging, pulping and manufacturing processes are expected to conform to the environmental regulations of the country of origin.

A catalogue record for this book is available from the British Library.

Library of Congress Cataloging-in-Publication Data
McDonough, Frank.
    The Conservative Party and Anglo-German relations, 1905–14 / Frank McDonough.
        p. cm.
    Includes bibliographical references and index.
    ISBN-13: 978–0–230–51711–0 (cloth)
    ISBN-10: 0–230–51711–0 (cloth)
        1. Great Britain – Foreign relations – Germany. 2. Germany – Foreign relations – Great Britain. 3. Conservative Party (Great Britain) – History – 20th century. 4. Great Britain – Politics and government – 1901–1936. I. Title.
DA47.2.M258 2007
327.4104309′041—dc22   2007060003

10 9 8 7 6 5 4 3 2 1
16 15 14 13 12 11 10 09 08 07

Printed and bound in Great Britain by
Antony Rowe Ltd, Chippenham and Eastbourne

To the memory of my father Francis McDonough

Contents

Preface

The book has taken many years to finally reach publication. The delay does not reflect any lack of hard work on the part of the author, but more the intrusion of many other projects and publication commitments. The book began life after a conversation with the late and great R.A.C. Parker, my tutor, on his 'Special Subject' on 'British Policy and the Coming of The Second World War' at Oxford way back in the 1980s. He suggested that I undertake a doctorate with him on some aspect of appeasement. I thought it had all been said on that subject, most by R.A.C., but he felt that two areas had been neglected: the mass media and the evolution of appeasement before Chamberlain came to power. I began work on the press and appeasement and produced some articles in that subject. I also wrote a book on appeasement entitled, *Neville Chamberlain, Appeasement and the British road to war* (1998), and I have become associated with the Parker-inspired 'post-revisionist' or 'counter-revisionist' school. I decided to examine how the appeasers in the Conservative Party in the 1930s evolved their ideas during the early period of the twentieth century. The title of my thesis, at the outset, was 'The Evolution of Appeasement in the Conservative Party 1905–1937'. I even set up a database (actually it was then a card index) of all the Conservative MPs who sat in parliament from 1905 to 1937. I quickly realised a flaw in my over-ambitious plan: the vast majority of the Edwardian 'die hard' Tories never made it to the 1930s. Most of them never evolved at all. They simply got old, and like everyone else they died. I finally decided to undertake research on the Conservative Party's attitude to Germany as an Opposition party from 1905 to 1914. I soon found that no one had produced either a monograph or a doctorate on this subject. I was finally underway. After many years of research and a doctorate awarded on the subject in 2000, now finally comes the monograph.

I would like to take this opportunity to thank a number of people who have helped along this long journey: R.A.C. Parker, for sparking the idea to begin my research and Dr. Ruth Henig, my Ph.D. supervisor, at the time of completion – a great influence and inspiration. I would also like to thank Professor David McEvoy, Director of the School of Social Science, who helped me in carrying out most of the archival research for this project. I am also grateful for the generous support of the University's Research Committee. I would also like to single out for very special praise Dr Nick White, Reader in Imperial History, with whom I have shared a room at university for longer than we both care to remember and who pushed me to finish off the thesis and the book. In addition, he has provided me with much intellectual and academic stimulation and also a great many laughs over the years. My other colleagues in the History Department at Liverpool John Moores have also provided support and encouragement. But the whole project would not have been possible without the support, loyalty and love of Ann, my wife. Finally, I must mention my dear old dad, Francis, who died on 11 August 2006, aged 82, after a very long illness. I write this less than a month after his death. I could write many words about this man: he helped so many people as he passed along in his life and without the challenging intellectual stimulation he provided at home I would not be writing this and you would not be reading it. Quite fittingly, the book is dedicated to his memory.

6 September 2006
　　　　　　　　　　　　　Dr Francis Xavier McDonough
　　　　　　　　　　　　　Reader in International History
　　　　　　　　　　　　Liverpool John Moores University

Introduction

The relationship between Britain and Germany has been a notoriously difficult one. It has been characterised by a curious mixture of fear and admiration. There have been many well-meaning efforts on both sides to improve relations. Two prominent Conservative politicians were at the forefront of the two most high-profile attempts to gain a long-standing Anglo-German 'understanding'. Joseph Chamberlain had discussions concerning an Anglo-German alliance during the 1890s. During the 1930s, his son Neville sought to prevent war by attempting to solve German grievances through the policy of appeasement. Both Hitler and Chamberlain signed the 'Anglo-German declaration' which promised that the two countries would strive 'never to go to war with one another again'. Needless to say, these initiatives ended in failure. It is probably more important to emphasise that the two Conservative leaders who have adopted a consistently negative attitude towards the aims of the German Government have enjoyed the most enduring popularity among Conservative supporters. Winston Churchill built his enduring political reputation as Britain's most admired Prime Minister on the strong anti-Nazi stand he adopted before and during the Second World War. Margaret Thatcher's negative attitude to German unification and the role of Germany within the European Economic Community also proved popular among her supporters.

In modern-day Britain, the image of Germany has remained steadfastly negative. Journalists, comedians and politicians have all been prepared to demonise Germany more than any other nation. Offering crude stereotypes about Germany has almost become a socially acceptable pastime. In the words of A.A. Gill, a popular columnist on the *Sunday Times*, 'Admit it, we all hate Germans'. The traditional defence of such xenophobic utterances is that they are just part of the 'ironic' British sense of humour. If Germans attack British allusions to the 'darker aspects' of their past history such as the famous 'Don't mention the war' episode entitled 'The Germans' in the BBC comedy series 'Fawlty Towers', they are castigated as 'lacking a sense of humour'. According to the journalist Simon Hoggart, British people are 'just hard-wired to make German jokes. We just can't help it. We make [anti-] German jokes in the same way that cats kill small birds'.[1]

A similarly negative view of Germany's past has been regularly presented in films, newspaper articles, TV adverts and comedy shows. A recent public opinion survey of British children, organised by the Goethe Institute, asked who were the most famous Germans they knew. At the top was Adolf Hitler with 68 per cent, followed by Jurgen Klinsmann, the footballer (47%), and Boris Becker, the tennis star (40%). When asked what Germany was famous for, one fairly typical response was 'Starting Two World Wars and a football team'.

In fact, the England versus Germany football rivalry, certainly for many English fans and especially for the British tabloid press, has often resembled the extension of the Second World War by other means. During the 1996 European football championship, the *Daily Mirror*, invoking British Second World War propaganda, claimed in banner headlines before the England versus Germany semi-final: 'Achtung! Surrender. For you Fritz ze Euro 96 Championship is over'.[2] In a recent British Channel 4 programme, 'The 100 Greatest TV moments', England's 4–2 victory over Germany in the 1966 World Cup Final came top, and Winston Churchill won the BBC public phone vote of the 'Greatest Britons' by a similar landslide.

At British screenings of the recent popular Hollywood film *Saving Private Ryan*, which concentrates on the D-Day landings, it was reported in the British press that many young people cheered every time a German was shot or killed. In 2003, a video featuring Rik Mayall, the British comedian, was shown at the media launch of a British-funded campaign against the Euro. Mayall, dressed as Adolf Hitler, is seen in the video promoting the benefits of the Euro with the slogan 'Ein Volk! Ein Reich! Ein Euro!' (An obvious reference to the Nazi slogan 'Ein Volk Ein Reich Ein Führer'). The German Government expressed outrage at the crass link made between the modern democratic German Government's support for the Euro and the tyrannical Nazi regime. Boris Johnson, the Conservative MP, in true Basil Fawlty style, commented that the Germans lacked a sense of humour by complaining about a 'harmless, light-hearted commercial'.

But what has all this got to do with the Conservative Party and Anglo-German relations between 1905 and 1914? The answer, as will be explained in more detail in the chapters that follow, is a great deal. Any study, which examines one aspect of British attitudes towards Germany, must take account of the fact that British society has all grown used to 'being beastly to the Germans'. In the process, many myths on Anglo-German relations have become deeply enshrined not only within popular discourse but also within the existing historiography. One dominant historiographical myth suggests that Anglo-German antagonism really took hold during the Edwardian period and that the Conservative Party was one of the fomenters of this Germanophobia. This orthodox view will be challenged in the course of this study.

It is worth pointing out that being 'beastly to the Germans' was very much a new and by no means universally popular phenomenon in the early years of the twentieth century. In fact, a surprisingly friendly relationship had existed between Britain and the many German states, dating back to the eighteenth century. As a result of the 1701 Act of Succession, the dukes of Hanover were invited by the British Government to establish a royal dynasty after 1714. The presence of German kings on the English throne ensured that Anglo-German relations remained cordial. At the Battle of Waterloo, the British forces, under the command of that bastion of the Tory Party, Lord Wellington, were saved from defeat by Prussian forces. In 1840, Queen Victoria married the German Prince Albert of Saxe-Coburg-Gotha. Kaiser Wilhelm II was Queen Victoria's grandson, the nephew of King Edward VII and the cousin of George V.

Britain and Germany appeared to have scant reason for conflict throughout much of the nineteenth century. Germany was a land-based empire, with a very small navy. It had no colonies, and its interests lay firmly on the landmass of the European continent. What is more, Britain and the German states enjoyed cordial trading relations. In 1860, one-third of Prussian imports came from Britain. Both Germany and Britain were predominantly protestant countries and had strong cultural links. British music lovers admired German composers such as Beethoven, Mozart, Brahms and Wagner more than any others, and many Germans admired British writers and poets such as Shakespeare, Lord Byron and Sir Walter Scott.

Most of the Conservative Party welcomed German unification, which took place in 1871, following the German defeat of France in the Franco-Prussian War. The first German Chancellor, Otto von Bismarck approved of upholding a balance of power between nations on the European continent, something that British policy also supported. It is worth noticing that the two countries which were most often at odds with Britain during the nineteenth century were France and Russia. Britain was almost in perpetual conflict with France and clashed frequently with Russia in Afghanistan, Persia and India. It seemed almost inconceivable, even at the beginning of the Edwardian period, that Britain would line up in any form of alliance with France and Russia against Germany.

Yet in August 1914, Britain did go to war with Germany. This incredible course of events occurred primarily because of the stridently provocative policies of the German monarchy and the way in which the British Government and Opposition interpreted those policies. In 1888, the 'half-English' Kaiser Wilhelm II came to power, and he took two major decisions which had far-reaching consequences for Anglo-German relations. In 1890, he dismissed Bismarck, who had sought to maintain cordial relations between Britain and Germany and attempted to ensure there was a balance of power in Europe. Even more controversial was Kaiser Wilhelm's support for Weltpolitik ('World Policy'), which involved Germany expanding its colonial empire and, most alarmingly for Britain, building a navy to rival the Royal Navy.

As 'World Policy' was implemented, Anglo-German relations began to progressively deteriorate. But during the 1890s, Britain still remained on even worse terms with France and Russia, and Anglo-German antagonism was confined to the adverse impact on British industry of the rapid growth of German imports. In the late 1890s, the Conservative Government led by Lord Salisbury vigorously attempted to gain an Anglo-German 'understanding'. It was only when this effort failed that British policy began to move in an anti-German direction. To meet the German naval threat, a new state-of-the-art battleship HMS Dreadnought was launched in 1902. This more heavily armed, larger and faster naval vessel was designed to act as a deterrent to any potential naval rivals. In response, the German navy built its own version of the 'Dreadnought', and so began the heated Anglo-German naval race which soured relations between the two nations more than any other single factor.

From 1902 onwards, British foreign policy moved to make Germany's enemies its friends. Lord Lansdowne, the Conservative Foreign Secretary, signed the 'entente cordiale' with France in 1904, which although described as a 'colonial agreement' created fears of 'encirclement' in Germany. In 1905, the German monarch decided to test the underlying strength of the agreement by provoking an unnecessary quarrel with France over trading rights in Morocco. Kaiser Wilhelm II visited Tangier in March 1905, and he promised German support to the Moroccan administration in the event of French aggression. Throughout the protracted crisis, the British Government offered support to the French. In December 1905, there was a talk of war between Germany and France. In the end, the Germans decided to settle their dispute over trading rights at the Algeciras Conference. The French allowed the Moroccan police to retain autonomy but gained effective control over financial and political affairs. The whole crisis cemented Anglo-French friendship. In 1907, Britain signed the Anglo-Russian Convention which helped to gain closer discussion of colonial disagreements between the two countries. This led to press talk of a Triple Alliance between Britain, France and Russia.

Between 1908 and 1910, Anglo-German naval rivalry reached a peak of intensity, and Anglo-German relations plummeted to an all-time low. In 1911, relations deteriorated further when a second Franco-German crisis re-ignited in Morocco. Civil disorder in Morocco during the spring of 1911 had prompted military intervention by French and Spanish troops. In May, French forces entered Fez. In June 1911, in a move perceived by the British, Russian and French Governments as highly provocative, the Kaiser sent the German gunboat Panther to Agadir. In July 1911, David Lloyd George, the British Chancellor of the Exchequer gave a high-profile speech at the Mansion House in which he hinted that if war broke out over the Agadir crisis, Britain would certainly side with France. The Russian Government pledged similar support to France, and Germany was forced to compromise. In 1912, the German Government accepted the French right to rule in Morocco. Yet the whole crisis had soured relations between Germany on the one side and France, Britain and Russia on the other. Anglo-German relations had by this time deteriorated to an all-time low. It is all these events which lay at the heart of the issues that are examined in this study.

Not surprisingly, the existing historiography on Britain's role in the outbreak of the First World War concentrates on the part played by central decision makers in the Liberal Government, and key policy advisers in the foreign office, the navy and the army.[3] These studies portray British foreign policy as the special realm of Sir Edward Grey, the Foreign Secretary, and chief advisers at the foreign office. This standard view also suggests that those individuals in charge of British foreign policy before 1914 were not significantly influenced by the domestic political situation, and formulated policy towards Germany in the light of external events, most notably, the escalation of German military and naval power in Europe, and the erratic nature of German foreign policy. On this view, British foreign policy in 1914 was determined to prevent a German domination of Europe.[4] This Primacy of *Aussenpolitik* ('the primacy of external factors') explanation of why Britain went to war in August 1914 views the state as a cohesive and independent actor in diplomatic decision making, with a dominant interest in safeguarding national security. It offers a comprehensive account of the motives behind the behaviour of state officials during the unfolding European crisis. The most important sources used to bolster the 'primacy of *Aussenpolitik*' interpretation are the painstakingly catalogued state papers of the Foreign Secretary, the Foreign Office, the Cabinet and the diplomatic service. A study of these documents does shed light on Britain's decision to go to war in 1914.

However, many historians prefer an alternative approach to explain the outbreak of the First World War, one that takes account of the broader context of the society in which the major decisions were taken. Fritz Fischer, the renowned German historian developed a model to study foreign policy which examines the overall domestic balance of social, political and economic forces.[5] This *Primat der Innenpolitik* ('the primacy of domestic factors') interpretation pays close attention to the domestic factors which influence foreign policy decision making.[6] It is now accepted that the relationship between internal and external factors in explaining the outbreak of war is extremely complex.[7] As Zara Steiner, an consummate exponent of the 'high politics' approach to foreign policy, concedes:

> there was an obvious connection between the political life of the
> country and its diplomatic stance, between the actions of states-
> men and the prevailing climate of opinion. The Foreign Secretary
> was a product of his time, and worked within a particular political
> and bureaucratic framework; his policies were shaped by Britain's
> economic and strategic position which were in turn controlled by
> other men.[8]

However, one major gap in the historiography of Britain's role in
the origins of the First World War is a thorough analysis of the stance
of the Conservative Party towards Anglo-German relations from 1905
to 1914. Hence, the first major aim of this study is to remedy this
omission by examining how the Conservatives reacted to the
German threat. By focusing on the role of the most important British
Opposition party towards Anglo-German relations, it is possible to
assess the continuing importance of the 'primacy' controversy to the
study of Britain's role in the outbreak of the First World War.

The existing research on Edwardian political history has concentrated on the struggle of the Liberal Party to maintain its ascendancy
on the centre-left of British politics in the face of a growing Labour
movement, heightened class conflict and industrial turbulence.
There have been many biographies of leading Liberal politicians. The
views of leading Liberal thinkers and policy makers have been extensively scrutinised. The relative vigour of the Liberal and Labour
parties has also been probed at national and regional levels. At the
same time, the rise of the Labour Party has received enormous historical attention. As a consequence, the study of the Conservative
Party in the Edwardian period has been, until recent years, a neglected
area of study.[9] During the 1960s and 1970s, the small amount of
research on the Conservative Party in the Edwardian period
focused on three domestic areas: first, the inner divisions within
the Conservative Party over the policy of tariff reform; second, the
'Die Hard' opposition to the 1909 People's Budget, which culminated
in the two General Elections of 1910; and third, the bitter Conservative
opposition between 1911 and 1914 towards the proposed introduction
of Irish Home Rule.[10]

The election victory of Margaret Thatcher in May 1979 and the
conquest of 'new right' ideas during the 1980s influenced the growth

of research into the right of the political spectrum. The Edwardian period became a key focus of this fresh interest among British historians into right-wing politics.[11] This new research into the pre-1914 right in Britain shifted scholarly attention away from the 'high politics' of the Conservative Party towards the study of the 'extraparliamentary' deeds of the 'radical right', defined as consisting of groups and individuals who became disheartened with the leadership and organisation of the Conservative Party, and surged 'around and beyond the older Conservative Party structures and programmes', in search of 'progressive' and 'constructive' solutions to social, economic and international problems.[12] Recent research into the so-called revolt from the right in the Edwardian period has focused on patriotic pressure groups, jingoistic imperialist propaganda and right-wing economic interest groups. In addition, some very thought-provoking comparative work on the pan-European phenomenon of right nationalism has also appeared in recent years.[13]

The myriad domestic problems of the Conservative Party in the Edwardian period have been fashioned into the notion of a 'crisis of Conservatism'.[14] However, the attempt to comprehend the 'crisis of Conservatism' in terms of a grass roots rebellion by an unsatisfactorily defined 'radical right' has encountered methodological problems.[15] As Martin Blinkhorn quite accurately points out, 'the definitions, typologies and taxonomies beloved of social scientists tend to fit uncomfortably the intractable realities which are the raw material of the historian'.[16] Many of the individuals often described as members of the 'radical right' often displayed a 'quite illogical amalgam of modernising and anti modernising attitudes'.[17] The neat pigeonholing of right-wing 'Conservatives' into expedient sub-groups such as 'Die Hards', 'Whole Hoggers', 'scaremongers' and 'social imperialists' shrouds the complexity of right-wing attitudes and ignores the fact that many individuals on the right wing did not maintain unchanging positions on most of the key issues. Eric Hobsbawm has suggested that the idea of an organised 'extreme right' in the Edwardian period is a flawed 'what might have happened theory' rather than a precise explanation of what did happen.[18] These methodological problems are increased when it is understood that many of the actions of the 'radical right' can be interpreted as expedient propaganda exercises designed to weaken the Liberal Party rather than the outward manifestation of deep ideological beliefs.

As a result, most studies of 'radical right' pressure groups have examined the response of Conservatives at the grass roots level towards the German threat, with little reference to the views and policy of the upper stratum of the Conservative leadership.[19] Indeed, the views of the 'radical right' towards Germany are often regarded as the views of the Conservative Party. Not surprisingly, it is commonplace to argue that the Conservative Party from 1905 to 1914 consisted primarily of 'anti-German' scaremongers who reacted to Germany, whether in connection with trade rivalry, the naval arms race, foreign policy and conscription in a hostile fashion that contributed to the growth of Anglo-German antagonism. However, Paul Kennedy, the most highly esteemed authority on Anglo-German relations in the Edwardian period, has argued that the most neglected aspect of the study of the pre-War right in Britain is a detailed examination of how the 'official' Conservative Party reacted to the German threat, and to the supposed Germanophobia of the patriotic leagues.[20] The second key objective of this study, therefore, is to scrutinise whether the Conservative Party did consist of anti-German scaremongers who share some responsibility for the growth of Anglo-German antagonism.

The existing research on Anglo-German relations has attempted to explain the diplomatic, economic and strategic reasons for the growth of Anglo-German antagonism.[21] The one interpretation which has come to dominate the subject is advanced by Paul Kennedy, who argues that the growth of German economic and naval power, combined with the craving of the German-governing elite to use that power to attain great power status, was bound to come into conflict with Britain's need to uphold the existing balance of power within the European order. Kennedy concludes that unless 'Germans surrendered their desire – and their inherent capacity to halt the existing order in Europe or overseas; or unless the British were prepared voluntarily to accept a great change in that order, then their vital interests remained diametrically opposed'.[22] But, it is worth emphasising that Kennedy's massive comparative study of the growth of Anglo-German relations covers the period from 1860 to 1914 and does not scrutinise any one British or German political party in any great detail. It is a vast macro-study of the social, economic, cultural, diplomatic and strategic reasons for the growth of Anglo-German estrangement. Even so, two very important aspects of Kennedy's study will be critically examined in the course of this study. The first is Kennedy's methodological approach, which he defines as a 'lumping process', involving the examination of a wide range of views from British and German society. It is argued here that this indiscriminate lumping together of different views on Anglo-German relations fails to explain the position towards Germany of any single political party or economic group in any significant depth.[23] Indeed, this study will interrogate whether the interpretative load which Kennedy attaches to economic factors for explaining the growth of Anglo-German antagonism can be applied to the response of the Conservative Party towards Germany between 1905 and 1914. In particular, Kennedy's view that tariff reform and anti-Germanism went 'hand in hand' will be subjected to detailed examination in the chapters which follow.[24]

But this study is not chiefly intended to dispute the work of other historians in the field.[25] The primary objective is to provide the first ever in-depth examination of the views of the Conservative Party towards the key aspects of Anglo-German relations from 1905 to 1914. The book will concentrate on how the Conservative Party at Westminster formulated the party view towards Germany and how those views were articulated within parliamentary debate, propaganda, elections and pressure-group activity. A detailed examination of how the Conservative Party responded to the German threat from 1905 to 1914 provides an original and valuable input to historical debates over Britain's role in the origins of the First World War, the condition of the Conservative Party in Opposition from 1905 to 1914, the pre-war right in Edwardian Britain and the study of Anglo-German relations.

It is also important to highlight at the start of this book that the study of British Opposition parties and foreign policy in the Edwardian era is a neglected area of study when compared with the vast amount of books which deal with British foreign policy. Most British political historians are more at ease in the well-organised and chronologically catalogued world of Government foreign policy formation, rather than the more loosely structured terrain of Opposition political activity. As a result, this study faced complex and difficult methodological problems in deciding how to approach this subject. It was important to hit upon a methodological approach that avoided Kennedy's drawback of lumping together 'Conservative' views in a generalised manner. Most of the 'high politics' studies of the Conservative Party in

Opposition from 1905 to 1914 offered hardly any guidelines, primarily because they concentrated exclusively on the private views and tactical manoeuvrings of Conservative leaders towards domestic policy. These studies took not much interest in the effects of opposition policy on parliamentary debate and the electorate. Most of the existing studies of the Conservative Party in opposition are not very different in approach and methodology from the study of a party in Government. Indeed, there is very little awareness in the studies of the 'high politics' of the Conservative Party in the Edwardian period that an Opposition can only really make a major impact on political events and hope to replace the sitting Government by proving effective in public debate. This gives the public statements of an Opposition and the broader structural political context in which most Opposition political activity takes place much greater significance than is generally understood.

It was decided to adopt a distinctive thematic and comparative methodological approach in this study that avoided 'lumping' together Conservative views in a random manner and one which acknowledged the distinctive role of an Opposition party and one which also allowed the Conservative response to Anglo-German relations to be examined in a number of distinct spheres of Opposition political activity, namely, the nature and organisation of Opposition foreign and defence policy, party leadership, parliamentary debate, electioneering, propaganda, pressure-group activity and policy making. By concentrating on the Conservative response to the German threat in these differing spheres of political activity, it is possible to present a complex and broad-ranging interpretation of the response of Conservative Party to the German threat from 1905 to 1914. The methodological structure adopted for this study is not calculated to uphold a particular line of argument, but to establish a broad analytical framework in which Conservative views in a variety of differing public and private contexts can be analysed. To limit the framework of analysis to manageable proportions, the study concentrates on Conservative views in four key aspects of Anglo-German relations, namely, foreign policy, naval rivalry, the commercial relations between Britain and Germany, and the conscription controversy. These four issues were chosen for analysis because they were the ones which dominated the discussion of Anglo-German relations within the Conservative Party from 1905 to 1914.

Assembling a broad-ranging analysis of the views of the Conservative Party towards Anglo-German relations from 1905 to 1914, which is credible, has required the use of a number of different types of sources. To explain the private views of the Conservative leadership and to outline the policy structure of the Opposition on the key aspects of Anglo-German relations, the private papers of all the leading Conservative politicians have been consulted. However, most Conservative politicians were primarily concerned with the cut and thrust of domestic politics and were only concerned with the German threat sporadically. As a result, the amount of relevant material found in private papers was not extensive, and much effort was expended in the archives for relatively little reward. The most helpful collection of private papers, relevant to this study were those of A.J. Balfour. He was one of the very few Conservatives who took an unrelenting and detailed interest in Anglo-German relations. The papers of Andrew Bonar Law, which are not used in most other studies of foreign and defence policies in the pre-1914 period did provide a good deal of valuable information for this study. The papers of J.S. Sandars, Balfour's private secretary, who was in close communication with most of the leading Conservative front bench figures, also provided a good deal of relevant material. The papers of Lord Selborne and Austen Chamberlain also yielded some useful material for this study. In most of the papers of the other leading Conservatives, however, there was precious little mention of Anglo-German relations. The Conservative Party archive at the Bodleian Library was also examined at length. Although Central Office records for the period 1905 to 1914 are extremely patchy, the election addresses of parliamentary candidates, party publications and election propaganda material were available in large measures and provided some very good material. Unfortunately, there was hardly any material directly relevant to Anglo-German relations found in local Conservative Party records. There was also an attempt made during the course of research for this book to locate the private papers of every Conservative MP at Westminster from 1905 to 1914. Indeed, a database of every Conservative MP who served at Westminster from 1905 to 1914 was established. Several research trips were made to local archives containing the papers of obscure backbench Conservative MPs. However, this proved a largely fruitless exercise, which produced very little useful information. Most of the private papers of the backbench MPs consulted were obsessed with domestic, local and personal matters.

It soon became clear that to examine a wide range of Conservative views towards Germany required the examination of many previously neglected sources. Finding relevant material resembled prospecting for gold, and the slim length of this study should not detract from the fact that what is presented here represents the vast bulk of the sources available. The parliamentary debates of the House of Commons and the House of Lords, generally neglected by political historians, provided some very valuable information and enabled a very useful comparison between the views of the Conservative leadership towards Germany and the views of the party rank and file at Westminster. The leading newspapers and, especially, the periodical press were exhaustively trawled during the research for this study. These sources did provide a good deal of relevant information on such issues as the naval arms race, the conscription controversy and foreign policy. In addition, information gathered from specialised Conservative Party publications helped to clarify the differences between the Westminster framework of activities and the public presentation of Conservative policy towards the key aspects of Anglo-German relations outside parliament.

For the examination of pressure-group activity, the private papers of Lord Roberts, the leader of the National Service League, L.J. Maxse, the editor of the right-wing *National Review*, and the papers of H.A. Gwynne, the editor of the *Standard*, were all consulted. These papers were useful in explaining the inter-face between the 'radical right' and the organisational framework of the Conservative Party. In addition, the specialised periodicals, and pamphlets and leaflets of the Imperial Maritime League, the Tariff Reform League and the National Service League were also examined, and some very useful material was gleaned from them. For the study of electioneering, the papers of Sandars, Bonar Law and Balfour proved useful, but the election petitions of Conservative candidates, party periodicals, and Conservative leaflets and pamphlets provided even more useful and relevant material.

The argument presented in this study, which receives more elaborate discussion in each of the following chapters, can be briefly summarised. It is argued here that the response of the Conservative Party towards Germany, whether in connection with foreign policy, trade rivalry, the naval race and the conscription controversy, showed a high level of restraint and displayed a marked absence of open hostility towards Germany. The leadership of the Conservative Party was determined to avoid giving offence to the German Government, in order to bolster the publicly restrained attitude towards Germany, adopted by Sir Edward Grey, the Foreign Secretary, in the interests of bi-partisanship. It will also be emphasised that the bi-partisan consensus on foreign policy between the two major parties was able to operate even during the bitter turmoil of the inter-party struggle over domestic issues. The Conservative Party rank and file at Westminster was encouraged by the party leader to keep harsh private views about the German threat under stringent public restraint. On the issue of commercial rivalry between Britain and Germany, it is argued here that the Conservative case for tariff reform was not linked specifically to the German commercial threat, but focused instead on the intransigence of free trade Liberals who opposed the policy. In many instances, Conservative supporters of tariff reform depicted Germany as a role model and defended the German way of life from Liberal attacks primarily for the tactical and domestic purpose of winning the electoral battle with the Liberal Party over the future course of British economic policy. It is also emphasised that Anglo-German naval rivalry was the principal reason for the growth of fear about Germany within the Conservative Party. The hostility between Britain and Germany during the naval race was the most important factor which pushed the majority of the Conservative Party in a pro-French direction in the years which led to the outbreak of the First World War. On the question of conscription, it is argued that the widespread approval within the party for military service, which grew in response to fears about the growth of the German navy, was held in check by the realistic and pragmatic view of the party leadership which opposed conscription because of its supposed electoral unpopularity. Overall this study suggests that outright 'scaremongering' against Germany was an extra-parliamentary phenomenon. It was the sanctuary of 'outcasts' on the extreme right of extra-parliamentary 'Conservatism' who had little influence over the Conservative leadership. The new evidence presented here will make it easier to understand why the 'radical-right' pressure groups had such a limited impact in persuading the Conservative leadership to adopt a more strident Germanophobic approach. Overall, the study provides a powerful and long overdue corrective to the traditional depiction of the Conservative Party as a chief source in fostering Germanophobic views in Britain and thereby contributing to the growth of Anglo-German antagonism and the anti-German popular mood which still persists in some section of British society even today.

1
The Nature and Organisation of Conservative Foreign and Defence Questions at Westminster

In August 1914, the Liberal Government entered the war with Germany with the full support of the Conservative opposition. In the circumstances, Opposition support had been vital to prevent the fall of Asquith's administration. Yet very little has been written about the policy-making and information-gathering mechanisms of the Opposition on foreign and defence matters between 1905 and 1914 or on the organisational context in which Conservative views towards Anglo-German relations took place or even who were the most decisive figures in the decision-making process on these issues. It must be emphasised at the outset that foreign policy was viewed by the two major parties, the Conservatives and the Liberals, as a subject unsuitable for consideration from a purely party standpoint.[1] Lord Rosebery, the former Liberal Prime Minister, said in a speech in 1888: 'I have always held that the Secretary of State for Foreign affairs should speak, whenever possible, with the united voice of the English nation, without distinction of party'.[2] A.J. Balfour, the Conservative leader between 1902 and 1911 was another firm supporter of the principle of bi-partisanship on foreign policy. In 1911, Balfour told the House of Commons that 'Never in the history of Opposition has so much trouble been taken to keep ... the defence of the Empire as far as may be outside the area of party controversy'.[3] Lord Lansdowne, a former Foreign Secretary and the leading Conservative spokesman on foreign affairs in Opposition also believed that 'foreign policy in this country should be a continuous policy, and not be deflected by the eddies of party political opinion'.[4] Even the bitter party political struggle over the Parliament Bill in 1911 could not persuade Balfour to abandon support for bi-partisanship. On the contrary, Balfour assured Asquith, the Liberal Prime Minister, that he could depend on the support of the Opposition on any question of national honour.

Lansdowne believed that a Foreign Secretary should always speak with 'the united voice of the English nation', and he urged the Conservative Party to offer 'unqualified support for Grey', the Liberal Foreign Minister.[5] The *National Review* commented in 1911: 'The Opposition have consistently bolstered the foreign policy of Sir Edward Grey in the interests of continuity'.[6] Yet Conservative support for bi-partisanship was conditional on the Liberal Government continuing with the main lines of policy established by Lansdowne, while he had been Foreign Secretary. The main plank of that policy was the Anglo-French Entente, signed in a blaze of publicity in April 1904. It was viewed by most Conservatives as the one brilliant success of the ill-fated Balfour Government, which had sustained one of the worst Conservative electoral defeats in 1906.[7]

In spite of all the well-documented internal divisions that troubled the Conservatives in opposition from 1905 to 1914 over tariff reform, Ireland, the party leadership, and the constitution, the bi-partisan consensus between Government and opposition kept foreign policy insulated from the domestic political struggle. In February 1909, Balfour commented, 'I think the House will admit that during this parliament, and in the years preceding this parliament, there has been a steady resolve, to withdraw foreign affairs from the arena of controversial politics'.[8] In 1911, Balfour, who had frequently caused irritation within his own party because of his often ambiguous statements on key domestic issues claimed that his frequent statements in support of bi-partisanship, 'were no mere fair weather enunciations of an easy morality; they were not merely doctrines stated at a time when the temperature of party differences was low, and when the political horizon was free from cloud. They were genuinely meant, and they will be faithfully carried out'.[9] The constant support given by the Conservative leadership for bi-partisanship left it in a very curious position. It had no responsibility for the foreign policy of the Government, but its leaders had what can only be described as an official mindset which restrained them from criticising the foreign policy of the Liberal Government.

A small 'inner circle', consisting of the party leader, the ex-foreign secretary and a small group of trusted former Cabinet ministers controlled opposition foreign and defence policy. An exclusive 'inner council' had been a key feature of the conduct of foreign and defence matters while Lord Salisbury had been Prime Minister, and it was continued by Balfour as both Prime Minister and Opposition leader. This small group conducted policy primarily by correspondence with the party leader and between each other.

Balfour used this elite group as a policy think tank, free from parliamentary or party control. As Prime Minister, Balfour had decided policy after taking detailed advice from trusted ministers and selected 'experts' he respected in the navy and army.[10] In 1904, Balfour had set up the Committee of Imperial Defence (CID), a body which gave naval and army experts a role within the machinery of Whitehall decision making. The CID was directly accountable to the Prime Minister and the Cabinet. Balfour believed it could become an important advisory group that could inform Government policy on defence and foreign affairs.[11] Within this framework, Balfour thought that parliament and public opinion should not play a significant role. As Prime Minister, he had consistently opposed parliamentary debate on foreign and defence policy. Votes on the naval and army estimates were not taken on the grounds that they endangered state secrecy and cordial foreign relations.[12]

In Opposition, Balfour continued to rely for policy advice on defence policy on two key sources of information within the defence establishment. The first was Admiral 'Jacky' Fisher, the First Sea Lord, a firm supporter of the 'Blue Water strategy', who remained wedded to the view that naval power was the key to British defence. Fisher was a very important adviser to Balfour in opposition, and he supplied him with a great deal of confidential information on naval policy. A second key adviser to Balfour on defence matters and foreign policy was Lord Esher, who had been a leading figure in the CID and another firm supporter of the view that Britain's security rested on the strength of the navy. Esher provided Balfour with a great deal of confidential information on the defence strategy of the Liberal Government.

In addition, Balfour received unsolicited information on admiralty affairs from Lord Charles Beresford, who was a firm and often vitriolic opponent of Fisher's leadership of the admiralty. However, the

Conservative leader did not attach much weight to this advice. In fact, Beresford told a close friend that Balfour was, 'the greatest enemy I had' during his much publicised battle with Fisher over the administration of the navy.[13] In a similarly marginal role was Lord Roberts, a leading army figure and a firm supporter of the need to introduce conscription. Roberts often passed on unsolicited information to Balfour on the state of the army, but his influence over the Conservative leader was as minimal as that of Beresford. Whereas the views of Fisher and Esher were listened to by Balfour, the views of Beresford and Roberts were tolerated but not acted upon.

The practice of using 'experts' as key sources of information to guide opposition defence policy fitted in with Balfour's view that the interests of national security were best served by sheltering national defence from close parliamentary scrutiny. Balfour was even opposed to foreign office ministers being required to answer supplementary questions in parliament because 'it is impossible, if such a practice is to prevail, to carry on the difficult and delicate negotiations in which an empire of this magnitude is consistently engaged'.[14] Balfour even questioned whether a Foreign Secretary should even sit in the House of Commons on the grounds that 'No man can effectively discharge, in conjunction, especially at a time of crisis, the duties of the Foreign Department and those attending the Commons'.[15]

Given Balfour's preference for exclusiveness in foreign and defence policy formation, it is not surprising to find that, in true aristocratic fashion, he saw high social prestige as a pre-requisite for appointment to the post of opposition foreign or defence spokesman.[16] This certainly explains why the leading Conservative front bench spokesmen on foreign and defence policy were recruited from that narrow and privileged elite within the landed aristocracy and gentry which was later dubbed 'The Establishment'. The majority were elderly peers from ancient aristocratic families. Balfour felt members of the aristocracy were a group that could be relied upon to keep the secrets vital to success in foreign and defence policy.[17]

The two most important members of the opposition's inner circle on foreign and defence policy from 1905 to 1914 were the party leader and Lord Lansdowne, the former Foreign Secretary. It was these two figures who directed the opposition attitude on foreign and defence matters. They corresponded with individual Shadow Cabinet spokesmen, took expert advice when necessary and cooperated closely with each other before key parliamentary debates. The party leader was the decisive figure in this relationship because he selected the leading Shadow Cabinet spokesman on foreign policy and defence, and he had the final say on the position to be adopted by the opposition on any given issue.

By 1905, it was an established principle of Conservative organisation in parliament that a person who had attained Cabinet rank in Government should retain that role in Opposition.[18] Balfour followed this convention in the selection of his Shadow Cabinet spokesman, and all former Cabinet members with front bench responsibility on foreign and defence matters had some previous ministerial experience. Most had long-standing personal links with Balfour dating back many years. Lansdowne had been Balfour's 'fag' at Eton. Lord Selborne, the leading opposition spokesman on naval affairs, was a close relative and was addressed by Balfour in correspondence, in all seriousness, as 'my dear Willie'. Three other notable Shadow Cabinet figures, namely, Lord Curzon, who spoke on Indian Affairs, Lord Midleton, the leading spokesman on army issues in the Lords and George Wyndham, who performed the same role in the Commons, had all been members of a group known as the 'Souls', a tight-knit aristocratic intellectual splinter group, which Balfour led during the late nineteenth century.

The essential characteristics, therefore, for entry into the 'inner circle' on opposition foreign and defence policy were close relations with the party leader, an aristocratic background and a public school-Oxbridge education. Of the leading opposition spokesmen on foreign and defence affairs at Westminster, eight were peers, or the sons of peers. Apart from Arthur Lee, who spoke on defence matters in the Commons, all had attended public school, and eight of them were old Etonians. Apart from Lee and Ernest Pretyman, who sometimes spoke on naval questions, all were Oxford or Cambridge graduates, with most having a hereditary title and a large country estate.[19]

In managing parliamentary debate, Balfour created another 'inner circle', consisting of Alexander Acland Hood, the Chief Whip, Wilfred Short, his personal secretary and J.S. Sandars, his private secretary. The last two mentioned conducted most of his correspondence and consulted with his parliamentary colleagues. H.O. Arnold-Foster described the Whip's room in the House as 'A sort of private club where, everyone except Sandars and a few other cronies are regarded as intruders'.[20] Walter Long commented to Balfour, 'The selection of topics for debate, and even speakers from front and backbenchers has been entirely in the hands of Alec Hood and Jack Sandars'.[21] Balfour added to the elitism and aloofness, which characterised his leadership of the Conservative Party at Westminster, by rarely mixing with backbench MPs.

It can be said, with a great deal of confidence, that the role of the Shadow Cabinet on foreign and defence policy was relatively insignificant. The Shadow Cabinet consisted primarily of former Cabinet ministers, the Chief Whip and, after 1911, the party chairman. It was summoned by the party leader in the Commons (Balfour) and the Lords (Lansdowne).[22] It met periodically from 1905 to 1914 inside parliament, most often in the room of the party leader in the Commons. Meetings of the Shadow Cabinet also took place in Lansdowne's room in the Lords. Outside parliament, meetings occurred at Carlton Gardens, the home of Balfour, and at Lansdowne House, the ex-foreign secretary's London address. There were very few meetings of the Shadow Cabinet between 1911 and 1914 at Pembroke Lodge, the home of Andrew Bonar Law. As Arthur Lee put it, 'It was an incredibly dreary house and no-one on the front bench knew how to get there'.[23]

The first Shadow Cabinet, held in December 1905, was confined entirely to ex-ministers, but in 1911, F.E. Smith, Edward Carson and Arthur Steel-Maitland – who had all never sat in a previous Cabinet – were brought in.[24] The Shadow Cabinet had no research or secretarial support, and there is no recorded instance of the leader of the opposition being defeated by a vote taken in the Shadow Cabinet from 1905 to 1914.[25] Even so, the meetings of the Shadow Cabinet appear to have been conducted in the style of a real Cabinet. Memoranda were circulated for discussion, ex-ministers spoke on their own specialist areas of policy, and votes were sometimes taken. The decision to reject the 1911 Parliament Act was the agreed policy of the Shadow Cabinet.[26] It was only convened by Bonar Law in August 1914 after the opposition leader had discussed policy within his 'inner circle' and had already communicated his decision to support Grey's policy of intervention in the European War to the Prime Minister.

Even former ministers realised the limitations of the Shadow Cabinet as a policy-making body and especially as a restraining influence on the views of the opposition leader. As Balfour remarked of divisions over policy in the Shadow Cabinet during the House of Lords crisis in 1910, 'Had it been a real Cabinet – the dissenting minority would have resigned, or they would have silently acquiesced in the decision of the majority. There could be no question in the case of a Shadow Cabinet of resignation'.[27] Lord Balcarres, the Chief Whip, described the majority of Shadow Cabinet members as 'discredited politicians whose inclusion in a future Conservative government would create dismay and perhaps revolt among the rank and file'.[28] Balfour said of the acrimony within the Shadow Cabinet over the House of Lords issue,

> In a Cabinet, if there is a division of opinion the rule is that the majority must prevail; and if the view of the majority is not accepted; those who will not accept it have no alternative but to leave the government. But, here after a full discussion, a minority decline to accept my advice which commanded a majority of the shadow cabinet and the dissenting members have gone out into the world proclaiming their differences, and have embarked upon a policy of active resistance.[29]

Balfour once described it as a 'sham Cabinet',[30] and he asked Lord Stamfordham to dismiss from his mind the very thought that 'a shadow cabinet exercises a greater influence over the Leader of the Party than the real Cabinet does over the Prime Minister'.[31] Lansdowne shared the misgivings expressed by Balfour over the role of the Shadow Cabinet in Opposition policy formation. The ex-Foreign Secretary believed that proposing anything to the Shadow Cabinet meant 'considerable delay', and he thought its meetings were unsuitable during 'emergencies'. Lansdowne preferred confining important policy decisions of the Opposition to 'a few of our friends'.[32]

It is unwise, therefore, when analysing the activities of the Conservative Opposition from 1905 to 1914 to make a simple equation between membership and attendance lists at the Shadow Cabinet and a key policy-making role or substantial influence over the policy adopted by the party leader. Closer examination of those who had influence is required and that can only be discovered by extensive examination of private correspondence. There were very important defence spokesmen who rarely attended Shadow Cabinet meetings. There were some ex-Cabinet ministers who attended regularly, but had no influence at all. At the same time, there were ex-ministers who did frequently attend and were influential.

In the light of this, it is very important to put the leading spokesman on foreign and defence matters under closer scrutiny, in order to assess the amount of influence each had over the policy of the party leader. The most important member of the Balfour's 'inner circle' on foreign and defence affairs was undoubtedly Lord Lansdowne, the former foreign secretary. He had very close French connections. His mother was the daughter of Count de Flahaut, the son of Talleyrand. He was fluent in the French language and frequently visited France on holiday. During the 1890s, Lansdowne had been chair of a parliamentary committee which had discussed the possibility of a Channel Tunnel. He was Foreign Secretary when the entente-cordiale was signed in 1904. Despite all of this, Lansdowne did not view the Anglo-French agreement as a distinctly pro-French policy nor as a means of encircling Germany. As Foreign Secretary, Lansdowne had consistently refused to discuss the European implications of the entente, and he continued to view it, in the early years of opposition, as an important way to settle a number of long-standing and costly Anglo-French colonial disputes and thereby reduce the over-stretched defence budget. In 1905, Paul Cambon, the French Ambassador asked Lansdowne to outline the circumstances which would trigger British support to France in the event of war with Germany. In reply, Lansdowne only promised 'consultation' in the event of a German attack on France. In fact, it is clear that Lansdowne did not originally view the entente as a means of dividing Europe into two antagonistic blocs.

The close relationship which had developed between Balfour and Lansdowne on foreign policy in Government continued in Opposition. Balfour valued Lansdowne's experience on foreign affairs and his unquestioning loyalty. Though Balfour wanted foreign and defence policy to be guided by his own views, he always consulted Lansdowne. Lord Cawdor told Sandars that Balfour always relied on Lansdowne for his cool and detached ability in 'dealing with difficult questions'.[33] For his part, the ex-foreign secretary always took pains to seek permission from Balfour before making any key speech or taking policy action on foreign and defence issues. A typical example is contained in a letter from Lansdowne to Sandars, written before an important naval debate in the House of Lords in 1909, in which he writes, 'I must see the Chief and ask him the best manner of dealing with the Navy question in the House of Lords'.[34] Lord Selborne offered the following insight on Lansdowne's relationship with Balfour: 'If ever I had to make any criticism of Lansdowne, it would be that he is insufficiently self assertive'. Selborne wished that Lansdowne would 'act on his own judgement', more often during his discussions with Balfour on foreign and defence questions.[35] Even so, it cannot be denied that Lansdowne enjoyed a very significant influence over the opposition attitude towards foreign policy and an equally esteemed international reputation. Austen Chamberlain recalled that Sazonoff, the Russian Foreign Minister, told him during talks in Moscow in 1912, that the Tsar was concerned that Lansdowne might be replaced by the 'anti-Russian' Curzon as Foreign Secretary in a future Conservative Government. But Chamberlain assured Sazonoff that Lansdowne remained the most likely future Conservative Foreign Secretary.[36] Another great admirer of Lansdowne's judgement was King Edward VII who frequently sought his advice on foreign affairs.[37]

The two most important Conservative figures on naval policy also sat in the upper chamber at Westminster. Lord Cawdor had overall responsibility for Conservative naval policy from 1905 until his death in 1911. According to Walter Long, the leading Conservative front bench spokesman on naval affairs in the Commons, were expected 'to consult with Cawdor, who alone would be able to give approval or disapproval to their suggestions on policy towards the navy'.[38] But, this was not the whole truth as Cawdor did not act on matters of naval policy without first consulting with Balfour and Lansdowne. Cawdor was exceptionally loyal to the party leadership and was frequently accused by Long of 'always backing up and defending the Admiralty'.[39] Cawdor, taking his lead from Balfour, was also a firm supporter of Lord Fisher, who provided him with confidential information before key naval debates.[40] Balfour admired Cawdor's dutiful loyalty more than he valued him as a naval expert, and he viewed Lord Selborne as the leading Conservative policy expert on naval matters. But Selborne was high commissioner for South Africa between 1905 and 1910 and so could not play a leading role. Lansdowne was also a great admirer of Selborne's views on naval affairs, and he thought of Cawdor as a loyal and pliant deputy while Selborne was abroad. 'I wish Selborne were at home', Lansdowne told Sandars, 'because in his absence, our Front Bench is not up to much'.[41]

On many other occasions, between 1905 and 1910, Lansdowne would write to Selborne, outlining recent developments on naval policy and often told him that he would be 'glad when you resume your place on the Opposition Front Bench'.[42] It was not only Balfour and Lansdowne who bemoaned Selborne's absence. Cawdor actually drew on many of the policy papers, written by Selborne as naval minister, as the basis of many of his own speeches on the navy.[43] Contemporary observers, especially among the party rank and file, had serious misgivings about Cawdor's supposed status as the leading figure on opposition naval policy. F.S. Oliver, a leading member of the National Service League, remarked to Austen Chamberlain, 'I had a very pleasant chat after dinner with a nice old gentleman in the corner of the dining room, and told him all sorts of things he didn't know about the navy. Later on, I discovered it was Lord Cawdor'.[44] In the final analysis, Cawdor was really a cipher of Balfour's views on the navy and remained a member of Balfour's 'inner circle', not as a policy maker, but as a loyal and trusted friend of the leader.

After returning from South Africa in 1910, Selborne resumed his role as the leading Opposition speaker in the House of Lords on the navy. Selborne was a heart-and-soul big navy man, who summed up his own views on the proper priorities of national defence in the following way:

> I am all for having a small home army, thoroughly organised and trained, and that presumably is what Haldane is aiming at, but I have never been a believer, and I do not believe that Roberts is on the right track pressing for a greatly increased expenditure on the Home Army. If we are not sufficiently secure against invasion the increased expenditure ought not to be on the army but on the navy.[45]

Upon his return to Britain, Selborne quickly concluded that the Conservative Party lacked a clear and independent naval policy. Selborne believed 'success in politics is to believe something and to avow it. Men always follow a steady and consistent lead'.[46] It seems Selborne's decision to criticise Balfour's handling of naval policy was primarily caused by his irritation with Balfour's handling of the House of Lords crisis. In fact, during that struggle, Selborne became a leading figure in the Halsbury Club, which aimed to rebuild party morale and produce a 'fighting policy behind a fighting leader'.[47] The views of the Halsbury Club were supported by the *National Review*, which argued that 'the Opposition has had no policy whatsoever as regards national defence'.[48] In essence, Selborne wanted the Opposition to argue for much greater spending on the navy than the Liberal Government through the introduction of a 'Two Keels to One Standard' to keep ahead in the naval arms race with Germany. A combination of disloyalty to the party leader and his membership of the Halsbury club ensured that Selborne's influence over Conservative policy towards the navy became much less important after 1910, and Balfour, after he resigned, was to exert the greatest influence over the party on naval matters.

In the House of Commons, Arthur Lee and Ernest Pretyman were the most frequent front bench speakers on naval affairs. At other times, and much less frequently, Austen Chamberlain, F.E. Smith and George Wyndham spoke on the naval matters. Of all these figures, Arthur Lee, who was never a permanent member of the Shadow Cabinet, can be classed as the leading opposition speaker on naval affairs.[49] Yet Lee later acknowledged that he was always on the verge of the 'inner ring' that managed Conservative foreign and defence policy.[50] The chief whip in the House of Commons never approved of Lee, regarding him as 'over addicted to independence and not a true blue party man'.[51]

It seems snobbery concerning Lee's social background was one major cause of this mistrust. Lee had lived his early years in poverty. He had attended an elementary school and later married an American heiress, not for love, claimed his critics, but for the money and status he had been denied in his early life. As a result, Lee was treated as a classic outsider by the leading figures in the 'inner circle' surrounding the Conservative leader. Yet there is one perk British modern Prime Ministers enjoy because of Lee's generosity: in his will, he left the beautiful mansion at Chequers to the state.

Lee never addressed the House of Commons on any subject other than national defence from 1905 to 1914. He was highly regarded by Balfour, not as a policy adviser on naval policy, but as a rabble-rousing parliamentary debater, whose primary role in naval debates was 'to interject to embarrass the government'.[52] Lee later recalled that he was 'frequently incited and occasionally ordered to bait the Liberal front bench by A.J. Balfour'.[53] Yet his critics within the parliamentary party were always bemoaning his contribution in naval debates, questioning his loyalty to the leader and his lack of previous Cabinet experience. As Selborne told Ernest Pretyman, 'I have not always thought Lee's attitude in the House of Commons towards Admiralty questions has been judicious, but then he had nothing of the experience at the Admiralty you and I had'.[54] Selborne's attitude to Lee within the 'inner circle' was both typical and influential. But criticism also came from a few leading figures in the party rank and file. Lord Charles Beresford, a leading backbench figure on naval matters, said of Lee in 1914, 'Why Mr. Lee should arrogate to himself the position of the spokesman for the Army and Navy I am at a loss to know'.[55] Not surprisingly, the position of Lee as leading Opposition spokesman in the House of Commons on the navy was by no means uncontested. The alternative and obvious candidate was Pretyman, a country gentleman of so-called impeccable lineage. He had the added advantage of having served much longer at the admiralty before 1905. But Pretyman had lost his seat in the 1906 general election and was outside parliament. Then, in 1908, Pretyman won a stunning by-election victory at Chelmsford. On his return to the Commons he fully expected to be offered by Balfour the position of opposition spokesman on the navy. In such circumstances, Lee enlisted the support of Walter Long, a potential future leader of the party who had sat in the House of Commons since 1880 and had occupied the post of Chief Secretary for Ireland in the Balfour Government. Long felt that Lee had made a good impression on naval issues and explained his own view of the relative merits of Lee and Pretyman for the role of naval spokesman to Balfour in November 1908:

I had an interview with Arthur Lee. No one could be nicer or more loyal than he is in every respect. He does not want to press the matter, but he feels, and I think rightly, that unless something is done confusion and difficulty will arise. He has for three years now done the Admiralty work on our Front Bench and I'm bound to say that I think he has done it well. He thoroughly understands the position that we now take in regard to Admiralty questions ... The question is: is he to go on, or surrender the whole case into Pretyman's hands? It appears to me that it would be most unfortunate if we were to change horses at this moment ... It would be desirable for Lee to go on acting as he has done ... On the whole, therefore, I am inclined very strongly to recommend to you that something very definite be said to Pretyman in order to prevent further complications arising. It would be very awkward either in or out of the House to make statements in regard to Admiralty questions which were not in complete accord with the view which I think we all share on the subject.[56]

This intervention by Long, which displayed his confidence in Lee, had the desired effect on Balfour who retained him as opposition spokesman on the navy. With some reluctance, Pretyman agreed to speak in a supporting role to Lee during future naval debates. Austen Chamberlain commented on the dispute between Lee and Pretyman, before the navy estimates debates in 1909: 'I will debate the Navy estimates at seven, i.e. if Pretyman (who has "got the hump" because Lee is not superseded) thinks it infra dig to follow Lee'.[57] In South Africa, Selborne was not happy with this decision and made no secret of his own admiration for Pretyman. 'I am glad for the sake of the navy', he told Pretyman, 'that you are back in the House of Commons. I fully agree with you on naval matters'.[58]

Naval issues certainly caused in-fighting and controversy among the opposition, but on the whole they were a source of unity within a party that was divided on matters such as the constitution, tariff reform, social policy, the party leadership and organisation. Army issues also created similar levels of disunity, confusion and sometimes embarrass-ment. As Austen Chamberlain told L.J. Maxse, a passionate supporter of conscription, 'your army service league [National Service League] have a very definite policy [conscription]. We as a party have not'.[59]

In 1913, George Wyndham, the leading Conservative spokesman on the army in the House of Commons died suddenly. But such was the level of bitterness and tension within the party caused by the Home Rule crisis in Ireland, which had re-emerged as a key issue in British politics after the outcome of the two 1910 general elections that had left the Liberal Government dependent for its survival on the support of pro-Nationalist Irish MPs, that Bonar Law, then Conservative leader, could not think of a single MP who could replace Wyndham as army spokesman without causing him 'any embarrassment'.[60] In these circumstances, Law informed Lee that he wanted him to speak on both navy and army affairs in the House of Commons.[61]

Between 1905 and 1914, however, the two leading opposition spokesman on army matters were Arnold Foster, who died in 1909, and Lord Midleton. Both were unsuccessful and discredited former War ministers who did not command great respect within the party, and although they continued to barrage the party leader with policy advice, it was mostly ignored. The shortcomings of both were frequently discussed by leading party figures. Sandars, Balfour's influential private secretary, described Arnold Foster and Lord Midleton as 'worse than useless'.[62] In 1911, Lee advised Bonar Law that in any debate over army questions, the opposition would have difficulty, 'contrasting Haldane's performance unfavourably with those of Unionist War Ministers of recent date'.[63]

Arnold Foster frequently claimed 'the man who believes in invasion believes in conscription.' Up until his death in 1909, Arnold Foster did not believe in either invasion or conscription.[64] Midleton, on the other hand, did favour conscription, but he agreed not to diverge from the official party line of opposing the policy. Lord Balcarres, the Conservative Chief Whip believed that Midleton 'speaks above his ability' and he also thought, 'Most of our people distrust his judgement.' After a long conversation with Midleton on army issues in 1912, Balcarres, wrote in his diary, 'He feels the statesman all over, talks in mysterious ellipsis, swears one to secrecy on topics which are the talk of the town and ... leaves one hopelessly bewildered'.[65]

Even worse, Midleton wanted the opposition to take a clear and independent line on army policy, thus challenging the loyal adherence of the party leadership towards the bi-partisan consensus on defence policy. In 1909, Midleton told Balfour that 'Lord Roberts [the leader of the National Service League] is keen to have a meeting with Lansdowne, Cawdor, Milner and myself to try and get some understanding. At present, we are pulling in different ways on the army issue'. Balfour's reply to Midleton was clear and hard-headed: he opposed conscription and opposed meeting those openly associated with it in public.[66] In spite of this, the National Service League continued to gain many converts among the Conservative rank and file, particularly in the House of Lords. In July 1909, when Roberts proposed a National Service bill in the upper chamber, 98 Conservative peers supported it. But Balfour took a strong line over the proposal, and he immediately told Lansdowne to urge the Opposition front bench to oppose it.[67] Overall, the influence of Midleton over the party leader was relatively insignificant. Balfour consistently ignored his pleas for the party to adopt a more sympathetic line towards conscription, while Bonar Law preferred to seek the advice of Henry Wilson, a leading Army General, for 'expert' advice on army questions.

George Wyndham, who replaced Arnold Foster as leading Opposition spokesman on army affairs in the House of Commons, was yet another deeply discredited figure. On the surface, he had all of the chief characteristics of an ideal member of the 'inner circle'. He was very much part of the landed elite. But, he was ill equipped for the increasingly bitter nature of cut and thrust of party political debate at Westminster after 1906. Balcarres bluntly described Wyndham as 'the most indolent member of the Front Bench'.[68] Balfour always disliked the literary allusions Wyndham employed in most of his long-winded parliamentary speeches: 'I believe it's his natural way of talking, but it's a great bore for a person with a non-literary mind like mine'.[69] The Annual Register described Wyndhams's speeches as 'more eloquent than convincing'.[70]

After 1909, Wyndham publicly endorsed the aims of the National Service League, even though he believed that conscription could not be achieved without a cross-party agreement. He was also very careful in his public speeches outside Westminster to emphasise that his support for conscription was a 'personal view'. In the House of Commons, Wyndham supported the principles of bi-partisanship, and he spoke against conscription. In 1912, Wyndham claimed that 'no difference, I believe, in principle, divides the Government and Opposition in respect to the objects which we have as a nation to achieve if we wish to be safe and preserve our place amongst the great powers'.[71] To make his views even more confusing, Wyndham also opposed the idea of an opposition party 'producing alternative policies' and framing 'hypothetical estimates'. Wyndham was certainly a part of the inner circle, and he frequently discussed defence issues with the party leader, but his influence over the party leader was extremely limited.

It can be seen that even within the small inner circle of front bench spokesmen on foreign and defence matters, the amount of influence each spokesman had over the party leader varied greatly.[72] The party leader exercised a remarkable degree of control over foreign and defence matters within parliament and over the Shadow Cabinet. In essence, the party leader relied primarily on Lansdowne to decide the policy line, and took advice from several sources of 'expert opinion' in the party, the Admiralty and the CID. The most significant figure within the inner circle on foreign policy was Lansdowne. The influence of the spokesmen on naval and army questions offered a much more confusing picture. The party leader expected the leading naval spokesmen to consult with Cawdor and Lansdowne before making any speeches on naval matters. Leading army spokesmen were allowed to offer sympathy, even outright support for conscription outside parliament, but were expected to oppose the policy at Westminster, at elections, and even in speeches outside parliament to emphasise that they were expressing 'a private view'.

The view that an exclusive 'inner circle' surrounded Balfour was a prevailing theme of his backbench critics. As William Bridgeman, MP, told Balfour, 'It is well known that a feeling exists, rightly or wrongly, amongst a large section of the Unionist Party that you have been surrounded by men who are not in touch with the mass of the party.'[73] J.F. Remnant, MP, summed up the general feelings of backbench critics of Balfour's organisation of the party in parliament in a letter to the *Morning Post*:

> In the House of Commons the organisation is as defective today for practical purposes as it has ever been during the whole time I have had the honour to sit in the House. Advisers drawn from a very small section of the party beset the leader and the Front Bench who represent a still smaller section of the Unionist Party outside it. Consequently, the leader knows little or nothing of the opinion of the rank and file and nothing is ever done to encourage any member outside the select circle to take an active role. What hope is there for a party so governed? ... the future of the Empire must rest in the hands of advisers?.[74]

Balfour dismissed this attack as a 'profound illusion, though no doubt one of a kind which is common enough in the history of parties'.[75]

Yet Balfour's iron grip on how the opposition dealt with the discussion of the German threat in parliament and his firm support for a bi-partisan consensus on foreign and defence issues ensured that his critics were consigned to the periphery. This helps to explain why H.A. Gwynne, the editor of the *Morning Post*, thought that the majority of Tory MPs were 'silent and useless' on the German threat.[76] Henry Wilson, a Conservative MP, who took a great interest in defence issues, described the opposition response to Liberal naval cuts in 1907 thus, 'the Unionist benches were empty, and, except, for a vigorous speech by Mr. Lee and a mild protest from Mr. Balfour there was no response to what is really a revolution in naval policy'.[77] Maddison, a Labour MP, said of Conservative attendance in a key naval debate: 'there were not more than half a dozen on the opposition benches ... I should have thought that the representatives of the great imperial party would have been present in their full strength to defend the Empire'.[78]

The most outspoken and frustrated backbench critic of the restrained response of the party leadership and opposition front bench towards the growth of German naval and military power was Lord Charles Beresford, MP, who 'blamed Balfour more than anybody' for failing to alert the country to the German threat.[79] He also criticised Bonar Law for not taking 'the slightest note of my requests to stress the German danger'.[80] The decision of Law to offer support to Churchill as First Lord of the Admiralty from 1911 to 1914 produced the following private tirade from Beresford:

> Mr. Churchill has always proved himself, politically, a traitor. In 1904, when the Unionist Party was getting in low waters and difficulties, he traitorously left them, and joined our political enemies. In 1909, he led, recruited for, and reinforced the Little Navy Party ... Mr. Churchill perceiving he will get more votes for a big Navy than for a little Navy has again turned traitor, and deserted the army of Little Navyites, hoping their enemies (the Unionist) will support him ... The Unionist Party complains of the apathy of the public. What else can they expect? The people at one date hear the Leaders of the Opposition proclaim the Cabinet as traitors, felons, and guilty of corrupt practices, and a few weeks afterwards the same men state that one of these traitors (Mr. Churchill) is the 'hero of the stricken battlefield and as good a First Sea Lord as any Unionist' and ... 'A genuine patriot'. Of course, the ordinary thinking men in the Country thinks we are neither genuine nor sincere.[81]

The continuing frustration of Beresford over his lack of influence over the party leader over the Conservative response to the German military and naval threat is evident in the following comment: 'What is the use of me going on fighting the case, if Unionist leaders will not take it up.'[82] These feelings of frustration and marginalisation from Opposition decision making are also noticeable among Conservative supporters of the National Service League, who wanted Balfour to outline a clear policy on conscription. As Henry Page-Croft, the Conservative MP, put it, 'what we all think is so much needed is a definite statement of policy from Mr. Balfour. We are constantly asked our position and are in the dark'.[83] The usual response of Balfour to this sort of backbench criticism was to claim it was

> hardly justified. I am not aware of a single topic of public interest on which I have not made pronouncements as clear and as definite and as detailed as it is wise for any Opposition to make ... which they have not, while in Opposition, any power to pass into law.[84]

In private, however, Balfour's position on conscription was crystal clear: 'I have never been able to accept this policy – for a great many reasons, military and political, and if it ever fell to my lot to form a government again, I certainly should not ask anyone to join who, I thought might subsequently break on this question'.[85]

Significantly, there was hardly any criticism within the Conservative Party over the bi-partisan approach to foreign affairs. The major backbench critics of British foreign policy came from Liberals, the so-called 'Radicals against War' – and from a majority of Labour and Irish MPs.[86] They argued that the bi-partisanship on foreign affairs amounted to a 'Front Bench conspiracy', designed to stifle parliamentary debate. As Ramsay MacDonald, the Labour MP, put it,

> I am afraid that in respect to the pious opinion in favour of continuity of foreign policy I am something of a heretic. It all depends on what you are continuing. If the foreign policy you have inherited from your predecessors is a bad foreign policy, I am bound to confess I see no virtue in carrying it on ... His Majesty's Government has been too loyal in its dealings with Lord Lansdowne's policy. I think it has carried it to extremes.[87]

The critics of bi-partisanship claimed that the 1904 Anglo-French Entente and the 1907 Anglo-Russian Convention were anti-German.

This charge was vehemently denied by Sir Edward Grey who claimed that the diplomatic agreement with France and Russia did not represent a barrier to good relations with Germany.[88] This view was also supported by Lansdowne who claimed that, 'the whole policy of late government was quite inconsistent with the idea of coming to an agreement which should exclude the possibility of agreements with other powers or which should divide the European powers into two hostile camps'.[89]

In 1914, the whole question of the parliamentary discussion of foreign and defence matters was discussed at a parliamentary select committee. During the deliberations, Balfour denied there was a parliamentary straight jacket around critics of foreign and defence policy. He claimed that backbench MPs were 'allowed to put questions to ministers, they can express their views during a discussion of naval and army estimates debates, and invite other MPs to support them in a claim for a debate on foreign and defence matters'. To give MPs greater parliamentary powers over foreign and defence matters was, in Balfour's view, 'undesirable and unnecessary'.[90]

Even though the period from 1905 to 1914 is generally viewed as a period of bitter divisions within party politics, it becomes apparent that this conclusion did not apply to foreign and defence matters. The Conservative leadership consistently supported the principles of bi-partisanship in such matters. Balfour's handling of the constitutional crisis displayed a similar desire to put the nation before the party. The personal control exercised by the Conservative leader and his inner circle' of advisers and front bench spokesmen over foreign and defence matters at Westminster was the organisational mechanism through which the Conservative leader enjoyed a free hand in the realm of policy making and total and unchallenged control over the line opposition spokesmen would adopt in parliamentary debate. As a result, the Shadow Cabinet had no power to restrain the leader, while backbench critics in the Commons and the Lords who disagreed with the policy of the leader were effectively marginalised. For these reasons, the views of the leader towards Anglo-German relations were of primary significance because they determined the attitude which the Conservative Party adopted at key moments in the unfolding international crisis that led to the outbreak of the First World War.

2
Leadership: (1) A.J. Balfour and Anglo-German Relations

This chapter provides a comprehensive account of the views of A.J. Balfour towards Anglo-German relations. It explains how Balfour's views towards Germany were significantly transformed while the Conservative Party was in Opposition from 1905 to 1914. The chapter adopts a chronological approach, because Balfour was only deeply concerned with Anglo-German relations during brief and episodic periods, in particular, when Britain's relations with Germany dominated the political scene and at times of acute international crisis.

A.J. Balfour was born in 1848 into one of the leading aristocratic families which dominated the upper strata of the Conservative Party. Balfour's father, James Maitland Balfour, owned two large country estates in Scotland, but he died when Balfour was a mere seven years old. Balfour's mother, Lady Blanche Gascoyne-Cecil, was the sister of Robert Cecil (Lord Salisbury), the Conservative Prime Minister, who became the paternal uncle of A.J. Balfour, and the trustee of his father's substantial estate. Balfour's close connection with the Conservative 'establishment' was further enhanced by the fact that his godfather was the Duke of Wellington. Balfour's education also reflected his privileged background. He attended Eton College, then Trinity College, Cambridge. Balfour took a great interest in philosophy while he was an undergraduate, and he penned a number of books on philosophical subjects, most notably, *A Defence of Philosophic Doubt* (1879). In later years, Balfour's political critics claimed the title of his most well-known philosophic work summed up his outwardly diffident approach to politics.

The swift progress Balfour made up through the ranks of the Conservative Party was undoubtedly helped by his family link to

Lord Salisbury. A safe Tory seat was found in the Cecil family heartland of Hertford, which Balfour duly won at the 1874 General Election. When Salisbury became Secretary of State for India, his nephew acted as his private secretary. In 1878, Balfour attended the historic Congress of Berlin in the company of his uncle. The first important Cabinet post held by Balfour was the difficult and politically sensitive post of Chief Secretary of Ireland.[1] Balfour was praised by the Conservative Party for his unbending policy of 'coercion' against Irish Nationalists. Balfour's success in Ireland was a very important stepping stone to his elevation to the leadership of the Conservative Party. In 1891, he became Conservative leader in the House of Commons. When Lord Salisbury retired in July 1902, the nephew he had groomed for high political office succeeded him as Prime Minister. Balfour's appointment gave rise to a popular music hall joke of the day which suggested that anything was possible in British politics if 'Bob's your uncle'.

The period when Balfour led the Conservative Party from 1902 to 1911 is viewed by historians as the low point in the electoral fortunes of the party during the twentieth century. The impression of a party divided into different factions, without clear guidance from the leader and obsessed with domestic issues is a well-established feature of the existing historiography.[2] The five major biographies of Balfour give passing references to his keen interest in foreign and defence questions, but none focus in detail on Balfour's views on Anglo-German relations. All of Balfour's biographers express admiration for his abilities as an effective parliamentary debater and a competent administrator, but they portray him as a detached politician whose mind was wracked by 'philosophic doubt' on most of the major political issues of the day.[3] Many contemporaries provide evidence to support this traditional portrayal of Balfour. Lord Esher describes a visit to Balfour's home in Carlton Gardens thus: 'I called on Arthur Balfour this morning. He was in bed; a small brass bed, with an electric light over his head. He generally remains there till mid-day'. According to Beatrice Webb, a close friend, Balfour possessed 'an ever open mind, too open, perhaps, and on no issue has it been sufficiently closed by study'.[4] Admiral Sir John Fisher believed that Balfour 'saw too much of both sides of any argument'.[5] Even in contemporary cartoons Balfour is portrayed as vague, indecisive and aloof. He actively encouraged his generally negative public image by making statements such as 'I am a thick and thin supporter of nothing, not even myself'.[6] Yet this orthodox and rather unflattering presentation of Balfour as a detached philosophical statesman, dithering over every issue, does not fit his approach to foreign and defence questions. As a close confidante commented, 'The reality of his belief was much stronger than superficial appearance. There were profound convictions on a limited number of subjects'.[7] One of these subjects was certainly national defence. In this area of policy, Balfour's influence over Conservative policy was dominant, his authority unchallenged and his expertise highly respected.

Balfour believed the major aim of British foreign policy was to ensure that Britain remained a great imperial power. In Balfour's view, naval dominance was 'the very basis of our national existence'.[8] As a result, Balfour was convinced that Britain had to maintain an on-going programme of naval expansion and modernisation to keep ahead of rival naval powers. As Prime Minister, he introduced several key naval reforms, including improved officer training, the re-distribution of the fleet, in order to offer greater protection from invasion, improvements in the reserve fleet, the scrapping of numerous obsolete vessels and, most significantly, the building of the Dreadnought. Though Balfour regarded command of the seas as the major priority of national defence, this does not mean he viewed the role of the army as completely insignificant. For Balfour, the army was a vital supplement to naval power, but he consistently resisted the clamour within certain sections of the Conservative Party for the introduction of conscription.[9] As Prime Minister, Balfour allocated the greatest proportion of army expenditure to the British Army in India. As a committed supporter of the imperialist ideal, Balfour viewed British foreign policy, before the advent of the Anglo-German naval race, as linked primarily to the defence of the Empire, not with upholding the balance of power on the European continent.

Given Balfour's long-standing preoccupation with imperial defence, it was only natural for him to view Russia as the 'traditional enemy' of the British Empire. Balfour did not believe the Tsar wanted or was planning a war with Britain in Asia, but he did not trust him, and he was concerned that Russia's deep-seated economic problems and domestic turmoil might encourage the fragile Tsarist regime to engage in a programme of expansion in Asia.[10] Balfour believed that the Tsarist regime regarded a policy of conciliation on the part of

Britain as a severe sign of weakness.[11] To strengthen Britain's strategic position in Asia, therefore, Balfour supported the signing of the Anglo-Japanese Treaty in 1902. He even contemplated a war with Russia in 1904, after a merchant vessel was sunk at Dogger Bank by a Russian battleship. The event which eased Balfour's fears of Russian power in Asia somewhat was the spectacular Japanese naval defeat of Russia at Tsishima in May 1905. Only at this stage did Balfour cease to regard Russia as a mortal threat to India. This is not to say he completely ruled out, in the longer term, a revival of Russian military and naval power. In fact, it was Balfour's underlying fear of a Russian revival which helps to explain his negative attitude towards the Anglo-Russian Convention, signed by Sir Edward Grey in 1907, which was designed to reduce Anglo-Russian colonial tension in Asia. Balfour felt the agreement with Russia might serve to inflame the German Government and stood little chance of helping to lessen international difficulties, nor to resolve Britain's long-standing dispute with Russia over problems in Persia, Tibet and Afghanistan.[12] One of Balfour's most persistent fears was of a war involving Britain against France and Russia combined, which he believed might result in the end of British naval supremacy.[13]

For Balfour, the second-most dangerous rival to Britain's worldwide imperial interests was France, the alliance partner of the Tsarist regime. In January 1899, for example, Balfour described France as an 'incalculable quantity' and 'the most obvious danger to European peace'.[14] In public speeches on Anglo-French relations, Balfour alternated between making friendly comments about French people and disparaging comments about the 'decadent culture' of French society. By and large, Balfour believed, before 1905, that the French were generally hostile to British interests.[15] In 1903, when Balfour asked the Committee of Imperial Defence (CID) to investigate the possibility of a naval invasion of the British Isles, the French navy was defined as the hypothetical invader. The committee concluded, in line with Balfour's own thinking, that the Royal Navy could prevent a French naval invasion without any substantial support from the army.[16]

The signing of the Anglo-Entente, therefore, did not transform Balfour into a Francophile.[17] The Entente, signed in the aftermath of the ill-judged and poorly planned Anglo-Boer War, underlined the overstretched nature of Britain's defence forces. At the outset, Balfour viewed it as a means of ending long-standing Anglo-French colonial quarrels. He made no attempt while he was Prime Minister to convert the Entente into a military alliance. As far as Balfour was concerned, the Entente was designed to put Anglo-French relations on a more friendly footing. It was not designed, although many others thought differently, to divide Europe into two hostile camps or to underwrite a French war of revenge against Germany. Balfour's feelings of uncertainty about the wisdom of drawing Britain into closer alliance with France surfaced once more in June 1905, when Theophile Delcasse, the French Foreign Minister, and chief architect of the Entente, was forced to resign, under pressure from the German Government, in the aftermath of a Franco-German quarrel over trading rights in Morocco. On hearing of Delcasse's resignation, Balfour claimed that France, 'could not be counted on as an effective force in international politics'.[18]

In the early years of opposition, therefore, Balfour doubted that diplomatic agreements alone could provide any real deterrent against the outbreak of a major European war. In 1908, Balfour told a CID sub-committee on invasion that he did not believe the safety of the nation could depend on 'some paper instrument or a mere Entente, however, cordiale it may be'.[19] Nor, in 1906, did Balfour view Anglo-German hostility as a permanent feature of European relations. In fact, throughout most of the period before 1905, Balfour adopted a friendly and sympathetic attitude towards Germany. This 'open-minded stance' towards the growth of German power was a natural counterweight to his negative attitudes towards Russia and France. Balfour always denied that he was 'anti-German'. There is no evidence in his private and public statements on Anglo-German relations to deny the validity of that statement. He supported German unification, even though he did not approve of the 'militaristic methods' by which it was achieved. He was even sympathetic to German demands to create a colonial empire.

Balfour was convinced that a strong and stable Germany in central Europe, enjoying cordial relations with Britain, was likely to act as an effective balance to French and Russian imperial ambitions. His frequent travels to Germany convinced him that Britain could learn a great deal from German social and educational reforms. He admired German music, and he fully acknowledged the major German contribution to science, philosophy and history. Balfour described Kaiser Wilhelm II as, 'the only Royalty I ever met, that was in the least interesting to talk to'.[20] Given these generally pro-German views, it was only natural for Balfour to favour a close diplomatic understanding between Britain and Germany. Balfour thought an Anglo-German war would be 'perfect lunacy' and against the best interests of both nations.[21] Being hostile towards Germany was not something Balfour felt comfortable about. In April 1898, following a discussion with Lord Salisbury on the prospect of an Anglo-German diplomatic agreement, Balfour acknowledged that if an understanding with Germany was reached, 'I should wish to the be one that lent the cheek, not that implanted the kiss'.[22] In 1900, Balfour supported the signing of an Anglo-German trade agreement which dealt with mutual trade in China.[23] In December 1901, Balfour told Lansdowne that if Britain fought in a future European war alongside Germany, 'we should fight for our own interests.' Indeed, Balfour firmly opposed Britain signing any diplomatic arrangement in Europe which saw Germany, 'squeezed to death between the hammer of Russia and the anvil of France'.[24] During the period of the Anglo-Boer War, while most of the Conservative Party were putting forward anti-German views, Balfour continued to argue that the most sensible diplomatic move for Britain was to join the Triple Alliance.[25]

When Balfour became Premier in 1902, his appointment was warmly welcomed in Berlin. He also attempted to further the cause of Anglo-German understanding as Prime Minister. In December 1902, he initially supported an ill-judged Anglo-German naval blockade in Venezuela. He also gave British business the go ahead to cooperate with German engineers in building the Baghdad railway. However, these conciliatory moves, designed to improve Anglo-German relations, provoked a bitter outcry from the right of the Conservative Party, the popular Tory press and a growing 'anti-German' faction at the Foreign Office. A typical 'scaremongering' response came from L.J. Maxse, the editor of the right-wing *National Review*, who claimed that '10 Downing Street was becoming a mere annex of *Wilhelmstrasse*'.[26] Such was the ferocity of anti-German feeling, especially in the press, that Balfour agreed to withdraw British cooperation over Venezuela and from the Baghdad railway project. In spite of these set backs, Balfour still believed that opposition to improved Anglo-German relations in Britain was confined to a small minority of ill-informed 'scaremongers', and he was confident the British public would soon lose interest in 'the German bogey'.[27]

Even so, Balfour began to contemplate after 1903 the possibility of Britain being drawn into a European war to prevent a German mastery of Europe at some future date. In 1904, for example, he admitted that 'Germany is always contemplating the absorption of Holland'. He also conceded that if Germany launched an unprovoked attack on the low countries then 'France and England will have to fight Germany.'[28] In a memorandum, prepared by Balfour, just days after the surprise Japanese naval victory over Russia, he warned the Cabinet that the Russian defeat by Japan might encourage Germany to push ahead with its long-term military aim of dominating eastern Europe. During this German bid for European supremacy, Balfour expected another defeat for France at the hands of the German Army. Accordingly, Balfour recommended that in the event of France being 'suddenly attacked' by Germany, it would be in 'Britain's national interest to support the French'.[29] In the final weeks of 1905, Balfour accepted that in certain circumstances the Anglo-French Entente could develop into a military alliance, but he would 'regret it and would avoid it as long as possible'.[30] In surveying the state of Anglo-German relations at the end of 1905, Balfour acknowledged that a definite 'mistrust' of Germany now existed within certain sections of British society and was of recent origin. He offered three reasons to explain the growth of this Anglo-German antagonism. First, the Kaiser's aggressive actions with France over Morocco in 1905 left a 'painful impression' on public opinion. Second, the planned growth of the German navy had raised a 'genuine concern' that Britain's traditional supremacy at sea might be placed under threat. Third, German statesmen, and many articles in the German press, had started to repeat a constant refrain 'that Britain was standing in the path of German aims'.[31]

Though Balfour recognised that relations between Britain and Germany were worsening, he was unwilling to drag the Conservative Party in an overtly anti-German direction which inflamed relations between the two nations. Even at the end of 1905, Balfour refused to accept that a fundamental clash of interests existed between Britain and Germany, which made war inevitable. On the contrary, Balfour told Sir Frank Lascalles, a leading diplomat, who opposed the growth of anti-German feeling in Britain: 'I have, as you know, never at any time been anti German: and I have regretted the vehemence with which some sections of the English press have expressed their suspicions of German intentions'.[32] Even the growth of the German navy did not initially cause Balfour to lose much sleep. As Balfour remarked to Selborne, 'I find it difficult to believe that we have, as you seem to suppose, much to fear from Germany – in the immediate future'.[33] It is also worth emphasising that Balfour thought it was 'a complete delusion' to argue that Anglo-German trade rivalry was a key source of friction between the two countries.[34] Balfour had always believed that Britain and Germany had always been friendly trading partners, and he told Metternich, the German Ambassador, that most British businessmen were not jealous of German economic strength at all.[35]

During the first two years of Opposition, between 1905 and 1907, Balfour remained well known in public for his pragmatic and generally open-minded attitude towards Germany. He was the self-confessed opponent of the scaremongers. He continued to support cultural interaction between British and German people. To this end, Balfour became a leading patron of the Anglo-German Union Club, set up in 1905 to promote 'friendship between the two countries' and to promote 'the advancement of knowledge, science and art for the common good'. The Anglo-German Union club arranged meetings and dinners between British and German parliamentarians and sponsored a wide range of Anglo-German cultural and sporting events. Balfour attended many of the meetings, dinners and cultural events arranged by the Anglo-German Union Club.[36] Yet Balfour's continuing 'middle-of-the-road' stance towards Germany provoked some stern critical outbursts from leading 'right-wing' newspaper editors and from activists in 'radical right' patriotic pressure groups. These critics claimed that Balfour was failing to take the German threat seriously enough. Balfour did little to appease these right wing critics by dismissing the notion of a German naval invasion of the British Isles as 'an impossibility'.[37] In parliament, Balfour continued to urge caution on his front bench colleagues whenever they publicly discussed Anglo-German relations.[38]

Between 1906 and 1908, however, Balfour came under increasing pressure from his right wing critics to modify his view on the possibility of a German invasion. In public, Balfour attempted to pacify his critics by suggesting that his views on the question of invasion of the British Isles had been misquoted. He also insisted that naval defence had to be kept under constant review.[39] In private, however, Balfour did not regard a German naval invasion as even a remote possibility, as long as the channel fleet remained in a position of supremacy in the North Sea. There was, in fact, a clear consistency in Balfour's attitude towards invasion. In December 1902, Balfour informed the Cabinet that a 'sudden surprise barbaric attack' by 'alien aggressors' was 'completely out of the question'.[40] This view was repeated in most of Balfour's subsequent speeches on the subject. In reaching this conclusion, Balfour was greatly influenced by Admiral Sir John Fisher, the First Lord of the Admiralty and the leading naval 'expert' of the Edwardian period. Fisher was reportedly once told by his doctor that he had so much mental energy: 'he should have been twins'.[41] In November 1907, 'Jacky' Fisher, in a provocative speech, aimed at Balfour's right-wing critics, urged the British people to 'sleep quiet in your beds' and 'do not to be disturbed by these bogeys about invasion and otherwise which are being periodically resuscitated by all sorts of leagues'.[42] Although Balfour disapproved of the confrontational nature of Fisher's speech, he was fully in agreement with his point of view. Sir George Clark, another confidante of Balfour on naval matters, and a leading figure in the CID, warned the Conservative leader that his right-wing critics were trying to create 'a German scare' in order to raise doubts about Balfour's long-standing sceptical views on invasion.[43]

Lord Roberts, the 'most famous soldier' of the Edwardian age and the leader of the National Service League certainly did believe in a German invasion and he constantly pressed Balfour to lead the Conservative Party in a vigorous campaign to alert the public of the danger Britain now faced from the startling growth of German naval power.[44] In September 1906, Clark was anxiously informing Balfour that a majority of the Conservative Party now believed his 'invasion is impossible' speech was no longer credible.[45] Throughout the summer of 1907, Roberts, and his supporters in the National Service League, asked Balfour to put pressure on the Liberal Government to call a second inquiry on invasion.[46] Lord Midleton also pressed Balfour to support a new invasion inquiry, because 'the facts on which you made your celebrated statement, have either considerably altered, or are not applicable to Germany', adding, in a direct sideswipe at Fisher, 'I cannot sleep safely in my bed'.[47] By the end of 1907, Colonel Repington, The Times Military Correspondent, and a key adviser to Lord Roberts on the question of invasion, reported, in a triumphalist tone: 'We have been able to push Balfour much further than we dared hope'.[48] Balfour decided to support the demand by the right to re-open the invasion question for three reasons. First, he feared that the Liberal Government was taking the policy of 'naval economy' too far. Second, he was persuaded that the growth of German naval power required consideration by the CID. Third, and most importantly, Balfour was confident a new investigation into the question of invasion would confirm the validity of his original argument and thereby help to defuse the invasion lobby within the Conservative Party and weaken the position of his right wing critics in the popular Tory press.[49]

Asquith, lobbied effectively by Lord Esher, agreed to mount a new investigation of invasion by a sub-committee of the CID, whose meetings would be held in private and whose findings would not be binding on the Liberal Government.[50] The second sub-committee on invasion regarded Germany as the hypothetical invader and held its first meeting on 27 November 1907. Fisher was not best pleased with the decision to re-open the invasion question by what he called 'an irresponsible committee'.[51] Selborne believed that Fisher would use the inquiry as an opportunity to silence his right wing critics.[52] Only two days after the first session of the sub-committee had been held, the First Lord of the Admiralty was pleading with Balfour to give evidence to the sub-committee, in order to, 'smash the invasion bogey for good'.[53] In May 1908, Balfour gave detailed evidence. The views of Balfour, as presented to the sub-committee on invasion are very important because they offer a clear and behind-closed-doors expression of the Opposition leader's views on the German naval threat in the spring of 1908. Balfour began his evidence by denying he had ever said the invasion of the British Isles could be prevented by naval power alone. He said a new investigation of invasion was necessary because of the rapid growth of German naval power. Even more significant was Balfour's admission that his previous 'open-minded' attitude towards Germany had undergone some change. He expressed apprehension about the immense preparations made by the German navy, and although he considered himself 'one of those most reluctant ever to believe in the German scare', he now accepted that 'every German thinks the enemy is England'. This clear acceptance by Balfour of the danger posed to British naval supremacy by the German fleet did not, however, lead to any change in his fundamental views on invasion. On the contrary, Balfour rejected the view of Lord Roberts, who had earlier told the sub-committee that it was possible for Germany to mount a 'bolt from the blue' attack on the British Isles. Balfour did not believe such an attack was possible, not because he did not take the German naval threat seriously, but because he was aware of the logistical difficulties involved for any potential naval invader of the British mainland. As a result, Balfour dismissed the idea that Germany could, or would, mount an unprovoked invasion before war had been declared.[54] In conclusion, Balfour told the sub-committee that a German naval invasion of the British Isles was 'an impossible operation', given the present strength of the Royal Navy.[55] Lord Esher informed the King that members of the sub-committee were 'astounded by Balfour's command of the subject'.[56]

Balfour's view that Royal Navy was too strong for any foreign power, including Germany, to mount a successful invasion was the major conclusion of sub-committee report, published in November 1908.[57] However, Balfour's impressive presentation of his views on invasion to the sub-committee on invasion did recognise the long-term threat which German naval power posed to British naval supremacy.

It is worth emphasising that the rapid growth of the German navy from 1906 onwards was the root cause of the transformation of Balfour's views towards Germany.[58] He began to have major philosophical doubts about the underlying aims of German policy. He started to accept the view that the extension of the German naval programme was essentially a provocative attempt to challenge British sea power. At the end of 1908, Balfour was predicting that German shipyards would be in a position to produce battleships at a faster rate than in Britain within four years. Balfour's growing alarm over the German naval threat at the end of 1908 was witnessed by Lady Selborne who found Balfour, 'much pre-occupied by the German scare' and seemingly convinced: 'the Germans are determined to sweep us out of the way'.[59] In October 1908, Kaiser Wilhelm added to Balfour's growing anxiety by excitedly telling a *Daily Telegraph* reporter that there was a 'widespread hatred' of Britain in Germany.[60] In January 1909, Lord Balcarres, the Conservative Chief Whip, commented of Balfour's growing anxiety about the growth of German power, 'the chief is ... nervous about the state of the navy, really frightened about the actual disposition of the fleet, still more about its prospects for the future'.[61]

Throughout the early months of 1909, Balfour, greatly influenced by the deterioration of Anglo-German relations during 1908, adopted an uncharacteristically aggressive tone towards the naval spending plans of the Liberal Government. In March 1909, a full-scale row between the two major political parties over naval spending was triggered off during the naval estimates debate, when Reginald McKenna announced that the Liberal Government would only sanction the building of four new dreadnoughts now, and four later, if the need arose, but would not order the eight new battleships which the Admiralty felt were necessary to keep ahead of the German ship-building programme.

During the naval estimates debate of March 1909, Balfour led a vigorous Conservative campaign designed to put pressure on the Liberal Government to immediately sanction the building of all eight battleships.[62] Balfour, departing from his usual faithful adherence to the bi-partisanship on defence questions, accused the Liberal Government of compromising naval defence.[63] Asquith dismissed the Conservative naval agitation in the House of Commons as 'scaremongering'. In private, Esher told Balfour that he was 'pushing at an open door' by demanding that Asquith agree to build all eight ships.[64] To keep the naval agitation going, therefore, Balfour called for a motion of censure against the naval policy of the Liberal Government, which was held on 22 March 1909.[65] In the debate on the censure motion, Sir Edward Grey accused Balfour of unashamedly pandering to the scaremongers in his own party by 'dragging the navy into the arena of party politics'.[66] In response, Balfour claimed that if Asquith had agreed to build all eight ships, he could have relied on the loyal support of the Opposition. By refusing to do so, claimed Balfour, especially during a 'dangerous phase' of the Anglo-German naval race, the Liberal Government was responsible for the bitter Government–Opposition dispute on the navy.[67] The motion of censure, however, was rejected by 353 votes to 135, and the 'naval panic', which had dominated British politics for over a fortnight during March 1909, soon burned itself out. Once the dust had settled, Balfour told Esher that a matter as serious as the Anglo-German naval race should not have been allowed to degenerate into 'a daily diet of scare stories in the press'.[68]

During the naval panic of 1909, Balfour was voicing his own growing private anxiety about the German naval threat which had built up throughout 1908 rather than making political capital out the naval issue. Balfour was also attempting to pressurise Asquith to resist the demands of 'little navy group' within the Liberal Party for further naval cuts. In July 1909, the Liberal Government decided to build all eight ships. Liberal radicals claimed that Asquith had given in to 'the coercive policy' of the Opposition. Balfour was delighted by the decision, because it seemed to vindicate his own strong stand during the naval debates and helped to restore the bi-partisan consensus. In July 1909, in a speech in the House of Commons, Balfour praised Asquith for the decision to build all eight ships and concluded that the defence of the Empire was once more 'in safe hands'.[69] The naval estimates debate of 1910, which saw the Liberal Government announce increased naval expenditure, was held in a calm and restrained atmosphere. By July 1914, Balfour was advising Lord Selborne that he had no reason to attack the Liberal Government in the forthcoming naval estimates debate 'because nothing has come to my attention at the Defence Committee to suggest cuts in the navy'.[70]

By the end of 1909, however, Balfour's views on Germany had been transformed from the open-minded attitude of the early years of the century, alluded to earlier in this chapter, to a well and truly established fear of German aims. One further illustration of this view is a detailed and very important secret memorandum written by Balfour in December 1910 on the current state of Anglo-German relations.[71] In the memorandum, which Balfour circulated to leading members of his 'inner circle' and to Bonar Law, he admits that he had become suspicious of the 'unscrupulous diplomatic methods and aims of Germany's foreign policy'. However, the economic and military growth of Germany in the late nineteenth century did not cause him anxiety, or enmity, because German power at that time was based on a formidable army, with foreign policy aims concentrated in Europe. It was the growth of the German navy, accompanied by the provocative policy of *Weltpolitik*, which indicated to Balfour that the British Empire had been selected by Germany's rulers as the major obstacle in the path of Germany's desire for a world-wide Empire. This interpretation of the aims of German foreign policy seemed justified, argued Balfour, because the Kaiser had continually rejected every British and European offer to limit the growth in naval armaments and constantly stressed that war between Britain and Germany was

'inevitable'. In Balfour's view, the only plausible and logical explanation for German naval construction was to mount a challenge to
British naval supremacy, with the ultimate aim of eclipsing it. The
growth of Germany's costly fleet of battleships led Balfour to conclude that 'Germany is preparing for war', and to a firm conviction
that 'Germany wants war'. As a consequence, Balfour predicted that
Germany could be expected to try and divide France and Russia and
also to make strenuous efforts to undermine the Anglo-French
Entente. By the end of 1910, therefore, Balfour was convinced that
German foreign policy threatened Britain's long-term interests and
was leading inexorably towards war.

The Agadir crisis of 1911, which raised the possibility of Britain
being drawn into a war over Franco-German differences in Morocco,
served to intensify Balfour's existing fears about German aims. During
the Agadir crisis, Balfour concluded that the chief aim of British
foreign policy must be to uphold the balance of power in Europe.[72] In
September 1911, Balfour assured David Lloyd George, the Chancellor
of the Exchequer, that if the Agadir crisis developed into war 'the
Opposition will certainly not cause you any embarrassment'.[73] Balfour
felt that support for Grey during the Agadir crisis was a 'patriotic
duty', and he did not request any privileged information in return. In
fact, Balfour claimed, 'it came as a shock of surprise – I am far from
saying of disapproval – when I found how rapidly after I left office,
the Entente had, under the German menace, developed into something resembling a defensive understanding'.[74] He told Count Albert
von Mensdorf, the Austro-Hungarian Ambassador to London that at
times of international crisis the Prime Minister and Opposition leader
did meet to exchange information, but at these meetings he never
requested any privileged information or attempted to influence the
foreign policy adopted by the Government.[75]

Balfour's resignation as Opposition Leader in November 1911 did
not greatly reduce his powerful influence within the Conservative
Party over foreign and defence matters. He remained an influential
adviser to Bonar Law, who always consulted him on questions related
to national defence and foreign affairs. Balfour's views on foreign and
defence issues were also sought by the leading figures in the Liberal
Government. At the end of May 1912, for example, Balfour had
dinner with Winston Churchill, the First Lord of the Admiralty, and
told him that such had been the transformation of his views on

Germany that he now favoured the Anglo-French Entente being turned into military alliance. When Sir Edward Grey, the Foreign Secretary, heard this startling news, he instantly wrote to Balfour and invited him to prepare a detailed memorandum outlining his views on the current state of European relations.[76]

Meanwhile, during the summer of 1912, Balfour decided to make public his growing anxiety about the German threat. For Balfour, who had always assiduously avoided stoking up the fires of Anglo-German antagonism, this was quite a dramatic move. In June 1912, Balfour wrote an article entitled 'Anglo-German relations', which appeared in a leading German periodical called *Nord and Sud*. In the article, Balfour explained to his German readers that the recent actions of Germany in Agadir had led the 'average Englishman' to believe that German foreign policy was inevitably leading in the direction of war.[77] The German press attacked Balfour for putting all the blame for the deterioration of Anglo-German relations on the shoulders of the German Government while ignoring the scaremongering activities of many Conservative newspapers, politicians and pressure groups. In response, Balfour complained that the German press had blown up, out of all proportion, what he felt were quite reasonable comments about the current state of Anglo-German relations.[78] Maxse wrote of the controversy over Balfour's *Nord and Sud* article in the *National Review*,

> Mr. Balfour has never been anything but an optimist, and he has habitually treated wars, and rumours of wars, as the stock-in-trade of sensational journalism and as unworthy of the notice of responsible statesmen. This makes his contribution to *Nord and Sud* all the more remarkable, and it may be some consolation to the readers of the *National Review*, – who must at times ... wonder whether its editor ought not to be shut up as an irresponsible person who had got 'Germany on the Brain' – to find that Mr. Balfour's views in all essentials coincide with the opinions of German policy which has been set forth month after month and year after year in *National Review* since the opening of the century.[79]

In July 1912, Balfour gave a speech in the House of Commons on the current state of tension in Europe, in which he claimed that Germany was 'steadily and remorselessly' menacing the Royal Navy.

Even more startling was Balfour's blunt admission that he now welcomed the rigid division of Europe into two power blocs consisting of the Triple Entente and the Triple Alliance because he felt that, 'no power would be so stupid as to involve itself in an offensive war in a cause which it had no quarrel'.[80] This speech illustrates how far the ex-Conservative leader's views had moved in a pro-French direction in response to the German naval threat and the provocative actions of the Kaiser during the Agadir crisis.

In November 1912, Balfour informed Grey that he now thought the Anglo-French Entente was now a 'totally unsatisfactory' device to contain the German threat. The best way to persuade the Kaiser that Britain was deadly serious in its commitment towards France, argued Balfour, was to establish a firm military alliance between the two countries, which would help to improve military planning and obstruct any German attempt to undermine the existing Anglo-French agreement. The only condition which Balfour believed should be inserted into his proposed Anglo-French alliance was for British participation in a European war to be conditional on an unprovoked attack by Germany on French territory.[81] Hence Balfour now believed that the key aim of British foreign policy was to 'save France from destruction' by German military power in Europe.[82] In December 1912, Balfour informed Bonar Law of his support for an Anglo-French military alliance.[83] However, the proposal was not supported by Lord Lansdowne unless Grey was also willing to support the idea.[84] In the end, Grey decided not to transform the Entente into a formal military alliance. This decision was accepted by the Conservative leadership without further comment. Balfour agreed to keep private his own support for an Anglo-French alliance in the interests of upholding the bi-partisan consensus on foreign policy.

Another indication of how firmly Balfour felt that Britain's national interests were bound up with those of France was the strong support he gave between 1911 and 1914 for the British Expeditionary Force to be sent to France immediately upon the outbreak of a European War. In November 1912, Balfour told Bonar Law that the major task of the British Army was no longer be the defence of India, or even the defence of the British Isles against invasion, but to supply a fully equipped expeditionary force whose main aim was to defend France and the Low Countries from a German attack.[85] To all these increasingly pro-French sentiments by Balfour should be added the observation of the German Ambassador, who noticed that Balfour openly expressed decidedly pro-French views during his own frequent conversations with the former Conservative leader between 1911 and 1914.[86]

The bi-partisan consensus on foreign and defence policy, which Balfour had done so much to encourage as Conservative leader, was enhanced still further by Asquith's decision to invite Balfour to join the third CID sub-committee examination of the question of invasion, which took place between January 1913 and April 1914. It was quite a unique development for a sitting Government to invite a member of the Opposition into the secret discussion of the technical details of defence strategy. The third invasion inquiry concentrated on the question of whether new innovations in naval technology had made the possibility of a German invasion more likely. Balfour once again played a deeply influential role. Sir Maurice Hankey, the secretary of the CID described a typical meeting of the sub-committee in the following way: 'Suddenly the door opened, and Balfour's loose figure sauntered into the room, and he sat down beside the P.M. He almost immediately grasped the point at issue and there and then set about drafting the paragraph which brought the committee together'.[87] The final report of the sub-committee reflected Balfour's view that new advances in naval technology gave much greater protection to defensive forces, thereby making a German invasion a 'contingency not to be expected'. However, the final report added weight to Balfour's idea of an Anglo-French military alliance by stressing that an invasion of the British Isles was more likely if Britain ended up at war with German without any French support.[88]

By the summer of 1914, therefore, A.J. Balfour, who had considered himself 'the last person to believe in the German threat' in 1905 and who had constantly emphasised that Britain should not be animated in its relations with Germany by 'jealously or enmity', was fully prepared to support France in the event of an unprovoked attack by Germany in western Europe.[89] The single-most profound cause of the transformation of Balfour's attitude towards Germany was the expansion of a German navy, deployed in the North Sea, which represented a clear challenge to Britain's naval supremacy, and ultimately to Britain's national and imperial interests and Germany's provocative actions during the Agadir crisis. As a result, it is important to stress that Balfour's view of Germany was transformed between 1905 and

1914, to a very large degree, by his own negative interpretation of German actions and by a growing conviction that German policy aimed to challenge the maritime balance of power, en route to threatening Britain's security by challenging the balance of power in Europe. In Balfour's view, only by maintaining naval supremacy and saving France from military defeat by Germany could the British Empire hope to survive. Given these views, Balfour was highly likely to support British involvement in a European war which aimed to prevent German domination of Europe at any time after the latter months of 1910.

3
Leadership: (2) Andrew Bonar Law and Anglo-German Relations

Andrew Bonar Law is a mysterious and enigmatic political figure whose career as Conservative leader was sandwiched between two more well-known contemporaries, Balfour and Stanley Baldwin, and overshadowed by the dominating figure of David Lloyd George. Even the titles of two of the major biographies of Law, *The Strange Case of Andrew Bonar Law* and *The Unknown Prime Minister*, reinforce the elusive nature of his political career.[1] Even his biographers make no grandiose claims about his contribution to the history of the Conservative Party. Taylor suggests that there is scant evidence of 'inspiration' in Bonar Law's political career,[2] while Blake concludes by stating that Bonar Law, 'never had a brilliant or original mind' and followed 'the Party's instincts' on most of the important issues of the day.[3] To examine Bonar Law's views on domestic politics is to enter a neglected area of historical research, but to analyse his views and policy towards Anglo-German relations between 1905 and 1914 is to enter a historiographical wilderness.

The election of Bonar Law as Conservative Leader in November 1911 was something of a surprise but was not completely unexpected. He had only been elected to parliament in 1900, had not been a Cabinet minister, and he was only promoted to the Shadow Cabinet in 1911. In the leadership contest, the front runners were Austen Chamberlain, a prominent supporter of tariff reform, and Walter Long, the representative of the landed interest, with views on tariff reform not greatly different from the increasingly unpopular Balfour. It was the mutual animosity between Austen Chamberlain and Walter Long that allowed Bonar Law to gain the leadership as the compromise candidate.

The issue which most concerned Bonar Law during his time as Opposition leader between 1911 and 1914 was not foreign or defence policy, but the bitter Conservative opposition to the introduction of Irish Home Rule. As Opposition leader, he developed a blunt and uncompromising debating style, dubbed by his Liberal opponents as the 'New Style' to distinguish it from the detached leadership style of Balfour. But Bonar Law's aggressive approach to domestic issues was underpinned by a deep sense of patriotism, which showed itself more fully when he dealt with foreign and defence questions.

The background and early life of Bonar Law was certainly very different from that of Balfour. Andrew Bonar Law was born on 16 September 1858 in New Brunswick, Canada. He was the son of James Law, an Ulster born, Presbyterian minister, who died in 1877 and Elizabeth Annie Kidston, who came from a wealthy Scottish family of iron merchants. Law's mother died suddenly in 1860 when he was only two years old. Janet Kidston, his aunt, travelled to Canada after hearing the news of her sister's sudden death in order to assume the role of surrogate mother to young Andrew. In 1870, when James Law re-married, he allowed his sister-in-law to take Bonar Law, with whom she had obviously developed a very close relationship, to live with her family in Helensburgh, a small, close-knit village, 25 miles north-west of Glasgow. The Kidston household consisted of the successful businessmen William and Charles Kidston who were partners in William Kidston and Sons, leading merchant bankers to the iron and steel trade.[4] Bonar Law attended the prestigious Glasgow high school.[5] During his time at school, he took an active role in political debating societies and revealed above average ability in both language studies and history. At 16, he left school to pursue a commercial career in the Kidston family business.

Bonar Law is often portrayed as 'a successful industrialist' or as a 'businessman in politics', but his successful commercial career owed much more to family patronage than any original business talent.[6] He was no 'self-made man', and he prospered through nepotism as much as Balfour. To begin with, the junior partnership that Bonar Law was offered in 1885 from William Jacks and Company, a firm of Glasgow iron merchants, was arranged for him by the Kidston family. Even Bonar Law's financial independence, which allowed him to undertake a career in national politics, was constantly boosted by family bequests totalling £63,000, which was a very hefty sum of money in the late Victorian age. In 1891, he married Annie Pitcairn Robley, the daughter of a prominent Glasgow shipbroker.[7]

Bonar Law was a dour, sober, family man, who drank nothing stronger than milk and had few really close friends. He was the essence of the no frills career politician from a business background. In 1900, he was elected Conservative MP for the Blackfriars constituency in Glasgow at the comparatively late age of 42.[8] Yet he rose rapidly, primarily because his speeches on trade issues displayed an impressive grasp of economic facts and figures. In 1902, he was appointed as parliamentary secretary at the Board of Trade, a post which he held until the Conservatives left office in December 1905.

The dominating issue of Bonar Law's political career before he became Opposition leader in 1911 was tariff reform. 'At the time I entered the House', he confessed in 1914, 'the very essence of my political belief was belief in Mr. Chamberlain'.[9] After the election defeat of 1906, it was his expert knowledge of tariff reform which enabled him to emerge as one of the most prominent figures among the generally dispirited Conservative opposition. As party leader from 1911 to 1914 it was the opposition to Irish Home Rule that became his central preoccupation.

Given this, it is often routinely argued by historians that Bonar Law was completely uninterested in foreign affairs.[10] In actual fact, Bonar Law took a very keen interest in the economic and the defence aspects of Anglo-German relations. What is not widely known is that he was a fluent speaker and reader of the German language. In the 1890s, as the Chairman of the Glasgow Iron Trade Association, he developed close relations with German traders, bankers and engineers. At William Jacks, he built up a thriving Anglo-German trade for the company. It was during the 1890s that Bonar Law observed at first hand the remarkable growth of German imports. He saw the German economic threat as a real one, which had affected the profitability of his own business and his determination for Britain to follow the German lead by introducing protectionism to protect British industry provided the stimulus for his support of tariff reform. Such was the depth of Bonar Law's interest in Anglo-German trade relations that he took out annual subscriptions to most of the leading German trade and economic periodicals. He also became an avid reader of the works of the leading contemporary German economists. J.L. Garvin, the editor of the *Observer*, once visited Law and found him reading an obscure book by Adolph Wagner, a major German economic thinker, in the original German edition.[11]

In 1911, Bonar Law admitted, 'I have many German friends, I love German books, almost as much as our favourites in our own tongue, and I can imagine few, if any, calamities which would seem so great as a war, whatever the result, between us and the Germany people'.[12] At Westminster, he engaged in many cultural and diplomatic interactions with German diplomats, business people and parliamentarians. He was an active member of the Anglo-German Union Club, and he attended many of the meetings which the club arranged between British and German businessmen. Law was also a frequent guest at many of the Anglo-German dinners arranged by the German Embassy. In addition, he was also actively involved in a number of Anglo-German charitable projects. He was, for example, the guest of honour at a special dinner for the opening of an Anglo-German hospital at Dalston in 1913.[13] In his key-note speech at this function, he emphasised to his Anglo-German audience his long-standing admiration for the commercial abilities of the German people, and he led a toast 'to the health of the Kaiser', whose views he said 'were often mis-represented as antagonistic towards Britain' by certain 'irresponsible' sections of the popular press.[14] Of course, these friendly comments about Germany can be interpreted as the despairing attempt of an ardent tariff reformer to correct the general impression that most supporters of protectionism within the Conservative Party were anti-German scaremongers. In Bonar Law's case, however, this interpretation cannot fully explain the consistency of his friendly comments about Germany, his continuing friendly interaction with German people and his deep interest in German economic affairs. Bonar Law was a blunt, but honest man and certainly no scaremonger in public on the German threat. He did genuinely admire the German economic system, he did have many German friends and he was genuinely in favour of friendly relations between Britain and Germany. War, he believed, was definitely bad for business.

It was the economic relations of Britain and Germany which most consistently engaged Bonar Law's attention whenever he discussed Anglo-German relations. During the early stages of the Tariff Reform League, between 1903 and 1905, the growth of German imports and alleged 'unfair' German trading practices, most notably, dumping and cartel arrangements, featured most prominently in his speeches on tariff reform. After 1906, however, Anglo-German trade rivalry ceased to be a dominant theme of most of his speeches on the tariff question. Instead, Bonar Law's presentation of the Opposition case in favour of tariff reform in parliamentary debate concentrated on the 'folly of the Liberal Party for remaining committed to free trade' within a world market becoming dominated by nations with protectionist policies.[15] It was an argument designed to rouse the Opposition and attack the Liberal Government. To this end, Bonar Law greeted every new tariff increase by a 'foreign' or colonial Government as part of a world-wide economic trend in favour of tariff reform which he felt Britain should follow.[16] Bonar Law's attitude towards Germany in these speeches was surprisingly conciliatory, and he did not use trade rivalry to inflame Anglo-German relations, and he frequently insisted, 'I have no ill will towards Germany'.[17]

Bonar Law's many public speeches on Anglo-German trade relations from 1905 to 1914 were full of friendly, constructive and positive comments about German social and economic methods. Bonar Law also frequently dismissed the Liberal Party claim that free trade equalled cordial Anglo-German relations, while the adoption of tariff reform would serve to intensify Anglo-German antagonism.[18] In Bonar Law's view, what most harmed the friendly relations between Britain and Germany were the frequent negative and disparaging remarks made by leading Liberals concerning the German way of life. Many leading figures in the Liberal Government, in highlighting the benefits of free trade, often claimed most Germans lived in what amounted to a military training camp and enjoyed a very poor standard of living, often existing on a meagre diet whose staple constituents were 'black bread and horsemeat'. In response, Bonar Law claimed that German 'black bread' had a much higher nutritional value than British white bread.[19] The important point to stress, therefore, is that Bonar Law depicted the German fiscal system and the German way of life as a role model and a positive advertisement for the policy of protective tariffs.

The use of statistical comparisons between important aspects of the British and German standard of living was another key feature of Bonar Law's presentation of the Opposition case in favour of tariff reform. In this numbers game, Bonar Law always portrayed Germany in positive terms.[20] In particular, he claimed that the condition of the working class in protectionist Germany was 'incredible', with wage rises for the average workers 'greater than in any other country' and with an unemployment rate which stood 4 per cent below the British level.[21] He also claimed German productivity levels were also higher. In December 1908, for example, he pointed out that while the German production of iron and steel between 1905 and 1908 had increased sharply by 50 per cent, British production during the same period had completely stagnated.[22] It was also typical of Bonar Law to praise German business for transforming the German economy from being an exporter of raw materials into a modern high-tech producer of manufactured goods.[23] In putting forward these friendly views, Bonar Law's main aim was to win the tariff reform versus free trade argument within the British domestic political debate. Even so, what he said did not inflame Anglo-German relations.

When Bonar Law became Conservative Leader in November 1911, he was forced to examine the broader aspects of Anglo-German relations and to examine them outside the framework of the party political cut and thrust of domestic politics. He did not allow his admiration for German economic methods to influence or determine his attitude towards the diplomatic, naval and military aspects of the Anglo-German relationship. His preoccupation with Anglo-German commercial relations, combined with his lack of detailed knowledge of foreign and defence matters ensured that on those issues Bonar Law needed to seek advice and to consult more fully with leading members of the Conservative 'inner circle' on foreign and defence policy bequeathed to him by Balfour. A few days after being appointed leader, Law admitted to Balcarres that he felt a great 'sense of responsibility' whenever he discussed foreign and defence affairs as 'he had never heard these issues discussed in Cabinet'.[24]

Bonar Law is best described as a 'realist' on foreign affairs and defence questions, who believed that 'the only security for peace is that each country should recognise the strength of the other, and should realise too, that ... each nation is prepared to defend to the last her rights and her honour.'[25] In his very rare public speeches on foreign affairs as Conservative leader, Bonar Law also displayed a very friendly attitude towards Germany which differed little from the point of view he expressed on tariff reform. In January 1912, Bonar Law summed up his view of Anglo-German relations in the following way:

> I do not think there is a man inside the House, or out of it, who is
> more anxious for a good understanding with Germany than I am,
> and I do not think there is anyone who would look with more
> horror than I upon a war between the two countries.[26]

Away from the public gaze, Bonar Law expressed some anxiety
about the German naval and military threat, and he reluctantly
accepted that the Anglo-French Entente was a necessary means of
upholding the balance of power on the European continent.[27] By the
time he became leader, he fully recognised that British foreign policy
had made a 'clear and unmistakable' commitment to France in the
event of a European war.[28]

If those on the 'radical right' of the Conservative Party outside
Westminster expected Bonar Law to adopt a belligerent 'scaremongering' approach to the German threat when he became leader, they
were very soon disappointed. Bonar Law never allowed the acrimony
which he displayed on domestic issues such as Ireland to spill over
into public discussions of Anglo-German relations. It soon became
clear the principle of bi-partisanship on foreign affairs, which had
been such a central feature of Balfour's approach to foreign policy,
was fully supported by his successor. In his very first speech on foreign
affairs, he promised the Conservative Party under his leadership
would never 'try to gain party advantage from the discussion of
foreign affairs'. He also promised that the Opposition would not criticise Government foreign policy 'if we believe there is any danger of
our criticism weakening our position among the other great powers'.[29]
Indeed, Asquith, the Prime Minister, often wished that Bonar Law
would transfer his restrained language on foreign and defence matters
to his often rough handling of domestic issues.[30]

At the same time, Bonar Law, who had assumed the party leadership
after the Conservatives had sustained a third successive electoral
defeat, was fully aware of the high level of criticism which had existed
over Balfour's subtle, evasive and elitist handling of party affairs. One
of the features of Conservative Party affairs in 1911 was the growth of
splinter organisations, outside the formal party machinery, including
groups such as the National Service League and the Imperial Maritime
League which were concerned with Balfour's even-handed handling

of foreign and defence affairs. One of the most frequent criticisms of Balfour by both of these groups, and among many backbench MPs, was his alleged failure to consult the party on its general attitude towards foreign and defence policy.[31]

In the early days of Bonar Law's leadership, therefore, there was pressure for the new leader to listen more to the party rank and file opinion on all issues. A great deal of uncertainty still existed within the party over the Anglo-French Entente. Was it a purely colonial agreement? or as many desired, 'a vital means of keeping war-mongering Germany encircled and powerless?'[32] Leopold Amery, a Conservative MP, later recalled that although there was general support for the Anglo-French Entente, very few Conservative backbench MPs had any real understanding of how loose Britain's obligations were to France in the event of a German attack.[33]

Even more uncertainty existed within the party over the Anglo-Russian Convention, the second pivot of Grey's foreign policy. Lord Lansdowne observed that most ordinary Tory MPs were 'inclined to look at its details with a critical eye'.[34] After the Agadir crisis in 1911, however, many Conservatives started to look more favourably on the agreement with Tsarist Russia. One prominent supporter of this view was Austen Chamberlain who believed that Conservative support for the Anglo-Russian agreement was a vital counterbalance to constant Liberal hostility towards it.[35] The most significant Conservative critic of the agreement with Russia was the former Viceroy of India, Lord Curzon, who suggested that Britain had already made far too many concessions in Persia in return for a 'very vague and ill defined promise' of Russian 'good will'.[36] Similarly, Mark Sykes, a Conservative MP argued that a pro-Russian foreign policy would damage British trade and help to drive Turkey into the hands of the German Empire.[37]

In the face of such uncertainty within the Conservative Party over the details of British foreign policy and in a move designed to placate backbench opinion over the perceived elitist approach on foreign and defence matters of his predecessor, Bonar Law instructed Lord Balcarres, the Conservative Chief Whip to consult the parliamentary party, with a view to defining its general attitude towards foreign affairs. After sounding out all sections of backbench opinion, Balcarres reported to Bonar Law that there was universal support among Conservative MPs for the Anglo-French Entente and a generally supportive, though somewhat more sceptical, attitude towards improved relations with Russia. Balcarres summed up the general attitude of the Conservative Party on foreign affairs in the following way:

> We have supported Grey for six years on the assumption he continues the Anglo-French Entente which Lord Lansdowne established, and the Anglo-Russian Entente which Lord Lansdowne inspired. Without our help he would have retired a long time ago. We are entitled to ask for assurances that he adheres to our generally agreed policy.[38]

The very idea of consulting backbenchers on foreign policy, something Balfour would never have even contemplated clearly illustrates that Bonar Law wanted to demonstrate to the Conservative Party at Westminster that whenever he spoke on foreign policy he was articulating a generally agreed attitude rather than articulating a view of the leader and his 'inner circle' which the party was expected to accept without dissent. Yet the act of consultation by Bonar Law with the party rank and file should not be interpreted as a sign that his views on foreign policy as leader were ever determined by backbench pressure. On the contrary, Bonar Law habitually disregarded backbench pressure when deciding the Opposition line on foreign and defence policy, and his penchant for greater consultation was really a shrewd tactical device designed to unite the party and give the impression of greater party democracy on foreign and defence policy than really existed in practice.

It was not backbench pressure that determined Bonar Law's approach to foreign policy but the advice of Lord Lansdowne. He also continued with Balfour's much criticised practice of managing foreign and defence matters through a small 'inner circle' of ex-ministers and close advisers. It was really 'business as usual' as far as foreign and defence matters were concerned. Even the composition of Bonar Law's 'inner circle' on foreign and defence policy was exactly the same as under Balfour. It became even smaller, because when Lord Cawdor died in 1911 and George Wyndham died two years later, they were not replaced. Under the leadership of Bonar Law, therefore, the articulation of Opposition policy on foreign and defence matters was conducted much more by peers in the House of Lords than had even been the case under Balfour.

Bonar Law, aware of his own lack of experience, relied heavily on the advice of Lord Lansdowne on foreign and defence affairs. He commented of his relationship with the ex-Foreign Secretary on foreign affairs thus: 'I shall, of course always consult him, as I have consulted him today, before making any statement on foreign affairs.'[39] All the available evidence suggests the advice of Lansdowne on foreign and defence matters was the most decisive influence on the line which Bonar Law adopted. In Lord Lansdowne's view, foreign policy had to be decided by the Conservative inner circle in private and 'the party and the public could make of it what they will'.[40] This was certainly the approach which Bonar Law adopted prior to the delivery of his first major speech on foreign policy in November 1911, but more generally, it explains his general conduct of policy making on foreign and defence policy as Opposition leader. Before making his key speech in the famous Agadir debate, Bonar Law asked Lansdowne to prepare for him a detailed set of briefing notes, outlining the central elements of Conservative foreign policy. In reply, Lansdowne wrote, 'The Entente does not, strictly speaking, bind us to more than mere support of the French government', but he added that 'it would be inconsistent with British interests, and dangerous to the peace of the world and to the balance of power to allow a friendly nation like France to be crushed'.[41] To ensure no embarrassment was caused by the Opposition to Sir Edward Grey, the Foreign Secretary, in the Agadir debate, Bonar Law actually discussed the content of his speech with Sir William Tyrell, Grey's private secretary at the Foreign Office. This was a ringing endorsement of the bi-partisan consensus which Balfour has established.[42] What is even less well known is that Tyrell met Bonar Law regularly from 1911 to 1914 and kept him fully briefed 'off the record' on important foreign policy developments. Bonar Law claimed he was 'astounded' by the amount of secret information which Tyrell passed on to him about foreign and defence policy developments at these meetings.[43]

During the Agadir debate, Bonar Law emphasised that the Conservative Party would 'never under any circumstances attempt to gain party advantage from the discussion of foreign policy'. He also emphasised that the entente 'had been of immense value to this country' because it had acted as 'deterrent' to the outbreak of war.[44] Even so, Bonar Law never promised the Liberal Government in public or in private that the Opposition would support a war to save France 'in all circumstances'. On the contrary, he stressed the leadership would decide on the circumstances surrounding any particular conflict and then decide if British intervention was in the 'national interest'. Law also insisted that if a major war did eventually break out between Britain and Germany, it would not be due to 'irresistible forces' but to 'the want of human wisdom'.[45]

The major focal point of Anglo-German rivalry was, of course, the naval arms race. On this central issue, there is no evidence that Bonar Law's views differed greatly from those of Balfour. During the 1909 'naval scare', Law had favoured the Conservative Party mounting a 'strong agitation' against Liberal cuts in the naval building programme.[46] In March 1909, he made one of his very rare interventions into the debate over Anglo-German naval race. In response to a speech by Admiral von Tirpitz, the German Naval Minister, who claimed that the German navy would only have 13 Dreadnoughts in 1912, not the 25 which Balfour had claimed in a speech during the naval estimates debate, Bonar Law asked the House of Commons, 'Why should we believe a man who could very soon be our enemy?' This very uncharacteristic public indiscretion on Anglo-German relations, which was widely reported in the German press, led Balfour to rebuke Bonar Law for unnecessarily inflaming relations between Britain and Germany. He never did it again.[47]

Not surprisingly, many within the rank and file of the Conservative Party at Westminster expected that Bonar Law would adopt a strong independent line on naval affairs. To this end, Lord Selborne pressed Bonar Law to adopt a 'two keels to one' naval standard. Selborne suggested this new standard, which aimed to build two dreadnoughts for every one built in German shipyards, would help to 'stop the progressive increase in German shipbuilding', because 'it would make it profitless for them to go on building'.[48] Austen Chamberlain added his influential support to Selborne's proposal as he thought such a 'simple and easily comprehensible formula', would be popular with voters.[49] Selborne even promised Bonar Law that he would, 'not allow Germany to be mentioned in connection with the standard, but simply the next largest European navy'.[50] The ever-cautious Lansdowne did not disagree with the policy 'in principle' but evidently worried about a possible breach in the bi-partisan consensus and he informed Bonar Law privately of his doubts about whether, 'it was desirable that we should, when we are in Opposition, commit ourselves to the details of naval policy'.[51] The final decision rested with Bonar Law, who told Selborne, 'I know how much better you are acquainted with naval matters than I can possibly be', but he admitted, in agreement with the advice of Lansdowne, that he did not like the idea of the Conservative Party, 'being committed in advance to this standard.'[52] As a result, the 'two keels to one' standard never became opposition policy. The whole episode reveals that Bonar Law was unwilling to abandon the bi-partisan consensus on naval policy and adopt a 'fighting independent naval policy'.

Overall, there is little sign of a 'New Style' in the conduct of policy or debate over the navy under Bonar Law. Bonar Law adopted the sort of 'constructive opposition' which had been favoured by his much maligned predecessor. In fact, the period from 1911 to 1914 was characterised by a surprisingly high level of harmony on naval affairs between the Government and Opposition front benches. Bonar Law offered consistent support to Winston Churchill, as the First Lord of the Admiralty, and he frequently praised Churchill for his steadfast determination to meet the German naval threat. Lord Charles Beresford, the renegade Conservative MP, often attacked Bonar Law for praising Churchill as 'a genuine patriot' and 'as good a First Sea Lord as any Unionist'.[53]

One important reason why Bonar Law's underlying fears concerning the German naval threat were eased after 1911 was due to secret information on the German naval programme communicated to him by George Armstrong, the former editor of the right wing *Globe* and a noted expert on Anglo-German naval relations. Armstrong had maintained close contact with influential German naval figures. In February 1912, Armstrong prepared for Bonar Law a detailed memorandum of his conversations with Commander Widenmann, the German Naval attaché in London. The purpose of these conversations, on the German side, was to persuade the Conservative Party to exercise caution when Germany's programme of shipbuilding was discussed at Westminster. The German naval attaché told Armstrong that German naval leaders 'entertained no hope of being able to defeat England at sea', and they agreed with Balfour that a naval invasion of the British isles was 'impossible'.[54] Bonar Law was so impressed by these backstage assurances from a leading German naval official that he circulated Armstrong's memorandum to all the Conservative members of the Navy Committee in the House of

Commons. In March 1912, Armstrong told Bonar Law that Captain Watson, the British naval attaché in Berlin, had discovered that Widenmann's comments on the navy were a very accurate reflection of the views of Admiral Tirpitz. As a result, Armstrong advised Bonar Law that a restrained approach by Conservative Party during the naval estimates debate was likely to weaken German fears of 'encirclement' and lessen the demands of the German Navy League for increased naval expenditure.[55] This advice appears to have had a significant impact on Bonar Law. During the naval estimates debates in March 1912, the Conservative front bench showed a quite remarkable amount of restraint when discussing Anglo-German naval rivalry. In December 1912, Bonar Law gave the following summary of his own position towards naval issues: 'I have never made the navy in any sense a party question. I have always desired to regard it as precisely something which should be left outside party politics'.[56]

Yet there was one issue which threatened to break the bi-partisan consensus on defence policy: conscription. Before Bonar Law became Opposition Leader, he had expressed some 'sympathy' for conscription, but he never openly endorsed the aims of the National Service League. In September 1908, he informed Fabian Ware, the editor of the *Morning Post*, that he was 'not opposed to compulsory service', but he did not feel the Conservative Party could adopt the policy because of its unpopularity with British voters.[57] As the years went by, Bonar Law became increasingly more sympathetic towards national service. In October 1912, General Sir Henry Wilson, the Director of Military Training and a key adviser of the Opposition leader on army questions, recorded in his diary that Bonar Law was 'absolutely clear' about the need to introduce conscription to meet the German threat.[58]

In the early days of Bonar Law's leadership, therefore, hopes were very high, especially among the growing pro-conscriptionist lobby within the Conservative Party, that conscription might become official party policy. Such a move would have been a clear breach of the bi-partisan consensus. In May 1912, Lord Roberts, the outspoken and belligerent president of the National Service League, asked Selborne to persuade the Opposition leader to undertake a policy review on the question of conscription because 'My impression is that members are not satisfied with the existing condition of our land forces'.[59] In June 1912, Lord Midleton, a close friend of Selborne, asked Bonar Law to set up a sub-committee consisting of all the leading front bench spokesmen on foreign and defence policy to conduct a review of opposition policy towards the army. Bonar Law sought the views of Arthur Lee on Lord Midleton's proposal. Lee welcomed the idea of the Conservative Party putting forward a 'definite policy' on conscription, but he suggested to Bonar Law that confining the proposed policy review just to army policy would 'lapse into the old heresy of separating the different aspects of national defence into watertight compartments.' In place of a review of opposition policy towards the army, Lee put forward the more ambitious idea of a full-scale review of Conservative naval, foreign and defence policy because 'the problem of national defence as a whole has not been considered or discussed by the Unionist leaders since we went out of office in 1905'.[60] Bonar Law then asked Lansdowne to comment on the demands within the Conservative 'inner circle' for a policy review on army policy. In response, Lansdowne suggested it was necessary for the Opposition to 'make up our minds what line we propose to take on compulsory service ... so that if a general election were to come upon us we should sing the same kind of song', but he completely rejected Lee's idea of a full-scale review of Opposition foreign and defence policy as 'the scope of such an investigation would be immense. It would virtually involve a duplication of the committee of Imperial defence.' Instead, Lansdowne suggested a small sub-committee should be set up to review the question of army policy alone. On the question of conscription, Lansdowne commented, 'some form of compulsory service is inevitable: but such a proposal would, I am afraid, not be popular, and I am not sure that as a party we are prepared to take it up. We might, however, induce the country to accept some form of compulsory training in schools'.[61]

In the end, Bonar Law accepted the advice of Lord Lansdowne and set up a small sub-committee, consisting of Lord Salisbury, Lord Midleton, George Wyndam and Arthur Lee to investigate 'the condition of land forces'. In February 1913, the 'Committee on Land Forces' produced an eight-page report, which made three recommendations: First, the Conservative Party should make a public commitment to restore Liberal cuts of £1.4 million in army expenditure which had occurred since 1906 if elected.[62] Second, the opposition should seek a 'Concordat' between the major parties on conscription to 'take the whole question of compulsion out the party arena'. Third, the party should support the idea of compulsory military training being introduced in schools. This was not a very controversial proposal, as cadet training was already widespread in many public schools.[63] Bonar Law flatly rejected the idea of committing the Conservative Party to restore Liberal spending cuts on the army. The proposed 'concordat' between the two major parties on conscription, in spite of the strenuous efforts of Lord Curzon, came to nothing. The only recommendation which Law publicly endorsed – and which Lansdowne favoured – was to support cadet training in schools. Overall, Bonar Law accepted that it was not possible to introduce conscription without cross-party agreement, and he confined his efforts to win support for the proposal behind the scenes, and away from the public gaze. One notable example of this activity was the encouragement he gave to Sir Henry Wilson's efforts to build up support for conscription among the army general staff. Nevertheless, Bonar Law, realising the electoral drawbacks, was not willing to commit the Conservative Party to a deeply unpopular policy, no matter what its merits were to deal with the German military threat.

Although most historians emphasise sharp differences in style and policy between Balfour and Bonar Law,[64] when examining Bonar Law's response to the key aspects of Anglo-German relations, it can be seen there were many elements of similarity and continuity between the two leaders. The principle of maintaining a bi-partisanship approach to foreign affairs was continued by the new leader. Bonar Law also followed Balfour's restrained approach to the discussion of Anglo-German relations in parliamentary debate. In addition, he continued with Balfour's long-established practice of managing foreign and defence matters through a small 'inner circle' of ex-ministers and close advisers. The most obvious difference between the conduct of Opposition foreign and defence policy was that Bonar Law, because of his lack of experience, consulted with members of the 'inner circle' on foreign and defence policy more fully than Balfour had ever done. He even undertook reviews of Conservative foreign, naval and army policy, but it is clear this was done with the intention of giving the impression to the party rank and file of being willing to listen to new policy ideas, but not accepting any proposal that breached the bi-partisan consensus on foreign and defence matters.

What is equally apparent is that Bonar Law was not Germanophobic and was not publicly contributing to the so-called Anglo-German antagonism. On the contrary, he showed genuine admiration for the German economic system, its scientific methods, its military organisation, its social and educational reforms, and he was not opposed to friendly relations between the two countries. Even so, Law's outward public admiration for German methods was underpinned by an underlying private fear that the growth of German economic power needed to be halted by the introduction of protective tariff against German goods. In essence, Bonar Law feared about Germany what he also admired. As a result, he did not allow his admiration for all things German to influence or determine his attitude towards diplomatic alignments and the naval and military dimensions of the Anglo-German relationship. On the contrary, Law's admiration for German efficiency made him all the more concerned about the German military threat and led him to support measures which would strengthen the European system of deterrence against Germany. Law believed that naval supremacy had to be maintained whatever the cost, but he was unwilling to adopt policies which breached the bi-partisan consensus. This explains why he rejected the adoption of the 'two keels to one standard'. On conscription, Law was a political realist who was unwilling to commit the Conservative Party to a deeply unpopular policy, even though he strongly believed conscription was necessary to deal with the German military threat. As a result, he held the Conservative Party in check on the conscription issue in public, but continued to work behind the scenes to hammer out a cross-party agreement on the proposal.

Bonar Law accepted that Britain was bound to support France in the event of an unprovoked attack by Germany, because he believed a German victory in Europe would inevitably threaten British security and the Empire. But he never promised that the opposition would support a war to save France 'in all circumstances'. As a result, Bonar Law's attitude towards supporting a war against Germany was not predetermined. On the contrary, Bonar Law would examine the details of any major crisis which threatened a European war very carefully. He would consult with Lord Lansdowne and other selected members of his 'inner circle' before deciding to support what he thought was the most sensible course of action.

4
The Views of the Conservative Party at Westminster towards Anglo-German Relations, 1905–1914

The three preceding chapters have revealed how the Conservative leadership ensured the party rank and file at Westminster avoided making openly antagonistic statements about Germany in order to maintain the bi-partisan consensus on foreign policy.[1] As a result, many of the public views of the Conservative Party towards Anglo-German relations were constrained by party discipline and constricted by tactical and political calculations. In this chapter, the main aim is to assess how credible this interpretation really is, by placing under detailed scrutiny the private and especially the public views of Conservative MPs and peers towards three important aspects of Anglo-German relations: the naval arms race, commercial rivalry and the conscription controversy. It will be revealed here that the now routine depiction of the Conservative Party as a bunch of Germanophobes fostering open hostility towards Germany is deeply misleading.

Throughout this period, the private correspondence of Conservative MPs and peers does reveal evidence of a deep-seated and growing anxiety about the growth of German economic, naval and military power. It is clear that the startling growth of German power lay at the heart of these concerns. Between 1890 and 1914, the German population soared from 49 to 66 million, and the economy grew faster that any other European power. Germany's steel output was higher than

Britain, France and Russia combined. In the same period, German coal production was only bettered by Britain. The prominence of science and technical subjects in the school curriculum gave Germany a notable lead in new 'high-tech' industries such as arms production and chemicals. The German army, organised on the basis of conscription, was tactically sophisticated, highly trained and well equipped. German naval expansion ensured that the German fleet rose from the sixth largest to become the second largest in the world behind the Royal navy.

As a result, fear of Germany became a live issue in British politics in the period before the outbreak of the First World War. As Joseph Chamberlain commented, 'Why do people not realise that Germany is making war upon us, and that her economic attack is just as surely an act of aggression as if she had declared hostilities?'[2] In 1908, Austen Chamberlain informed Leopold Maxse, the editor of the right-wing *National Review*,

> I do not share the view that the majority of Germans, or the Kaiser himself wants war with England, but I believe they have persuaded themselves or me that such a conflict is inevitable. If that is their view, then I do not see how we can underestimate the danger their past history indicates.[3]

Arthur Lee also expressed equally pessimistic private views about the likely course of Anglo-German relations. In February 1905, while the Balfour administration was still in office, he triggered a major Anglo-German diplomatic row by claiming, in a much-publicised speech, that a naval war between Britain and Germany was 'inevitable' and by adding it would be a good idea if 'the Royal navy struck the first blow.' This inflammatory public outburst on the naval arms race by a prominent Conservative, was extensively reported in the German press and led to a strong diplomatic protest from the Kaiser and an apology from Lee who was severely rebuked by Balfour who told the junior minister he had inflamed Anglo-German relations 'for no good reason'.[4] The incident served as something of a lesson for Lee who accepted he could not make openly antagonistic comments about the German naval and military threat in future. In private, Lee continued to be 'pre-occupied with the German menace and our unparadness to meet it'. He made several fact-finding visits to Germany between 1905 and 1914 in order to assess German naval strength at first hand. In September 1912, he returned from an informal visit to a number of important German naval dockyards and warned his colleagues: 'The prospects for European peace look more precarious than ever'.[5]

Lord Selborne expressed similar private worries about the rapid growth of the German navy. In 1902, he warned the Cabinet: 'I am convinced that the new German navy is being carefully built up from the point of view of war with us'.[6] From 1905 onwards, the term 'German menace' was a frequently mentioned phrase in all of his private correspondence concerning Anglo-German naval rivalry. During the famous 'naval scare' of 1909, Selborne adopted a very pessimistic view about the aims of German naval policy. In his correspondence with leading figures in Balfour's inner circle, he constantly urged the leading Opposition front bench spokesman to take, 'a very strong line about the navy'.[7] The growing colonial ambitions of the German Government in Southern Africa were a further source of irritation. 'If the Kaiser ever found himself at loggerheads with Britain on any issue', he told Midleton, 'he might attempt to cause trouble by supporting the Boers in a further conflict against the British Empire'.[8]

As the leading member of the Conservative front bench in the House of Lords, and the most important Opposition spokesman on foreign affairs, the attitude of Lord Lansdowne towards Germany was critical. Throughout the period 1905–1914, Lansdowne looked at Anglo-German relations in the most balanced and objective manner of any member of the Conservative front bench. Cool, reserved and extremely level headed, Lansdowne disliked the idea of British foreign policy being directed towards 'a profound dislike of any singly nation'.[9] He also felt it was the 'national duty' of the Conservative Party to avoid inflaming Anglo-German relations by making hostile public statements. It was 'preposterous', he argued, for anyone to maintain that it was in Britain's interest 'to provoke a quarrel with Germany'.[10] He never viewed his own foreign policy in the Balfour Government as being in any sense 'anti-German' or designed to drive Europe into two hostile and antagonistic power blocs. Yet Lansdowne became concerned enough about the German threat to confess in 1911 that it was inconsistent with British interests, 'to allow a friendly nation like France to be crushed.'[11]

Behind closed doors, in private conversation and in correspondence, most Conservatives expressed high levels of anxiety and a growing concern about the military, colonial and naval objectives of the

German Government. Many pessimistically believed that a war with Germany, at some unspecified date in the future, was a distinct possibility. But it is one thing to suggest the Opposition were 'scare-mongers' on the German threat in private, but quite another to suggest they carried these views into public debate and stoked the flames of the Anglo-German antagonism. It was for this reason that the Opposition's public statement on Germany, particularly in the sphere of parliamentary debate took on much greater significance as it was only open public statements that were contributing to any real or imagined Anglo-German antagonism.

In public discussions of matters related to Anglo-German relations by Conservatives in parliament, three issues dominated: (1) the naval arms race, (2) trade relations, and (3) conscription. Of these, the Anglo-German naval race, which focused on the speed at which Dreadnoughts could be built in British and German shipyards was the most frequent topic of debate. The sensitivity in British society concerning the naval issue covered a wide spectrum of public opinion. The navy was not only crucial for the defence from invasion of the British Isles, but it also safeguarded the complex territories that made up the British empire and the various British trading and financial interests Britain had accumulated over several centuries. Fear of Germany was also accentuated by a turn-of-the-century feeling, expressed by politicians, writers and even novelists such as H.G. Wells suggested that Britain's future in the twentieth century was likely to be characterised by industrial and imperial decline. It is no exaggeration, therefore, to suggest that Conservative estrangement from Germany during the period 1905–1914 was primarily not due to the growth of German economic and trading power, but, most importantly, to the expansion of the German naval fleet and its deployment in the North Sea.

Of course, Conservative support for the maintenance of British naval supremacy was traditional. Naval scares were a fairly familiar phenomenon in British party political debate. In 1883, there was a passionate Conservative agitation concerning the possibility of a French naval invasion. In the 1890s, there were also fears expressed by Conservatives about the growth of the Russian and Japanese fleets. The usual symptoms of an impending naval panic were a reduction in naval spending, followed by the growth of a determined rival in close geographical proximity to the British Isles or an important British imperial possession. As the editor of a leading Conservative

Party periodical commented, 'The Navy has always been a cause of the Conservatives'.[12] Most Conservatives were in full agreement with Selborne's view that the chief aim of national defence was for 'a navy that was definitely and indisputably strong enough for defence against invasion, the defence of the empire, trade and commerce'.[13]

What made the Anglo-German naval race much more heated than any of the many previous 'naval scares' was that Germany, the most powerful military power in Europe, and a nation that had never before possessed a major naval fleet, was building a fleet a few hundred miles away from the British coastline. Even so, Conservatives, rather than inflaming Anglo-German antagonism, went out of their way to suggest that their public concern about the growth of German naval power implied no hostility or criticism of the German monarch, the German Government or the German people. Conservatives were also quick to point out that their views concerning the Anglo-German naval race were constantly being distorted by Liberals, radicals and socialists in parliament and by certain hostile sections of the British media. Selborne was quick to reassure the German Government in public debate that Conservative excitability on the naval issue was 'a national duty' and was not engaged in with 'a spirit of hostility towards Germany'.[14] Cawdor also explained that the desire to maintain naval supremacy was 'a long standing and unalterable Conservative principle', designed to maintain 'the safety of our shores and protect commerce', not to 'inflame foreign relations'.[15]

In fact, a detailed examination of Conservative speeches on the naval race at Westminster shows that hostile comments about Germany were surprisingly few and far between. Instead, Conservatives used very mild language when discussing the Anglo-German naval questions. Most Conservatives turned their attack on Liberal Government for failing to maintain naval supremacy. As George Wyndham put it, 'the Opposition had every right to question whether naval security was adequate'.[16] Lord Beresford, a rather outspoken backbench peer on most political issues of the day, claimed that most Conservatives were primarily concerned with global strategic interests when discussing naval questions and were not seeking a 'quarrel with Germany'.[17] Gilbert Parker, a backbench MP, claimed that most Conservative speeches on the navy were designed to ensure the preservation of 'supremacy at sea' and were not designed, 'to inflame cordial relations between nations'.[18]

But Conservative parliamentary speeches on the naval race between 1905 and 1914 could not avoid comparing British and German ship-building programmes or discussing the possible implications should Britain lose the naval race. Arthur Lee frequently explained to the House of Commons that the Conservative Party had traditionally considered naval questions on the basis of comparative analysis which compared 'British naval building with the spending plans of other naval powers'.[19] Most leading peers in the House of Lords made similar claims. Lord Brassey argued that only by measuring British naval strength against that of the German building programme could the full extent to which the Royal Navy was falling behind in the naval arms race be fully evaluated.[20] Similarly, Lord Lovat explained that because the most potent threat to British naval supremacy came from Germany, it was logical to use that power as 'the most effective barometer to evaluate the Britain's naval preparations'.[21]

Most Conservatives were also keen to emphasise they were not making party political capital over the Anglo-German naval arms race. According to Sir Robert Cecil, the Conservative Party had a duty to 'King and Country' to criticise the naval policy of the Government when they believed the ideals of continuity were being infringed.[22] Viscount Helmsley, another Conservative MP, observed that from 1905 to 1909 he could not recall 'a single instance' when a Conservative had ever used the navy for 'purely political purposes' in parliamentary debate.[23] Similarly, William Peel, MP, insisted that Conservatives were merely reflecting public concern on the navy and were not seeking to manipulate the issue for party political purposes.[24] One of the most important reasons why Conservatives spent so much time explaining their 'patriotic' motives when discussing the naval race was to counteract the Liberal charge that Conservatives were using Anglo-German naval rivalry as a jingoistic issue, designed to improve their flagging electoral popularity. In response to this charge, Lee claimed that the Conservative discussion of the naval race was guided by patriotic motives within the framework of continuity. In a similar way, Cawdor insisted that the Conservative position towards the navy was based on the principle of 'national needs not mere party considerations'.[25]

During the great naval scare of 1909, Lee took pains in parliamentary debate to stress that Conservative grievances concerning the strength of the navy were not directed at Germany, but aimed at 'our own government for neglecting naval supremacy'.[26] Viscount Helmsley, MP, claimed that it was the failure of the Government to match German naval spending which had sparked the naval scare in the first place.[27] As a result, Conservative speeches in parliament during the famous naval estimates debate of March 1909 concentrated on attacking the Liberals for not upholding naval supremacy. George Wyndham was convinced that if Conservative concern for the maintenance of naval supremacy remained restrained it 'would not inflame Anglo-German relations'.[28] Most Conservatives viewed the growth of the German navy as a logical consequence of the emergence of Germany as a major European industrial power. Alfred Bigland, MP, claimed that 'the navy built by Germany, which has exercised so much argument and so much thought in this country, is not intended as a menace to this country but was created to ensure that when major international questions arise the voice of Germany will be heard'.[29] Gilbert Parker, MP, claimed that no Conservative had any quarrel with the ambition of Germany to become a great naval power.[30] Lee constantly insisted that the Conservative Party had 'no grievance against Germany' over its decision to build a large navy, because the German Government had 'made no secret of their intentions and had acted strictly within their own rights'.[31] Only a very small minority of Conservatives discussed German intentions in a manner that could be viewed as 'scaremongering'. Sir Robert Cecil, the Conservative MP argued that in any balanced discussion of the naval race, the 'foundations of German policy' had to be discussed. According to Cecil, at the heart of Anglo-German naval rivalry was the fact that the Germans wanted a large fleet, while the British required naval supremacy. As a result, there was 'very little hope of finding common ground'.[32] The most extreme version of this, rather mild viewpoint was that of Sir William Peel who commented that any study of history 'showed that Germany always achieved its aims by cunning diplomacy and force'.[33] Similarly, Lord Brassey, a Conservative peer, insisted that any expansion of German naval power was bound to come into conflict sooner or later with the British desire to maintain naval supremacy. However, Cecil and Brassey, who both expressed the gloomiest interpretations of German aims in parliamentary debate, are difficult to be pigeonholed as 'scaremongers'. Cecil was opposed to British intervention in the war against Germany in August 1914 and he later went on to found the League of Nations Union during the inter-war period. Lord Brassey was actually a member of the Executive Committee of the

Anglo-German Friendship Committee and took part in many social and cultural events with German businessmen and politicians.[34] Overall, Conservative views on the Anglo-German naval race in parliamentary debate showed a quite remarkable level of public restraint and a very surprising lack of hostility towards Germany. This is not to suggest most Conservatives did not have genuine private concerns about the German naval threat, but to emphasise that they decided not to air these at Westminster and did not inflame Anglo-German relations. The lack of antagonistic comments by Conservatives about the German Government even on the highly charged issue of Anglo-German naval rivalry reveals how the party leader's advice to MPs and peers to avoid making openly hostile statements about Germany at Westminster was adhered to by the majority of the parliamentary party.

The second issue discussed by Conservatives concerned with Anglo-German relations was commercial rivalry. It was the penetration of British and imperial markets by German goods which had led to this conflict. British concern about German 'dumping' of cheap imports in the British market began towards the end of the nineteenth century. In the early 1890s when German imports to Britain increased, a small group of Conservative backbenchers led by Howard Vincent, MP for the steel-making city of Sheffield, complained in parliament about such trivial matters as the high tariff Germans levied on British goods, Whitehall civil servants using German pencils, the admiralty buying German lifeboats and the import of goods made in prison by German convicts.[35] Fear of the impact of German imports on the British economy had been given the most impetus in 1886 by publication of the best-selling and deeply influential book *Made in Germany* by Ernest Williams, who claimed, 'Germany has entered a deliberate and deadly rivalry with Britain, and is battering might and main for the extinction of her supremacy'.[36] However, Lord Salisbury, then Prime Minister condemned the 'Made in Germany' scandal and he rejected the argument of protectionist supporters in the Conservative Party who argued that the rapid growth of German imports heralded the 'downfall of British trade'.[37] Indeed, most Conservatives dismissed the 'Made in Germany' affair as a sort of 'midsummer madness', which quickly faded. By November 1896, the *Daily News* claimed that the British public had completely forgotten about the 'German scare'.[38] In 1899, the *National Review* suggested that the American 'trade peril' was an even more potent one.[39] Hence, complaints about the impact of various foreign imports on the British economy, even from the protectionist wing of Conservative Party, were already broadening beyond a singular concentration on Anglo-German commercial rivalry before Joseph Chamberlain launched the Tariff Reform League in 1903. Even so, those historians who have examined the impact of tariff reform on the deterioration of Anglo-German relations from 1903 to 1914 have viewed tariff reform as an 'us and them policy' singularly obsessed with German commercial rivalry.[40] It has also become equally commonplace to pigeonhole the average Conservative supporter of tariff reform as 'bitterly anti-German', without any serious examination of their public views.[41] Of course, it is hard to deny that after 1900 fear of German economic penetration of British and imperial markets was a very important topic of Conservative political debate. It is equally difficult to suggest the economic threat from Germany did not feature prominently in Tariff Reform League propaganda. 'Herr Dumper', portrayed as a plump and bearded German shopkeeper, in horn rimmed spectacles, who sold cheap German imports in his 'Dump Shop', was a rather unflattering, if humorous, anti-German stereotype used very prominently in the leaflets and posters of the Tariff Reform League. However, when discussing the whole question of Anglo-German trade rivalry, a clear distinction must be drawn between the propaganda of the Tariff Reform League, outside of parliament, much of which could be viewed as outspokenly anti-German, and how the Conservative Party at Westminster dealt with the issue of Anglo-German trade rivalry. It must also be appreciated that the drive to introduce tariff reform became part of a broader right of centre movement which sought to make Britain more 'nationally efficient' by introducing a range of 'social-imperialist' policies, most notably, protectionism and social reform, and the introduction of conscription in order to meet the challenge of Germany in Europe, but most importantly, to save the British industry, the empire and the export trade.

A major feature of the Conservative language on tariff reform at Westminster was to use the term not 'German' but 'foreigner' to describe all countries with protectionist policies. It was, in fact, a very rare occurrence for a Conservative MP or peer to blame foreign nations which attempted to prevent British goods entering their own market. Austen Chamberlain, one of the strongest advocates of tariff reform, claimed that foreign countries did not use protectionism to inflame international relations but in order to provide 'their own people with the greatest amount of employment'.[42] Balfour insisted that passionate support for tariff reform should not be accompanied by antagonism towards any foreign country. It was not the external challenge posed by foreign trade competitors on which the Conservative case in favour of tariff reform revolved, but on what Balfour claimed were 'wild free traders in Britain who refuse to put on the armour at their disposal'.[43]

In evaluating the reaction of the Conservative Party rank and file to Anglo-German trade rivalry, therefore, the first point which needs to be emphasised is that it was surprisingly restrained. It must also be emphasised that Liberals, in their passionate defence of free trade, expressed the most deliberately hostile and antagonist comments about Germany. In comparison, most Conservative MPs regarded themselves as 'positive towards Germany', and they claimed that it was 'Liberal lies about Germany' that contributed most to the growth of Anglo-German tension. Arthur Du Cros commented that while the great majority of Conservatives viewed German progress in a positive light, most Liberals portrayed the Germans as a beleaguered people, living under a militaristic regime, in very poor economic conditions, with a very poor standard of living.[44] Edward Goulding, claimed that one of the major features of the Liberal campaign during his by-election at Worcester in 1908 was a poster campaign which declared 'A vote for Goulding is a vote for rye bread and horsemeat'.[45] Many other Conservative MPs shared these views. William Peel said that nothing soured Anglo-German relations more than 'frequent Liberal claims about the poor diet of the average German'.[46] It was the Conservatives who ended up defending the German way of life in parliamentary debate. A fairly typical pro-German comment was that of F.E. Smith who argued that 'this horse nourished country [Germany] had managed to preserve their national agriculture at a time when ours has been perishing'.[47]

It is also worth pointing out that the Conservative crusade for the introduction of tariff reform from 1905 onwards had broadened considerably beyond a singular concentration concerning Anglo-German trade rivalry. A detailed examination of all parliamentary questions put by Conservative MPs and peers at Westminster at Question time from 1905 to 1914 reveals no singular obsession with Anglo-German trade rivalry. On the contrary, Conservatives complained at Question time to the Prime Minister and other leading Liberal Government ministers about the following trading issues: imports of American cars, tin-plate, steel, wheat and tram rails, French limes, wine and cars, Japanese fraudulent use of British trade marks, imports of Dutch cheese, increased Russian tea duties and imports of low-quality Chinese tea. Conservatives called for curbs on the imports of hops, malt, sugar and every other imaginable import from a bewildering variety of countries around the world. As H.H. Marks, the Conservative MP put it, 'the Tariff question was one of world politics'.[48] Many Conservatives argued that Britain was being left behind in a world-wide conversion towards protectionism. 'I am convinced', said Lord Milner, 'that in the next twenty years we shall have duties in this country'.[49] Lansdowne who claimed that 'one country after another is endeavouring to shut Britain out of its markets' endorsed this view, in a more moderate tone.[50]

Of course, there were many ardent supporters of tariff reform in the Conservative Party who viewed the introduction of tariffs on foreign imports as the best means to finance increased defence spending in order to meet the German threat. George Wyndham believed that the extra revenue required to build new Dreadnoughts could only be provided by means of the increased revenue which would flow from the introduction of tariffs.[51] In a similar way, Lord Milner argued that tariff reform was not an isolated question concerned with the domestic economy and the unity of the Empire, but was an 'essential part of a great national imperial defence policy'.[52] For these Conservatives, tariff reform was a vital means of maintaining British markets, maintaining naval supremacy and limiting the economic and naval ambitions of foreign rivals.

But any analysis of Conservative views on Anglo-German commercial rivalry must also point to the far larger number of Conservatives who held very insular views on trade questions and were primarily concerned with how specific foreign imports affected the economic life of their own constituencies. There were certainly some Conservative MPs in constituencies hit by German imports, such as Howard Vincent in Sheffield who frequently highlighted the German commercial threat, but there were just as many Conservative complaints about French, American, Russian and Canadian imports when they impacted on the economic well being of their own constituents. Sir Arthur Fell often complained about the damaging effect imports of hops were having on the hop growers in his own constituency of Great Yarmouth.[53] This type of insular reaction to the impact of foreign imports was repeated in numerous speeches by Conservative MPs in constituencies dependent on a wide range of products and commodities, ranging from iron, steel and cotton to slate, wool and silk. Many of these attacks on the impact of foreign imports bore little relationship with Britain's diplomatic stance. Sir George Courthorpe, a very strong supporter of the Anglo-French Entente, frequently complained about the damaging impact the import of French cars was having in his own constituency of Rye in Sussex.[54] Similarly, Captain Craig, who also supported the Anglo-French Entente, claimed that the introduction of a tariff on French wine would greatly help wine producers in his constituency.[55] It must also be understood that there was a highly vocal group of Conservative MPs who frequently expressed fear about the 'American danger' to the British economy. As one Conservative MP commented, 'in 1905, 3,872,881 lb. of tinned American meat was imported and could only be curtailed by the introduction of a tariff'.[56]

It is also important to emphasise that most Conservatives at Westminster concentrated their arguments in support of tariff reform on the intransigence of 'free traders' in the Liberal Party who refused to introduce protectionism and portrayed Germany as an economic and social role model. It may be surprising to learn that it was, in fact, Conservatives who most strongly objected to frequent Liberal attacks on the German way of life. In fact, parliamentary debate on Anglo-German trade rivalry must be viewed as an integral part of the domestic electoral struggle with the Liberal Party over the future course of British economic policy rather than as a key ingredient in the growth of Anglo-German antagonism.

The third issue discussed in parliamentary debate by Conservatives concerned about the German threat was the role the British army would play in a future European war. Exactly how Britain might fight a future European war divided opinion within the Conservative Party. 'Navalists' tended to remain committed to the view that British survival depended on sea power, but 'Continentalists' argued that only a massive military commitment in Europe would ensure victory in any future war. Before the First World War, the British army was very small by continental standards, and it was recruited on a voluntary basis.

It was expected by British military and naval planners within the defence establishment that Britain's role in any future European War would be extremely limited, primarily concerned with maintaining control of the seas and mounting a successful trade blockade. The British contribution on land, in the event of a European war involving Britain on the side of France against Germany, would only consist of the six infantry and one cavalry battalion of the British Expeditionary Force (BEF). Most Conservatives doubted whether such a limited military contribution could prevent a German invasion and provide adequate support to the French Army. As fear of the German threat intensified after 1905, many Conservatives believed the introduction of conscription was the only way to really prevent the German mastery of Europe. In December 1910, for example, 177 Conservative MPs expressed 'sympathy' towards military service, and a total of 88 Conservative MPs were card-carrying members of the National Service League. The rapid growth of Conservative support for conscription was an extra parliamentary expression of the widespread private anxiety about the German military threat.

At Westminster, it was a very different story. Most Conservative MPs accepted the view of the party leader that conscription was a deeply unpopular policy which could not be advocated by one party alone.[57] Balfour, who remained a committed 'Navalist' refused to include in any future Conservative Cabinet anyone in the parliamentary party who refused to accept his line on the army question. Balfour told Grey that 'submarines and airships were far better protection against invasion than conscription',[58] and he advised Bonar Law after he became Conservative leader that the 'experts Conservatives should follow are sailors not soldiers'.[59] A large number of informed Conservative military experts at Westminster also raised objections to conscription. In Earl Percy's view, Lord Roberts' scheme of limited military training specifically for 'Home Service' was misleading because owing to the probable high casualty rates in any prolonged European war most conscripts would be expected to serve overseas anyway.[60] The Duke of Bedford claimed that the introduction of conscription would simply divert expenditure from the navy and the financing of the BEF.[61]

These divisions within the Conservative Party over conscription help to explain why the leading opposition spokesmen on army questions concentrated in parliamentary debate on the less controversial issue of the existing strength of the Territorial Army (TA).

Lord Midleton claimed the voluntarily recruited TA could not be expected to keep at bay 'a well armed German invasion force'.[62] In fact, few Conservatives believed the TA which had been created by Haldane's army reforms in 1907 as an auxiliary force of part-time soldiers was adequate enough to meet the German threat.[63] As Amery put it, 'the TA was a lamentable corps with which to cope with a German offensive'.[64] Yet it was very difficult for Conservatives to admit openly, given party policy, that the only way to meet the deficiencies in the strength of TA was to introduce conscription. In Lord Milner's view, the chief reason why Conservative 'sympathy' for conscription from 1905 to 1914 was never translated into action was due to the hardened prejudice of British people against the idea. 'These were facts', said Milner, 'which no political party could ignore'.[65]

As a result, the strongest arguments put forward in support of conscription at Westminster came from Roberts and Milner.[66] Lord Roberts, dubbed in the press as 'the most popular soldier of his day' and whose war record included stints in India and South Africa frequently claimed not to be attached to any political party, and he presented his views in the House of Lords as an 'independent Peer'. The alleged 'independence' of Roberts at Westminster enabled the Conservative leadership to endorse some of his milder claims on the strength of the British army and to distance itself from his more controversial views on conscription. Roberts was often a useful kite flyer, but more often he was treated as a loose canon by the party leadership. Even so, the views of Roberts are important because he spoke far more openly about the German military threat than any Conservative MP or Peer ever dared to. Roberts claimed that Germany was not only Britain's fiercest competitor in trade and shipping, but also the one power whose desire for a place in the sun conflicted with the British desire to preserve the status quo. He questioned whether the diplomatic agreements with France and Russia, with their vague commitments, combined with a singular reliance on naval power could prevent a German invasion of the British Isles in the event of a future war.[67] The only feasible solution to Britain's severe military deficiencies, according to Lord Roberts, was for all able-bodied men between the ages of eighteen to thirty to undergo four months tough military training in order to create 'a virile national army'.[68]

In private, Roberts expressed even more outspoken fears about the German threat. He frequently congratulated L.J. Maxse, the 'scaremongering' editor of the *National Review* for 'going on about the German peril and the absence of our defence against it'.[69] But even Roberts, supposedly free of any political restraint from the Conservative leadership, claimed his frequent utterances about the growth of German military strength implied 'no hostility and no fear of the Kaiserreich'. He also praised the German Government for greatly improving the quality of its armed forces in most of his speeches on army questions,[70] and he also attempted to reassure the German Government that the military position of foreign countries had to be taken account of when considering 'what ought to be our own arrangements' towards national defence.[71] In spite of this, the 'straight talking' of Roberts on the German military threat in the House of Lords often alarmed the Conservative leadership which was quick to distance itself from his views. Balfour even asked King Edward VII if he would plead with Roberts to stop making inflammatory references to Germany during his key speeches on army questions in the House of Lords.[72] Balfour also instructed Lansdowne to speak in firm opposition to the many various private member National Service Bills that Lord Roberts attempted to introduce in the House of Lords.[73]

Another open Conservative supporter of conscription at Westminster was Lord Milner, who frequently castigated the timidity and restraint of the Conservative front bench when speaking on Anglo-German relations. Milner summed up the dilemma facing any Conservative who spoke openly on the German military threat at Westminster in the following way: 'If anyone attempts to raise the question of the efficiency of our land forces at a time when the international horizon is clear, he is pooh-poohed as an alarmist. If anyone raised the subject when the horizon is clear he is branded a mischief-maker' . However, Milner, who did support conscription quite openly, also admitted that the German military system was enforced in a manner 'which will never be tolerated, and I am glad would never be tolerated in this country'.[74] In 1914, the Earl of Errol complained bitterly that the muddled nature of the Conservative position towards the conscription issue had contributed to public apathy on the true extent of the German threat. As a result, Errol claimed that the British public was 'psychologically unprepared for war'.[75] In a similar manner, Earl Percy remarked that while the German people had been directed by their political leaders towards the idea of a future war with Britain, the British people had been encouraged by the two major political leaders to view a war between Britain and Germany as a remote possibility.[76]

Overall, a surprisingly high level of caution was maintained whenever Anglo-German relations were discussed in parliamentary debate. Few provocative statements, or moral judgement towards Germany more generally marked the Conservative response to Anglo-German naval rivalry, in spite of the brief panic exhibited in 1909. The debate on tariff reform, included discussions of the German economy and standard of living, but it was more part of the domestic political struggle with the Liberals rather being linked to a vaguely defined 'Anglo-German antagonism'. The most radical proposal to deal with the German threat was conscription, but this was viewed as a deeply unpopular electoral policy which could only be implemented within a bi-partisan framework.

It appears the routine depiction of the Conservative Party as a group of anti-German 'scaremongers' who stoked up the fires of Anglo-German antagonism during the Edwardian era is really quite misleading. The charge of 'scaremongering' is particularly misplaced when applied to the approach Conservatives adopted towards Anglo-German relations in the Westminster sphere of political activity. As explained earlier, the public attitude of the Conservative Party towards Germany at Westminster, whether in connection with the naval arms race, trade rivalry and conscription, showed a high level of restraint and a marked absence of openly expressed hostility.

5
The Role of the German Threat in the Propaganda and Electioneering Tactics of the Conservative Party at the Two General Elections of 1910

For most of the period following the electoral Reform Act of 1884, the Conservative Party made opposition to Home Rule for Ireland and support for the Empire the two main planks of its appeal to voters. This proved a potent attraction at the 1900 'Khaki Election', which was fought at the very height of the Boer War, at a time when the Liberal Party was in turmoil. At the 1906 General Election, the mood of the electorate had changed dramatically. Jingoism lost the advantages it had enjoyed six years earlier. After Lord Salisbury's resignation in 1902, the party endured three years of bitter internal division over tariff reform and entered the election in a state of alarming disarray. During the election campaign, the Liberal Party offered voters a choice between a forward-looking modern party, espousing a 'New Liberalism' which was determined to uphold free trade and to implement social reform against a divided Conservative Party fighting to introduce protectionism.

In the aftermath of the cataclysmic 1906 election defeat, the Conservative Party, the traditional upholders of the status quo, seemed out of touch and searched for a 'positive' electoral appeal in order to provide an attractive alternative to the radicalism of 'New Liberalism'. Another background fear was the 'progressive' long-term appeal of socialism represented in infant form by the Labour Party. Most Conservatives recognised that jingoism, which appealed to nationalist feelings for the Empire appeared to have a limited electoral appeal to the average working class voter who seemingly demanded 'progressive' and 'constructive' policies to deal with social problems such as unemployment, low wages and poor housing.[1] As Sir Joseph Lawrence, a leading tariff reformer commented, 'It is no use to feed the empty stomachs of men with appeals to patriotism'.[2] With the benefit of hindsight, it seems political suicide for any British political party to have believed that protectionism would prove a vote winner at elections. In fact, jingoism has proved a more potent vote winner. Yet the Conservative Party fought two further elections in 1910 firmly committed to implementing tariff reform. Even though tariff reform proved a copper-bottomed vote loser, it did help to 'liberate the party from its previously negative attitude to policy making'.[3] It combined a patriotic appeal to unite the Empire, with promises to instigate social legislation and improved living standards from the custom duties levied on foreign imports.

But the electoral difficulties facing the Conservative Party after 1906 were not confined to the field of policy alone. There were several problems with the electoral machinery of the Conservative Party, which was poorly organised outside Westminster and lacked effective coordination. One of the major problems was the absence of clearly defined roles in the control of electoral strategy between Conservative Central Office, controlled by Sir Alexander Acland Hood and J. Percival Hughes, the Chief party agent from 1907 to 1912 and the more professionally organised National Union, controlled by John Boraston, the chief organising secretary of the Liberal Unionist Party. In essence, the Conservative Party had two separate and conflicting organisations involved in defining electoral strategy and party propaganda. Not surprisingly, this produced wasteful overlapping and competition between the 'Conservative' and 'Liberal Unionist' organisations at both the national and local level. *The Times* claimed that the relationship between Conservative Central Office, dominated by Balfourites, and the National Union, controlled by ardent Chamberlainite tariff reformers resembled, 'two motor cars driven side by side along a narrow road with the attendant risk of collision'.[4]

Even the electoral disaster of 1906 did not lead to a merger of these overlapping organisations. What emerged was a very uneasy compromise between the two groups. The National Union gained overall control over party propaganda, party publications and the selection of speakers during election campaigns, and control over the majority of local constituency organisations. Conservative Central Office paid a yearly grant of £8,500 to the National Union to operate as the 'servant of the party in parliament' for the publication and dissemination of party propaganda. In practice, the National Union between 1906 and 1909 made no attempt to coordinate electoral strategy or propaganda with Central Office.

These organisational deficiencies in the projection of Conservative propaganda were not compensated for by good relations with the press. The Conservative Party had the editorial support of a majority of national newspapers, most notably, *The Times, Daily Telegraph*, the *Morning Post* (now defunct), the *Daily Mail*, the *Daily Express*, the *Daily Graphic* (now defunct) and the major London daily newspaper, the *Standard*. A great many local newspapers also gave support to the Conservative Party. But, the electoral advantage of press support was greatly diminished by poor liaison between Central Office and the press. There was no blatant orchestration of the press undertaken by Central Office. On the contrary, relations between Central Office and the press were very loosely structured. Up until the end of 1911, when press relations were brought under the direct control of Sir Malcolm Fraser, Central Office manipulation of the Tory press consisted of an 'Editors Handy Sheet', which featured rather dull extracts from the speeches of leading Conservatives, which were circulated to the editors of pro-Tory national newspapers. The amount of coverage gained for the party by this method was extremely limited, even in those newspapers favourable to the Conservative cause. What Central Office failed to fully appreciate was that most editors had already received the contents of the public speeches by leading Conservatives from the Press Association, and they were unwilling to use party political material which duplicated this material or was supplied to every other rival newspaper.[5]

In general, most newspapers covered Anglo-German relations without any reference to the restrained views of the Conservative Party leader at Westminster. As a result, the Conservative press portrayed German aims in a constantly hostile manner, frequently highlighting naval and trade rivalry between the two countries, and the 'scaremongering' British press was viewed by the German regime at various times, most notably, during the 1909 naval controversy and the 1911 Agadir crisis as promoting Anglo-German antagonism. *The Times* described Germany as 'a new, crude, ambitious, radically unsound power'.[6] During the January 1910 General Election campaign, Lord Northcliffe, the proprietor of the *Daily Mail*, told the editor, a key aim of editorial line of the newspaper during the election campaign was 'to bring home to Englishmen the extent and nature of the German menace'.[7]

It seems that most right-wing newspaper proprietors such as Lord Northcliffe and many right-wing editors such as Kennedy-Smith at the *Daily Mail*, H.A. Gwynne at the *Standard*, and Ralph Blumenfield at the *Daily Express* believed the 'scaremongering' line they adopted towards Germany reflected the rank and file opinions of ordinary Conservative voters. Gwynne told Beresford most of the letters he received from the public showed enormous apprehension about the growth of the German navy.[8] Maxse, the editor of the *National Review*, believed that the Conservative Party at Westminster was so 'silent and useless' on the German threat that press agitation was a useful method of keeping the issue at the forefront of public debate. In a very real sense, blatant and public 'scaremongering' about Anglo-German relations was the independent preserve of pro-Conservative right-wing newspapers that put forward these views without the agreement of the Party leader and Conservative Central Office.

By the end of 1909, the absence of a coordinated Conservative propaganda message at elections was acknowledged by Central Office. This realisation led to J.L. Garvin, the editor of the *Observer*, being appointed as the chief party adviser on propaganda for the General Election of January 1910. One of the first things Garvin told Balfour was that most current Conservative propaganda was 'too abstract, academic and verbose' and required simplification in style and content in order to appeal to the average voter.[9] Garvin believed the Conservatives could not win the General Election 'on Tariff Reform alone' and needed to highlight other issues.[10] He urged Balfour to make the naval threat from Germany 'a new and dominating issue' during the campaign. In putting forward this view, Garvin was greatly influenced by the outcome of the Croydon by-election in March 1909. It had been fought at the height of the Anglo-German naval scare and had resulted in the Conservative share of the vote increasing from 3 to 19 per cent. Many Conservatives interpreted the Croydon result as evidence of the vote-winning potential of the German naval threat.[11]

Even so, Balfour was not prepared to make the Anglo-German naval race the key issue during the election campaign. Scaremongering was not going to replace jingoism. In fact, Balfour believed the naval issue might persuade many wavering lower middle-class voters in the south-east of England who had switched allegiance to the Liberals at the 1906 General Election to return to the Conservative fold, but he doubted whether it could gain votes for the Conservatives in solid working class industrial regions in the north, Scotland and Wales. Nor did Balfour agree with Garvin's view that the naval issue would 'breathe new life into the Party' and act as an 'electoral cannonball' which could bring the Conservatives an outright victory at the General Election.[12] In the end, Garvin reluctantly accepted Balfour's view that the Conservative campaign should not be fought as an uncompromising exercise in Germanophobia.[13] It was agreed by Balfour, Garvin and Central Office that the naval issue would rank in third place in the Conservative campaign for the January 1910 General Election behind the struggle against the Lloyd George's 'People's Budget' and support for tariff reform. Percival Hughes, the Chief Party Agent, implored all Conservative parliamentary candidates to mention the danger posed to the nation by Liberal naval cuts, but he also urged them to stress 'People's Budget' and to 'make tariff reform the key issue over everything else in the campaign', and emphasise that food taxes were not exclusively a patriotic policy directed against 'the foreigner' but a key 'solution to unemployment'.[14]

The General election campaign, which began in early December 1909 and did not conclude until the end of January 1910, was the longest in the twentieth century. An examination of the Election addresses of Conservative candidates shows that 100 per cent of Tory candidates mentioned tariff reform, 96 per cent national defence, 94 per cent the House of Lords veto powers, and 84 per cent Lloyd George's Budget.[15] These figures show that national defence and tariff reform did feature very prominently in the Conservative campaign. Most Tory candidates did stress 'tariff reform and national defence', but the dominant issue of all was 'The Peers versus the People'. After all, the Election had been called because the House of Lords had rejected Lloyd George's Budget.

Garvin was acutely aware that Tory propaganda during the campaign had to counteract the frequent Liberal charge that the Conservative Party was composed of a group of anti-German 'scaremongers'. To this end, a Conservative election leaflet was produced entitled 'Are the Unionists Scaremongers?'. It emphasised the restraint which Balfour had displayed on the German threat at Westminster and highlighted the consistent support given by Conservatives at Westminster to the principles of bi-partisanship on foreign affairs.[16] Yet the restrained approach towards the German threat which Balfour and Central Office urged candidates to adopt was often contradicted and severely undermined by much of the election propaganda produced by the National Union. In spite of the appointment of Garvin, there appears to have been very little effective coordination between the Central Office and the National Union over the presentation of Anglo-German relations to the electorate during the two General Elections of 1910.

This view is reinforced when the campaign material used by Conservative candidates and party workers during the General Election campaigns of 1910 is placed under closer scrutiny. Each local Conservative agent, candidate and canvasser was supplied by the National Union with a collection of essential campaign aids, which offered advice on campaign tactics and party policy on most of the key election issues. 'How to Canvass' was a 'confidential' small handbook, of handy canvassing tips, given to all party workers. It advised canvassers to always visit homes in their constituency in pairs, ensuring they carried with them all of the following: canvass cards, at least four election leaflets, a pencil, a box of matches and a Lantern for use in 'badly lighted districts'. Canvassers were also advised to enlist the support of a wife, if the husband was absent at the time of their visit on the grounds 'they are sometimes useful allies'. They were also advised not to waste time 'with a decided opponent'. The election issues which party workers were advised to highlight at the January 1910 General Election were carefully selected and placed in the following rank order: the 'unjust' nature of Lloyd George's Budget, the benefits of tariff reform, to promise voters that old age pensions would be retained and to mention the navy would be maintained 'upon such an adequate scale as will secure food supply being cut off from any hostile nation'. There was no mention made at all in 'How to canvass' on foreign policy or the conscription issue.[17] Two other widely used campaign aids were 'Notes for Speakers' and 'Gleanings and Memoranda', which both provided a detailed collection of extracts from the speeches of leading Conservatives on most of the key election issues.

The most comprehensive campaign aid produced by the National Union, however, was the 'Campaign Guide', which offered policy advice on every major and minor election issue. The language expressed in the 'Campaign Guide' on Germany is blatantly xenophobic and extremely hostile. In a very strident tone, the 'Campaign Guide' warned, 'Ever since the birth of Prussia the key stone of its international policy has been the sudden, but carefully prepared war of aggression'. On the naval race, the 'Campaign Guide' argued that naval supremacy had to be maintained because 'no other nation depends for its national existence upon a single defence weapon'. The attitude expressed in the 'Campaign Guide' towards Anglo-German trade rivalry is equally uncompromising, stressing that if tariffs are introduced, Germany would no longer be able to 'bully in the economic sphere'. This strong commitment by Conservatives to meet the German threat is contrasted with the Liberal desire to 'subordinate national defence to schemes of social reform', during a period when Germany was building 'the most powerful fleet ever possessed by any country, except Britain'. Yet no mention is made in the Campaign Guide about the need for conscription to meet the German threat.[18] On foreign policy, the Campaign Guide emphasised that foreign policy under Sir Edward Grey represented continuity with the policy of Lord Lansdowne and highlighted how diligently the Opposition at Westminster under Balfour had consistently refrained 'from offering criticism of foreign affairs'. The main pivot of Grey's foreign policy, the Anglo-French Entente is presented, not as a loose colonial arrangement, but as a firm deterrent against possible German aggression. What is more, German foreign policy actions are portrayed in the Campaign Guide as leading in the direction of a European war. Germany is denounced for acting like 'a dictator of Europe' in its dealings with Russia during the 1908 Bosnian crisis and is also charged with making persistent efforts to 'browbeat France into abandoning her alliance with Britain'.[19] Hence, while Balfour and Central Office were advising Conservatives to downplay Anglo-German antagonism during the campaign, most of the policy advice which candidates and canvassers received from the National Union presented Germany's actions in extremely hostile terms and put forward antagonistic views at odds with the moderate line put forward by the party leader and Conservative front bench at Westminster.

Despite Balfour's desire to downplay the German threat, the role of Germany featured very prominently in many of the pamphlets, posters and newspaper advertisements produced by the Conservative Party for the General Election of January 1910. The Conservative leaflet and poster campaign was a vast operation. The National Union distributed 50 million pamphlets and leaflets during the campaign in January 1910. Thousands of posters were displayed on giant billboards in most constituencies and advertising space was bought in most national and local newspapers. Most potential voters received pamphlets and leaflets on the issues of the navy and tariff reform. Very few Conservative leaflets were produced on foreign policy, and there was only one produced on the role of the army, and it did not even mention the dread word 'conscription'.

The rapid growth of the German fleet and the need to counteract it through increased naval spending featured very prominently in the Conservative poster and leaflet campaign. Under the jingoistic banner headline 'Britons Beware!', voters were warned in a widely used Conservative poster during the two General Election campaigns in 1910 that Britain faced a 'death fight for national existence' with Germany for naval supremacy.[20] But a more prominent message in most Conservative posters and pamphlets on the naval issue were strong attacks on the so-called unpatriotic radicals in the Liberal Party who had consistently supported cuts in naval expenditure. A typical Tory campaign leaflet asked, 'Can we trust the radical government to guarantee naval supremacy?'[21] In another widely used poster entitled 'Under Which Flag', the voters were given a stark choice: 'Are we to stand under the Union Jack, like our fathers before us, for the power and glory and welfare of Great Britain and her empire ... or ... Are we to hoist the Red Flag of Socialism, civil war, and national ruin at the bidding of Mr. Lloyd George?'[22]

This negative line of attack, which charged the Liberals with being 'friends of every country except their own' had been a familiar aspect of Conservative electoral propaganda ever since the days of Disraeli.[23] To this extremely familiar aspect of negative Conservative electioneering was added the view that Lloyd George and his 'radical friends' were allowing their passionate desire to introduce social reform to override, 'the additional needs of the navy'.[24] As one Conservative election leaflet put it, 'The sea-power of Britain is being sacrificed to socialism'.[25] In most of the Conservative campaign literature on the navy, it was suggested that the Liberal Government had 'made it possible for Germany to threaten Britain's naval supremacy without the help of any ally'.[26] The charge of a 'lack of patriotism' by Liberals was also extended to encompass supporters of the Liberal Government, especially within the Labour and Irish Nationalist parties. One widely circulated Conservative election leaflet quoted the view of Major McBride, an Irish Nationalist MP, who claimed that even if the Germans mounted a naval invasion of Ireland 'They would be welcomed with willing hearts and open minds.' The leaflet ended by asking potential Conservative voters 'Can you trust a party who look for parliamentary support from such allies?'.[27] To demonstrate to potential working class voters that support for a strong navy was not simply a return to the familiar pre-1906 jingoistic electoral tactics of the party, many Conservative pamphlets on the navy attempted to suggest that command of the seas 'is the only security working men have for the wages they earn and the bread they eat'.[28] By focusing propaganda on the navy towards attacks on the alleged lack of patriotism among their political opponents, the Conservative poster and pamphlet campaign was able to deny that its presentation of the naval issue was specifically anti-German.

But the issue of tariff reform took a far more prominent role than Anglo-German naval rivalry in Conservative election propaganda for the two elections of 1910. Voters were overburdened by the multitude of campaign literature delivered to their homes by the two major political parties. The Tariff Reform League produced over 80 million pamphlets to support the Conservative campaign, and the National Union cooperated with the Tariff Reform League throughout the campaign in order to coordinate their propaganda efforts.[29] Conservative canvassers were advised by Central Office not to present Germany as an economic threat but to emphasise that 'protectionist' Germany was a positive economic role model that was developing far more rapidly than 'free trade' Britain.[30] Many Conservative pamphlets and leaflets on tariff reform, which were often modified to fit the specific economic needs of particular constituencies, put forward a generally favourable picture of the standard of life in Germany. One widely used Conservative campaign leaflet entitled 'Ourselves versus Germany' claimed that 'protectionist Germany was making greater progress than Britain, with its people enjoying higher levels of exports, and lower levels of unemployment.'[31] In response, Liberal campaign literature depicted the average German as living in a paltry condition, eating a diet which consisted primarily of black rye bread and horseflesh. Conservative propaganda described these Liberal attacks on the German way of life as 'a great deception and an abuse of language'.[32] To refute the constant rude Liberal attacks on the eating habits of the average German, Conservative propaganda emphasised that German rye bread was far more savoury than dull British white bread and was put on the menu at most top class German hotels. On the question of Germans eating horseflesh, Conservative leaflets explained that horsemeat was eaten in Germany 'because Germans like it, ... like Scotsmen like Porridge'.[33] Each of the two major political parties used life in Germany for purely electoral purposes at the two general elections of 1910, with selected facts and figures used to confirm or deny a particular point of view whatever their true validity. The major reason why arguments about life in Germany formed such a key part of the Conservative campaign was primarily due to the need of the Conservative campaign to demolish the strong and persuasive Liberal claim that tariff reform meant increased bread prices and a lowering of living standards. This helps to explain why Garvin advised Percival Hughes, the Conservative Chief Agent, to ensure that Conservative propaganda stressed that tariff reform meant 'a British loaf – a big loaf.'[34] Garvin was also keen for Conservative propaganda to emphasise that the Liberals had introduced measures of social reform, such as old age pensions and social insurance based on German models, but had chosen to finance these reforms not with tariffs, as occurred in Germany, but by the use of increased indirect and direct taxation.

The question of how to present the issue of social reform produced divisions in the electoral strategy of the Conservative Party at the two 1910 elections. A simple negative and reactionary attack on free trade was regarded by many Conservative candidates, especially committed Chamberlainites, as inadequate. One of the chief consequences of the 1906 election defeat had been a severe loss of working class support. The Liberal victory had also shown that social reform was a popular policy. The growth of a solid body of Labour MPs revealed that the working class had recognised their potential power. Tariff Reform was viewed as a potentially popular policy among the working classes as it promised to 'tax the foreigner' in order to finance social reform. The most committed tariff reformers within the party wanted to emphasise that tariff reform offered an alternative means of uniting the Empire, ensuring Britain remained a great power, and to provide the revenue to finance social reform for the working classes. The more moderate 'Balfourites' were more non-committal about social reform and tended to project tariff reform as a policy which offered the safeguarding of British industry and greater job security for British workers, without making any specific commitment to implementing any wide-ranging programme of social reform. It is worth noting that only 40 percent of the Conservative candidates mentioned social reform in their election addresses for the January 1910 election.[35] Oddly enough, many of the most vociferous advocates of the idea that tariff reform meant social reform were 'die hard' peers in rural constituencies.[36]

By and large, most Conservative pamphlets and leaflets placed greater emphasis on the Balfourite view that tariff reform would bring greater security of employment in industry and agriculture by taxing foreign goods.[37] A total of 90 per cent of Conservative candidates presented tariff reform as a policy which would increase employment and wages.[38] To support this view, Conservative propaganda emphasised that 'foreign' competition was destroying local industry and agriculture. In the hop-producing region of Kent, a Conservative poster entitled 'No Hops' was displayed on billboards in local villages. It depicts a gloomy poor hop worker telling a farmer 'It's the workhouse for the wife and kids, while foreign hops are dumped here. What we want is tariff reform'.[39] A complementary leaflet argued that 'Free imports of foreign hops means more employment for the foreigner, and less employment for the British hopgrower, labourer and picker'.[40] Many similar posters and leaflets were targeted at a wide section of areas affected by foreign imports. In industrial regions, tariff reform was also presented as a policy which would protect local jobs. A fairly typical Conservative leaflet entitled 'A Word to the Working Man' claimed that tariff reform would protect British jobs by using 'an effective weapon against nations that have built up a tariff war against British goods'. It was also emphasised that taxing imports would enable a Conservative Government to remove taxes on tobacco, tea and a range of other goods imported from within the Empire.[41]

But a very important aspect of the Conservative propaganda was to engage in negative attacks on the 'foreigner' who 'dumped' goods on the British market at artificially low prices.[42] To end this practice, a widely used Conservative leaflet proclaimed 'Foreigners tax us. Let us tax them',[43] while another claimed 'Every vote for Free Trade means more work in Germany and more want in Britain'.[44] The Tariff Reform League added considerable weight to this negative propaganda tactic by creating mock 'dump shops' in many constituencies, which displayed the foreign goods that had allegedly destroyed British jobs. Any visitor to these shops could see the so-called foreigner mentioned in Conservative propaganda was, in fact, 'Herr Dumper', the stereotypical German shopkeeper, and most of the goods displayed in these shops were made in Germany. It is probably worth adding that many of these 'dump shops', created by the Tariff Reform League, were extensively vandalised in working class industrial areas.[45]

A further negative aspect of Conservative propaganda on tariff reform was to blame 'dumping', not only on the sharp business practices of 'Herr Dumper', but on the 'cosmopolitan interests' in Britain who supported free trade. Leopold Amery, a leading tariff reformer, admitted that his own chief hatred was reserved for the free traders in Britain whom he opposed 'with all the intensity which any Calvinist ever hated the church of Rome'.[46] These sentiments tend to reveal that the external threat of 'the foreigner' was often a convenient bogey used by many right-wing Conservatives to mask a deep and underlying fear of the immediate domestic threat from progressive forms of Liberalism and socialism. Indeed, there was an extreme strand of Conservative election propaganda, usually emanating from many pro-Conservative pressure groups, which combined xenophobia against 'foreigners' with attacks on 'socialists', 'aliens', 'cosmopolitans' and 'international financiers' in Britain who, it was alleged, were 'engaged in a conspiracy against the British Empire.'[47] There was a definite anti-Semitic tinge to some of this propaganda. Some Tory candidates in speeches expressed opposition to Jewish immigration, especially, in east London constituencies during the election campaign.[48]

However, it was not the Conservative propaganda campaign but the 'scaremongering' sections of the Tory popular press which often profoundly altered the course of the debate over key issues during the General Election campaign.[49] The most heated discussion of the German threat during the campaign for the January 1910 election was triggered off by a series of articles on the German menace by Robert Blatchford which appeared in the *Daily Mail* during December 1909.

Blatchford, who was a socialist, used bitter anti-German language and concluded that Germany was 'deliberately planning to destroy the British Empire'.[50] A pamphlet of Blatchford's articles on the 'German Danger' sold a staggering 1.6 million copies during the course of the campaign and another 250,000 were given away free by Conservative canvassers to potential voters. Blatchford's critical and negative views of German foreign policy aims were frequently discussed and endorsed in the speeches of a great many Conservative candidates during the campaign, without, of course, the approval of Balfour or the Central Office. Significantly, the Conservative campaign gained any real impetus only when the German naval threat became a key issue. Balfour's most significant speech in the campaign at Hanley on 4 January 1910 was on the naval issue. In the speech, the Opposition leader claimed that a great many British people agreed that 'a struggle between this country and Germany was inevitable', and he argued that the Liberals 'were squandering naval supremacy'. In such circumstances, the Conservative Party, Balfour argued, had to agitate for the maintenance of naval supremacy.[51]

The result of the general election of January 1910 was inconclusive. The Conservative Party did make a net gain of 105 seats and won a total of 273 seats, with a 46.9 per cent share of the popular vote. This was two seats behind the Liberal Party's total of 275 seats, gained on a 43.5 per cent share of the total vote and a net loss of 105 seats. The Conservative increase in seats was not matched in the share of the popular vote which had only increased by 3.3 per cent on the disastrous result in 1906. The Conservatives had secured a hung parliament, but the Liberal Party, which could rely on parliamentary support from the 82 Irish Nationalists MPs, at the price of offering Home Rule, and also from 40 Labour MPs, remained in power. The turnout in the election was extremely high at 86.7 per cent, which reveals how much passion the 'Peers versus People' issue had registered among voters. The results of the January 1910 election exhibit sharp regional differences in the swing to the Conservatives from the Liberals. The resurgence of Conservative support was confined to middle class and rural areas in the midlands and the south of England. Conservative support hardly increased at all in the north, Scotland and Wales. The average swing to the Conservatives in the north in the January 1910 contest was a mere 3 per cent, and in some industrial areas, it was less than 1 per cent. In contrast, the swing to the Tories from the Liberals in the south of England was a very impressive 8 per cent. The only major urban area in which the Conservative vote grew substantially was Birmingham, the home of the most radical tariff reformers. Of the 58 seats in which the Conservative Party polled over 60 per cent of the total vote, only one of them was outside the south of England.[52] Overall, the Conservative Party fared as well in south of England as they had done in the 1900 'Khaki Election'. At the same time, Liberal support held up remarkably well in its traditional heartland in urban and industrial Britain.

The Tory recovery in rural areas in the south of England was due to several factors. The appeal by the 'die hard' peers to defend the land of the aristocracy against 'New Liberalism' appears to have struck a chord with many rural Tory voters. As Lord Salisbury explained, 'I very much believe that we prevailed amongst the agricultural constituencies because the leaders of opinion in the upper & middle classes ... strove as they have never striven before to gain the support of electors'.[53] It seems tariff reform propaganda in rural areas which stressed how foreign competition was destroying agriculture proved equally attractive. Another explanation for Conservative success in the south of England is the prominence of the naval issue in the campaign there. The emphasis in Conservative propaganda on 'unpatriotic radicals' endangering national security by supporting naval cuts does seem to have benefited some Tory candidates in the south of England. Some of the most spectacular swings to the Conservative Party in the January 1910 contest, 19.8 per cent at Portsmouth and 17.2 per cent at Chatham, were in naval dockyard towns. The Conservative candidate at Chatham, who highlighted the Anglo-German naval race throughout the campaign, achieved a swing of 7.2 per cent, while the Conservative candidate at Woolwich, who campaigned on the issue of Liberal defence cuts at the Woolwich Arsenal, also scored an impressive victory. It is probably worth adding that 60 'radical' Liberals, many of whom had supported naval cuts between 1906 and 1909, lost their seats in the south of England to Conservatives at the January 1910 General Election. A *Times* reporter noted that most Liberal candidates avoided mentioning their support for naval cuts during the campaign.[54] It is clear the Conservative campaign in the south was much better organised and coordinated than in the north. The Conservative Party definitely won 'the battle of the pamphlets' with the Liberals in the south, but it was winning back former voters, worried about the navy, rather than winning new converts to the 'positive' appeal of tariff reform. Conservative Party workers also ensured that plural votes were used by middle class voters in more than one constituency in the south. Tory canvassers also persuaded more 'lodgers' to register to vote in the south than in the north. In general, it was only in very isolated dockyard constituencies in the south where the naval issue proved the 'electoral cannonball' that Garvin had suggested it might be. Throughout the rest of the country, the naval arms race with Germany did not have a very significant impact on the outcome of the election.

The most plausible explanation for the poor performance of the Conservative Party in the urban and industrial areas of the north, especially in the constituencies of Lancashire, Yorkshire and Scotland in January 1910 was the unpopularity of tariff reform and the preferment of the working classes for free trade. As the *Daily Telegraph* reported, 'Many working men have hazily gathered that Tariff Reform is the name of a plot between the Tories and the Peers, involving dear bread, black bread or the likelihood of no bread for the people'.[55] It is also noticeable how much the Conservative campaign in the north downplayed the naval issue, except in very isolated shipbuilding areas. In the Newcastle seat – which included the Armstrong and Vickers naval shipyard – the Tory candidate lost narrowly despite a rabble-rousing campaign that constantly emphasised the 'German menace'.[56]

The interpretation of the election results of January 1910 within the Conservative Party did not produce any clear consensus about the outcome. Austen Chamberlain flatly refused to accept that tariff reform had been a turn off for new voters, and he lost no time in informing his colleagues: 'Where we won, we won on and by tariff reform'.[57] A report on the Conservative campaign by party workers for the National Union in Yorkshire cited a number of reasons for the defeat, including, apathy among party workers, poor local organisation and speakers from London who did not tailor their speeches to the needs of local voters. On the issue of tariff reform, it was stressed that 'it was not sufficiently pressed' in the campaign in Yorkshire which became bogged down in the attempt of Tory candidates to contradict the Liberal claims that 'tariff reform meant dearer food'.[58] A report by the Liverpool Constituency Associations warned Central Office: 'We will lose another election through trying to force that vague, indefinite fog they call Tariff Reform'.[59] The Conservative campaign in the north, which had persistently stressed that 'protectionist' Germany enjoyed a higher standard of living than 'free trade' Britain did not prove attractive in either rural or industrial regions.

The second general election of 1910 took place in December. The short duration between the two elections meant that the Conservative pamphlets, posters and leaflets produced for the first election on the issues of tariff reform and the navy were simply recycled and used again. In the months between the two elections, there was also no attempt to reorganise the functions of Central Office and the National Union with regard to the control of propaganda. Nor was any effort made by Central Office to review party policy on most of the key issues. The National Union, however, did make a request to 'kindred organisations', including the Tariff Reform League, to consult more closely with the council of the National Union in order to prevent 'overlapping' and 'confusion' in the distribution of electoral propaganda.[60]

In a desperate attempt to weaken the persuasive Liberal argument that the standard of living enjoyed by workers in Germany was lower than in Britain, the Tariff Reform League, with the support of the National Union, sponsored a number of trips to Germany by British workers 'with an open mind' during the summer of 1910.[61] The reports of the 'Tariff Trippers' visits to Germany were included in the new edition of *How To Canvass* for the Unionist, which was used by canvassers at the second general election in December 1910. Canvassers were advised to contrast the Liberal view that Germans live on food that 'would not be given to a tramp in England' with the first-hand evidence provided by the ordinary workers who had visited Germany and who had reportedly seen 'no tramps, no loafers, and no ragged people'.[62] Garvin was not very impressed by the strength of the evidence produced by these visits, and he advised Balfour to downgrade both tariff reform and the naval issue at the second election. He wanted the campaign to concentrate on defending the House of Lords as 'the only bulwark against socialism'.[63] To water down the policy of tariff reform still further, Garvin suggested to Balfour that the Conservative campaign should promise electors that a Tory government would 'tax the foreigner, but ... not tax your food'.[64]

The general election campaign in December 1910 was less than a month in duration. The number of contested seats dropped from 571 in January to 485 and turnout fell by 5.6 per cent. The future of the House of Lords was the dominant issue of a very lacklustre campaign. As a result, concentration on the German naval threat by Conservative candidates declined quite dramatically. The heat and passion over the Anglo-German naval race had definitely simmered greatly in the months between the two elections. References to the German naval threat by Conservative candidates in December 1910 were noticeably less prominent and were much more restrained. A total of 74 per cent of Conservative candidates ranked the House of Lords as the key issue in December 1910, with only 17 per cent making tariff reform the top issue. Only 2 per cent of Tory candidates made national defence the most dominant issue, which was an incredibly steep decline from the January contest.[65]

To help boost the now faltering tariff reform cause in Lancashire, Bonar Law, dubbed by Liberals as 'the archangel of tariff reform', gave up his safe seat in Dulwich to fight Manchester North West. Bonar Law's campaign did attempt to refute Liberal claims that the German diet consisted of horsemeat and black bread, and he also repeated the now tired view that Germans enjoyed a higher standard of living than was the case in 'free trade' Britain.[66] Bonar Law halved the Liberal majority of Sir George Kemp in Manchester North West but failed to win the seat.

Balfour generally played down the tariff reform issue during the campaign, and it generally lacked the revivalist enthusiasm it had generated in January. The most significant important intervention by the Conservative leader during the election campaign came in speech at the Albert Hall on 29 November 1910 when he promised that an incoming Tory Government would not introduce taxes on foreign imports of food without a referendum. Everyone knew the British public would definitely endorse free trade in any referendum. So most of the Tory press felt Balfour's 'referendum pledge' would greatly help Conservative prospects at the election.

In the end, it made very little difference. The general election of December 1910 produced a virtual repeat of the January result. The Conservatives polled 46.8 per cent of the popular vote, ending up with 271 seats. The Liberal Party took 44.1 per cent of the votes and 272 seats, but with the promised support of 84 Irish Nationalists and 42 Labour MPs, the Liberal Government remained in power. A total of 55 seats changed hands during the election, but the Conservative

Party ended up with a net gain of just one solitary seat. The swing to the Conservatives was a mere 0.8 per cent nationally which goes to show how little voters minds had changed since the January contest. The highest regional swings in the election for the Conservative Party were in Lancashire (3.3%) and industrial seats in Wales (2.5%) which indicates that Balfour's referendum pledge on tariff reform did help to increase Conservative support in these areas.[67]

One fact that could not be ignored was that the Conservatives had suffered a third consecutive election defeat. One group of Conservatives ascribed the electoral difficulties of the party, not to tariff reform, but to the ineffective leadership of Balfour. Maxse summed up the views of a great many on the right when he stated, 'Balfour must go, or Tariff reform will go – that is the alternative'.[68] A second group blamed continued electoral failure on the problems of party organisation. As Midleton commented, 'All organisations were completely incapable of co-operating at the election'.[69] A group of 60 Conservative MPs, dubbed the '1900 Club', sent a petition to Balfour demanding an overhaul of 'the rusty old machinery'.[70] A local agent in Southampton reported that when he arrived in Southampton a fortnight before the December 1910 election 'not a single voter had been canvassed'.[71] These protests prompted Balfour to set up a committee to examine party organisation in February 1911, which recommended greater central control of the party. A party chairman, Sir Arthur Steel Maitland, was given total power over propaganda, finance and speakers. The National Union was placed under the control of the Principal agent, and its powers over party propaganda were completely curtailed. The chief whip, who had previously been responsible for the overall management of the party in parliament and in the country, was left to concentrate on party discipline at Westminster. Relations with the press were greatly improved by the appointment of Sir Malcom Fraser as Chief Press Officer, who set up the Lobby Press Service, which acted as a useful informal briefing mechanism for the Conservative Party to the editors of national and local newspapers. The main casualties of these organisational reforms were Acland-Hood and Percival Hughes, who both resigned. These organisational changes have been seen as 'landmarks in the party's transition into the world of modern politics'.[72] A third group within the party blamed electoral failure on the unpopular policy of tariff reform. In spite of all the propaganda, most electors did not believe that life in 'protectionist' Germany was better than in 'free trade' Britain. As Lord Galway told Austen Chamberlain, 'the electorate do not care a straw for tariff reform and you cannot win an election on that cry'.[73] The results of the two general elections of 1910 tended to support the view that tariff reform was not so much an electoral cannon ball but just a ball and chain. Bonar Law, although a firm believer in tariff reform, recognised when he became leader that the policy was not practical politics. From 1911 to 1914, tariff reform was relegated to virtual insignificance in the Conservative programme, as the issue of Irish Home Rule assumed an all-consuming dominance over the party.

The high point of Conservative electoral activity on the German threat, therefore, was the period immediately prior to the general election of January 1910. In this period, the naval and economic threat posed by Germany did play a significant role in the election-eering strategy and especially in the propaganda tactics of the party. There was no orchestrated plan on the part of the Conservative Party to create a systematic form of 'xenophobic propaganda' on the German naval or economic threat.[74] Official Conservative Party propaganda attempted to avoid outright scaremongering against Germany in favour of a negative attack on the Liberal Party. However, the attempt to confine the debate on the navy to a domestic squabble with Liberals over the proper level of naval spending proved impossible. The external threat from Germany was highlighted during the Conservative election campaign in order to illustrate to voters why the extra spending was required. Balfour and the Central Office found it impossible to stop Conservative candidates from making public their private concerns about the German naval threat, and the various scaremongering activities of the Tariff Reform League and the National Service League simply showed Balfour could not exert the sort of control over the Conservative Party message on Germany as he achieved at Westminster.

In the projection of tariff reform by Conservative propaganda at the General Elections of 1910, Germany also played a significant role. Conservative candidates often presented Germany as a model for Britain to follow but also as a threat to British industry and jobs. Even so, 'anti-Germanism' was not the chief characteristic of the language of Conservative election propaganda on tariff reform.[75] Conservative propaganda on tariff reform, supplemented by the Tariff Reform

League portrayed the German fiscal system as a model and presented the German way of life in positive terms. The projection of Germany as a protectionist wonderland in Conservative propaganda was linked to the needs of the domestic party struggle with the Liberals over economic policy. A great deal of Conservative propaganda on tariff reform presented a dual 'positive' and 'negative' image of Germany. The 'unpatriotic' policies of 'Liberal radicals' often intermingled with the equally underhand tactics of the German 'Herr Dumper'.

In general, the German threat played an ambiguous and rather confusing role in the electioneering strategy of the Conservative Party. Conservative propaganda presented the 'good' Germany of tariff reform and the 'bad' Germany of increased naval building side by side. At the same time, the Conservative leadership took pains to distance itself from the 'scaremongering' aspects of its own campaign and suggested the party did not want to openly inflame Anglo-German relations at a time of great international tension. To this end, Balfour and the Central Office did urge Conservative candidates to adopt a restrained attitude when discussing Germany during the election campaigns of 1910. However, most of the policy advice which candidates and canvassers received from the National Union, which was dominated by the radical tariff reformers and the propaganda produced by the Tariff Reform League, more often than not presented German foreign policy actions in extremely hostile terms and offered very little hope for future Anglo-German friendship. At the same time, the popular Conservative press presented Germany in a similarly hostile manner. The end result of all these internal contradictions and mixed messages was the external presentation of a confused image of Germany by the Conservative Party to the electorate which was both a model and a threat.

6
Extra Parliamentary Pressure Groups and Germany

Extra parliamentary pressure groups had been a prominent feature of British political activity outside Westminster ever since the days of the Anti-Corn Law League in the 1840s.[1] But most of the leading pressure groups of the Victorian era were dominated by Liberals and non-Conformist groups. Conservatives, the self appointed upholders of tradition, tended not to form or join such organisations. Only after 1880 did pressure groups dominated by Conservatives begin to appear – most notably, the Fair Trade League (1881), which supported protectionism, and the Imperial Federation League (1884), which advocated closer unity within the Empire. It was during the Edwardian period when Conservative pressure-group activity accelerated most dramatically with the founding of such popular bodies as the National Service League (founded in 1902), the Tariff Reform League (1903), the Imperial Maritime League (1908), the Anti-Socialist Union (1908) and the Budget Protest League (1909). As one Conservative commented, 'If past eras have been known as the stone age, bronze age and iron age, surely the present period in our history might be known as the league age'.[2] Pressure groups were part of a complex interaction between Westminster politics and society. These groups aimed to influence the Conservative Party to adopt their policies and to influence the public to support their aims through extensive propaganda activities.

It is, of course, tempting to view those pressure groups, whose membership lists were dominated by Conservatives, as safety valves for protesters within the Conservative Party during a period of extreme electoral crisis or as manifestations of the growth of a new 'radical right' which feared the growth of progressive forces at home, warned of external threats to British power and wanted to transform the Conservative Party into a 'progressive' political force fit and able to deal effectively with the rise of socialism, more progressive forms of Liberalism and the coming of mass democracy.

A study of the aims, membership and policies of the unprecedented number of pressure groups which existed from 1905 to 1914 would be a vast undertaking. For the purposes of this chapter, the study of pressure-group activity by Conservatives is limited to an examination of the views towards Germany of three important pressure groups: the National Service League, the Imperial Maritime League and the Tariff Reform League. The choice of these three organisations is not arbitrary. Unlike many of the other Edwardian pressure groups, which drew support from across the political spectrum and could legitimately claim to be 'non-party' organisations, the membership lists of these particular groups were dominated by Conservative MPs and peers, and they were overwhelmingly supported by members of the Conservative Party. The Tariff Reform League, as we have already seen in the previous chapter, used its vast financial resources to aid the electoral activities of Conservative candidates. In many constituencies between 1905 and 1914, the Conservative candidate owed allegiance to both the local Conservative association and the local committee of the Tariff Reform League. On the surface, the National Service League has a much greater claim to be termed a 'non-political' organisation because it functioned separately from the official Conservative Party machinery. But the membership of the National Service League was predominantly Conservative, boasting of 88 Conservative MPs as card-carrying members, compared with only three Liberals and hardly any Labour or working class member. Many prominent Conservatives, including Wyndham, Lee, Amery, Milner, Smith and Curzon were active members of the National Service League. The Imperial Maritime League, was a much smaller organisation, but it never even pretended to be 'non-political' and openly urged voters to vote Conservative at election time. Yet while it was acceptable for Conservatives to join the Tariff Reform or National Service League the same could not be said of the Imperial Maritime League, which was regarded by the Conservative leadership as a 'renegade' and extreme organisation that only gained support from a small number of very independently minded backbench Conservative MPs and peers and a number of right-wing newspaper editors, including Maxse and Gwynne. But all three organisations had one thing in common: they were all concerned with the naval, military and economic vulnerability of Britain to the challenge of German power.

The National Service League was set up in February 1902, with the central aim of educating the nation to 'an intelligent appreciation of military questions'.[3] It was the most important pressure group that campaigned for military training during the Edwardian period. The impetus for such an organisation grew out of the dissatisfaction felt by many leading Conservatives and army figures over the poor performance of British volunteers during the Anglo-Boer War. In the years following the South African war, the speeches and writings of military leaders resonate with words of pessimism about the condition of the British army. Most questioned whether Britain could maintain its position as a major world power in the face of the growth of a formidable rival in Europe such as Germany without the introduction of some form of compulsory military training.

The chief aim of the National Service League was to form a body of public opinion in favour of military training.[4] The leadership claimed that the organisation was a single issue, non-partisan pressure group, which was above the cut and thrust of party politics. It concentrated its efforts on persuading the political parties to adopt military service, but it did not adopt an electoral strategy and stood no candidates at national or local elections. In 1905, the public standing of the new organisation increased greatly when Lord Roberts, aged 73, and the most well-known Edwardian military figure, became the President of the infant organisation. Roberts had a gift for presentation and a persuasive tongue. He was the major driving force behind the demand for conscription in the Edwardian age. The argument he used in support of military training was simple and direct: the military resources of Britain were much too dependent on naval power and needed to be supplemented by service in the army for every man 'high or low, rich or poor', in order to repel a possible invasion of the British Isles by a foreign power. The vast majority of the membership of the National Service League recognised the German navy and army as the most likely invading force.[5] But, even Roberts realised his quest for compulsory military training was deeply unpopular among the British public. So to make it more palatable, he proposed only four months 'training' for all males aged between 18 and 21. This rather feeble training model was borrowed from Switzerland, a neutral country, which trained conscripts for short periods, unlike the two years which was normally served by German conscripts. The primary reason why Roberts emphasised the Swiss model was a tactical move that aimed to distance the National Service League from the charge that it wanted to transform Britain into a militaristic state along German lines. To further emphasise that 'military service' was a purely defensive measure, Roberts stressed that recruits would only be used for service within the British Isles.

The most significant factor which explains the growth in support for military service was fear about the potential of German military and naval power to dominate the European continent and threaten Britain's vast extra-European empire. In October 1904, the National Service League had a mere 1,725 members, including just five Conservative MPs.[6] In May 1909, with fears of the German naval threat running at panic levels, membership had grown to 35,000, located in 50 branches nation wide.[7] By 1914, the number of members stood at the very healthy figure of 100,000, and local branches had mushroomed to over a hundred.[8] Even more remarkable was the growth in support for the National Service League among Conservative MPs and peers. In December 1910, 88 Conservative MPs appeared on official membership lists, supplemented by over a hundred Conservative members of the House of Lords. This upsurge of parliamentary support for the National Service League led to the formation of a parliamentary committee of the National Service League in the House of Commons led by Sir Henry Craik, the Conservative MP.[9]

Despite the predominance of Conservatives within the membership of the National Service League, the organisation still attempted to win support from across the political and social divide. But close scrutiny of the membership lists of the organisation throughout its various branches dotted around the map of the British Isles reveals that the attempt to create a non-partisan mass movement was a complete failure. The vast bulk of the membership were existing traditional and long-standing middle-class supporters of the Conservative Party.[10] Most of the local branches of the National Service League were located in places such as the Midlands, the Home Counties, the south east and London where the Conservative Party support was already very strong. Membership was at its lowest level in areas where the Conservative Party was extremely weak, most notably, the industrial areas of the north, Wales and Scotland. Local branches of the National Service League in most rural areas were run by former military officers and members of the landed aristocracy. Even the traditional leaders of rural society in the south of England had great difficulty persuading local agricultural labourers that the National Service League was nothing more than an auxiliary Conservative organisation masquerading in non-partisan colours.[11] The recruitment drive in rural areas was far more successful than in industrial regions. A useful contrast can be drawn between the Essex branch, an existing Conservative stronghold in the south east, which saw membership increase from 560 to 1,000 between 1906 and 1909, and the Manchester branch in the 'free trade' stronghold of industrial Lancashire, which attracted a paltry 30 new members during the same period. During the summer of 1912, the National Service League put on a series of open air meetings, designed to overcome 'the apathy of the working man', in most of the industrial cities in the north. Lord Roberts, who spoke at several of these highly publicised events admitted by the end of the tour that the average working man 'continues to be apathetic to the National Service League'.[12]

The leadership of the National Service League was drawn from the extreme 'radical right' of the Conservative Party, and most of the leading activists in the organisation were deeply concerned about the German threat. One of the most influential was Lord Milner, the vice-president, who was the thoughtful son of a German professor. Milner argued that a pool of trained reserves was necessary to 'weigh in the scales of a Continental struggle with Germany'.[13] He described himself as 'a freelance' who was fighting on the side of the Conservative Party even though he professed, with some difficulty, to be independent of it. The National Service League, according to Milner, was as an 'Educational Agency' whose main objective was to change public opinion in Britain from opposition to support for conscription by means of a concerted programme of propaganda.[14] To Milner, therefore, the pressure-group activism and the energetic propaganda activities of the National Service League were a powerful antidote to the 'timidity' and 'lethargy' of the leadership of the Conservative Party at Westminster towards the German threat.[15] Milner viewed conscription as part of a grand plan to build a more technocratic and well-organised Government and military machine in Britain that would compete with the growing economic and military power of Germany and the USA. It is also worth adding that Milner was infatuated by Germany, with its strong and well-organised authoritarian state devoted to patriotic ends, with a leadership free of parliamentary control and a well-disciplined proletariat. This German model which Milner believed had contributed to the rapid growth of the *Kaiserreich* was one he wanted Britain to emulate, especially in the fields of military organisation and economic policy, and also in the creation of a powerful state machine devoted to ideals of 'national efficiency'.

But Milner's complex approach towards the German threat was by no means shared by many of the other leading activists in the National Service League. A great many are best described as hyper-patriots and ultra-imperialists who often displayed outright hostility and sometimes bigoted harshness when discussing the growth of German military and naval power. They all had an obsession with the military threat posed by Germany. Their correspondence bristles with over dramatic language about the 'German danger'. Most were ambivalent towards the traditional political parties, and they were all extremely frustrated with what they saw as the dilatory and the timid approach adopted by the Conservative Party towards the German threat. In essence, they wanted the Conservative Party to become a radical and modern right-wing alternative to the rising appeal of progressive forms of Liberalism and Socialism. A typical example of the king of person attracted to the National Service League is L.J. Maxse, the editor of the *National Review*, who even wrote a book entitled *Germany on the Brain* which chronicled his fear and loathing of almost every aspect of the *Kaiserreich*. He was fond of telling paranoid ripping yarns about German officers and spies roaming around the British countryside taking 'bicycles in all directions' and eagerly gathering intelligence for an 'inevitable invasion'.[16] The vitriolic language Maxse used in the *National Review* was deeply antagonistic towards Germany, and he carried his prejudiced arguments to the very extreme of right-wing intolerance of all things 'foreign' and 'alien'. He frequently stereotyped Germany as a 'bully' or a 'menace', led by a Kaiser with 'peace on his lips', but 'war on his mind', leading a population 'systematically trained by the powers that be, to look upon a war with England as a moral duty'.[17] He was firmly convinced that Germany could only be deterred from launching an 'inevitable bid for European supremacy', by introducing conscription. But he held out very little hope the National Service League could arouse:

> our political deadheads of either Party – to who Party (with a big P) stands for country (with a small c) – to any realisation of the German danger which is greater than the Spanish danger at the end of the sixteenth century, the French danger at the beginning of the eighteenth century or even the Napoleonic menace of a hundred years ago.[18]

In spite of Maxse's openly antagonistic language, he still denied, in the face of all evidence and logic to the contrary, that he was 'anti-German', rather unconvincingly. Even so, he claimed that his critics would be 'hard put to find a single sentence from the *National Review* which revealed prejudice against the German people'. Maxse suggested he reserved his strongest language for the 'irresponsible oligarchy called German Government', and he frequently castigated 'the tortuous duplicity of German policy'.[19] Maxse also contrasted a 'strong and vibrant Germany', building up its army and navy in preparation for an 'inevitable war' with a 'timid' Britain led by politicians absorbed by the narrow issues, as he saw it, of domestic politics and too afraid to champion conscription in case they lost electoral support.[20] In Maxse's editorials, speeches and in his private correspondence on Anglo-German relation, there is a massive conviction of the right-fulness of his views, mingled with desperation, bordering on a very bad case of paranoia. He fully recognised that he was regarded as 'disruptive right-wing' Germanophobe by Balfour, Lansdowne and the mainstream of the Conservative Party. To the Liberals, he was simply derided as a right-wing buffoon who soured Anglo-German relations for no good reason. Maxse's self-perception as an 'outcast' on the extreme fringe of the mainstream of political discourse is graphically illustrated by a typical editorial he wrote in the *National Review* in May 1912 on the German threat in which he compares Britain to a 'Titanic, obviously plunging at full speed towards certain disaster, because her so called statesmen refused to see the obvious or prepare against the inevitable'.[21] It is also evident in Maxse's description of the Conservative Party at Westminster as a 'bunch of Parliamentary syco-phants who are prepared to open their mouths and shut their ears and swallow whatever Mr. Balfour may give them'.[22]

The National Service League attracted many similar right-wing eccentrics. Leopold Amery, who wrote many of Lord Roberts' speeches and books, described the Conservative Party at Westminster as 'panic stricken sheep'.[23] F.S. Oliver, who came from a radical Scottish background, ferociously despised democracy and seemed to relish what he saw as the 'coming struggle' with Germany. 'Nothing will save us', he confessed, 'except the sight of blood running pretty freely, but whether British and German blood, or only British, I don't know – nor do I think it much matters'.[24]

All of these right-wing activists believed that a German invasion of the British Isles was imminent, and they exchanged details of the so-called secret German war plans and the activities of German spies in Britain. Even H.G. Wells' dire predictions about a future *War of the Worlds* seemed mild compared to the coming apocalyptic struggle with Germany these people imagined, not asleep, but awake in their beds. The power of their nightmares poured out in daylight in vitriolic prose. Colonel Repington, the *Times* Military Correspondent, another close adviser to Roberts on the question of a German invasion, often told a story – or was it a dream – about Count Metternich, the German Ambassador, whom he alleged often entertained between fifty and sixty exiled German officers every month behind closed doors at an Italian restaurant in London. After the spaghetti was eaten, the diners apparently drew up detailed plans for an invasion of the east coast. The story was obviously the figment of his fertile imagination. H.A. Gwynne, the editor of the *Standard*, obviously having similar nightmares he believed to be true, often relayed a story to fellow activists in the National Service League concerning his suspicion about a number of German-born hotel keepers in Aldershot, in the Isle of Wight and in several eastern coastal ports whom he claimed had created a secret and complex intelligence network which sent back details to Germany of the best coastal areas to mount a successful invasion.[25] Cecil Spring-Rice, a cantankerous ex-diplomat who had served for many years in Germany, often supplied Roberts and Maxse with pretty alarming reports of what he thought were German preparations for war. He was firmly convinced the German Government aimed to 'lull the English government to sleep, to make preparations in silence until it is too late for the government to take action'. He claimed that his information from Germany came from the 'highest sources', but he never revealed who they were, and all of his many invasion dates between 1907 to 1914 turned out to be completely wrong.[26] Not many sensible people took these far-fetched stories seriously at the time, and historians who make grandiose claims about the influence of the 'radical right' need to appreciate more fully how marginalised and plain 'loony' many of its leading figures were.

The chief propaganda aim of the National Service League was to convince the public of the danger of a German invasion. Lord Roberts who claimed that the National Service League had 'no desire to stir up an aggressive jingo spirit' did realise that the propaganda of the National Service League needed to 'grip the imagination' and 'stir the blood.'[27] To this end, the National Service League established its own monthly journal, *A Nation in Arms* (a title borrowed from a famous German military book). In 1908, *A Nation in Arms* enjoyed a fairly healthy circulation of 17,500.[28] In the pages of this journal, the military and naval danger posed by Germany looms very large, but it was often accompanied by admiration for German military progress. The Earl of Meath, a member of the executive council of the National Service League claimed that 'most Englishmen were inferior to Germans in intelligence, knowledge and practice not because we are an inferior race but because we neglect the military training of young men'.[29] Lord George Hamilton, another leading figure in the organisation, commented that if Nelson was alive he 'would have been on an National Service League platform'.[30] He also suggested that on the day military training was introduced, Anglo-German relations would immediately improve, because German leaders would realise 'they could not bully us with impunity'.[31] Most National Service League propaganda emphasised the possible social benefits of conscription. One National Service League supporter, who visited Germany frequently, claimed that it was army life which gave health, exercise and discipline to young Germans, even encouraging them to 'wash behind the ears'.[32] In another typical article, Miss H.S. Cheetham, a frequent contributor to *A Nation in Arms*, contrasted German 'thoroughness' with British 'slackness' and concluded, 'The German military system has been the making of modern Germany'.[33]

The most dominant theme of National Service League propaganda was the possibility of a German invasion. In those newspapers and periodicals that supported the conscriptionist cause, there were numerous articles devoted to the subject. A constant flurry of popular books, newspaper articles, pamphlets, magazines, plays, posters and comics brought the invasion scare constantly to the attention of the public. In comics, the German people were often described as 'sausage munchers' who were planning war. In weekly magazines and in many popular novels, it was suggested that German spies were already in Britain, collecting information, making detailed plans and even building elaborate underground ammunition stores in preparation for what was called 'a barbaric Prussian invasion'.[34] A great many of these invasion novels and articles were written by supporters of the National Service League, and many received sponsorship and endorsement from the organisation. The National Service League also financed a number of theatre plays on the theme of invasion. One such drama, which drew large audiences was called *A Nation in Arms* and was based on the best-selling book by Roberts. It graphically depicts a successful German invasion of the south of England. Roberts claimed the scenes in the play, 'are by no means an exaggerated picture of the scenes which would occur in England if an invading army was able to effect a landing on our shores'.[35]

For most of the leading activists in the National Service League, the strong emphasis on invasion was not a mere propaganda ploy, but represented the public expression of their own very real private anxieties about the growth of German military and naval power. As Lord Roberts explained in his evidence to the Committee of Imperial Defence (CID) sub-committee on invasion in 1908, 'Everybody in Germany – every school and University in Germany – is being educated to the idea of invading England'.[36] In support of these views, Roberts presented evidence to the sub-committee from the British ambassador in Berlin and from ten British consuls, based in German ports, who all warned of the preparations in Germany for a 'Bolt from the Blue' attack on poorly defended British coastal ports.[37] Roberts often compared Britain to 'a jeweller's shop', with a thin glass window, and Germany to 'a burglar waiting until the policeman [the Navy] turned his back and broke in.'[38] Yet Roberts realised that National Service League propaganda, which constantly warned of the German danger, had exerted precious little influence on a British people who 'shut their eyes to the dangers' and 'would take no steps to resist invasion'.[39] In spite of all the hype, much of it popular with certain sections of the public, and the useful additional support it received from many leading newspapers and periodicals, most notably, the *Observer, The Times*, the *Standard*, the *Daily Express*, the *Daily*

Telegraph, the *Morning Post* and the *National Review*, the National Service League never gained widespread public support. The Conservative Party, which gave the League its largest group of parliamentary supporters, believed it was electoral suicide to openly support the military service, while to support Liberals, Socialists and Irish Nationalists was miniscule. All this tends to emphasise that the overwhelming majority of the British public did not believe in the idea of a German invasion, and they preferred to rely on naval power to prevent it.

The Tariff Reform League, formed in 1903, was the most powerful and influential Conservative pressure group of all, but unlike the National Service League, it was intimately connected with the official Conservative Party machinery. The broadside against free trade delivered by the radical and imperialist Joseph Chamberlain on 15 May 1903, which demanded the introduction of tariffs on foreign imports outside of the British Empire, is traditionally viewed as the starting point of the formation of the Tariff Reform League. But Chamberlain's speech was really the rallying call of an already growing body of protectionists within the Conservative Party. In April 1902, H.H. Marks, a Conservative MP, and 24 leading industrialists met to consider the formation of a tariff reform pressure group. On 14 May 1903, the Protection League was established, which soon changed its name to the Imperial Tariff Reform League and finally to the Tariff Reform League on 21 July 1903. On the very same day, the first meeting of the new organisation was convened at the luxurious Westminster Palace Hotel, under the chairmanship of the Duke of Sutherland.

The Tariff Reform League claimed its principal aim was the safeguarding of 'the industrial interests of the Empire' through the introduction of taxes on imported goods and the creation of a colonial customs union. For Joseph Chamberlain, and most of the other leading tariff reformers, it was a two pronged policy, designed to halt British economic decline and to provide the Conservative Party with a 'progressive' policy in order to weaken the appeal of radical forms of Liberalism and the growing appeal of socialism. Even though the Conservatives had suffered a crushing defeat in 1906, the Tariff Reform League emerged in an extremely strong position within the party in opposition. Of the total of 157 MPs left after the defeat, 109 were 'Chamberlainites', 32 were 'Balfourites', and only 11 were 'free traders'.

To many of Chamberlain's supporters, tariff reform became similar to an evangelical religious sect which demanded total loyalty and devotion from its followers.[40] It was a very well-organised pressure group with its own policy think tank: the Tariff Commission, a popular monthly magazine, *Monthly Notes on Tariff Reform*, a nation-wide network of local branches, a trade union association, a powerful group of financial supporters and a modern and well coordinated programme of propaganda.[41] Richard Jay describes the Tariff Reform League as 'the most powerful propaganda machine that peacetime British history has seen'.[42] The membership of the Tariff Reform League, whose average age was 49, was strongest in the Midlands, Chamberlain's political heartland, and in London and scattered parts of the south east of England. Hard-core support for the Tariff Reform League was, in fact, rather middle aged and popular in areas with an already strong tradition of voting Conservative. But support was also strong in areas containing industries such as iron, steel, tin, glass, building materials and chemicals, all of which faced very stiff industrial competition in home and export markets. In rural areas, membership of the Tariff Reform League was much lower, except in those regions in which local agricultural producers faced foreign competitors.[43]

In the early propaganda of the Tariff Reform League, the German economic threat did feature very prominently. As already mentioned, in Chapter 5, one of the most potent images used in this propaganda was that of 'Herr Dumper', the rotund German shop keeper who sold cheap goods of so-called dubious quality to extremely 'gullible' British importers which resulted in the loss of British jobs. The early issues of *Monthly Notes* on Tariff Reform, the official journal of the Tariff Reform League, also feature many articles and reports which suggest that German industry used Britain as a dumping ground for its goods. The German bogey was also used in a satirical manner in cartoons and songs, most notably a popular music hall composition called 'Herr Schmit's advice', which featured the memorable line: 'Cobden [the famous Manchester free trader] vos a vondourous man'.[44] It is, however, important to recognise that German stereotypes were by no means the only ones used in Tariff Reform propaganda. A long list of 'foreign' stereotypes from around the world were frequently depicted in tariff reform literature.

To simply view the growth of the Tariff Reform League as primarily due to fears about Anglo-German trade rivalry is a gross over-simplification. Global economic development which affected British competitiveness and the influence of the domestic political situation were far more important than any singular obsession with the growth of German economic power. During the early years of the twentieth century, both the Conservative and Liberal parties realised that finding policies which appealed to the working classes were likely to become the deciding factor in future elections. Joseph Chamberlain and his supporters believed that the Conservative Party needed to find a popular policy which aimed to persuade industrial workers that economic and social reform could be financed by taxing foreign goods and not by increasing taxation for business, the landed aristocracy or the middle classes. To convince working class voters in industrial regions that protectionism did not mean a fall in their standard of living, it became vital to portray the economic and social condition of Germany, the most prosperous protectionist economy in Europe, not as a rival but as a positive model, worthy of emulation. This helps to explain why an endless stream of Tariff Reform League propaganda depicted Germany as place that combined protectionism with social reform for the benefit of the working classes. It also explains why the key enemies of Tariff Reform League propaganda were the Liberal free traders who allowed 'foreign' goods to be 'dumped' in the British market.[45] To appeal to the consumer interests of the average voter, tariff reform propaganda also suggested that free trade 'taxes the poor through duties on tobacco, spirits, beer and sugar', while 'foreigners' were allowed to send their goods into the British market tax-free.[46]

By and large, tariff reform propaganda presented Germany as an economic role model and a very prosperous society. Most pamphlets and posters of the Tariff Reform League suggest Germany had progressed at an incredible pace under protectionist policies, while Britain had fallen behind economically because of blind adherence to free trade. Tariff reform propaganda was extremely sophisticated by the standards of the Edwardian age, with specific groups of workers in a wide variety of industries having propaganda tailored to suit their needs. Railway workers were told wages for German rail workers had increased rapidly under protectionism.[47] Glass workers informed that while unemployment in their own industry was rising rapidly, it was falling in the German glass sector.[48] The sorry plight of the granite trade in Britain was blamed on the rapid growth of imports from Norway and Sweden.[49] Many other workers in a wide range of industries and trades were targeted in a similar manner.

Another major feature of Tariff Reform League propaganda was to urge potential supporters to dismiss 'bogey tales about Germany', put out by Liberal free traders, and to 'Look at Germany' where they would find the workers enjoying increased wages, reduced working hours, low rents, better education, welfare benefits and a much more nutritional diet than workers could afford in 'free trade' Britain.[50] Such arguments were an integral part of the long and protracted domestic debate between tariff reformers and Liberals over the standard of living in Germany. To help resolve this bitter struggle between the two parties, the Tariff Reform League financed several trips to Germany by 'ordinary workmen'. The most significant of these occurred in 1910, when the Tariff Reform League sent a large party of 'average' British workmen, 'of all political persuasions' on a free holiday to cities in Germany.[51] The national press dubbed them 'The Tariff Trippers'. The crucial aim of these trips was to use the evidence of the 'ordinary workers' in order to weaken the constant and seemingly persuasive Liberal claims that most Germans live on food, which Lloyd George had claimed, 'we would not give to tramps'.[52] In the summer of 1910, the 'Tariff Trippers', working on the principle that 'seeing is believing' spent over a month touring Germany at the expense of the Tariff Reform League. After returning home, these 'working men' told waiting reporters that the German worker was well educated, well dressed, well fed and very happy. They also mentioned that unemployment and the cost of living were much lower in Germany than in Britain. 'After what I saw', said one Manchester worker, 'I have become convinced that the German worker with protective tariffs, is far better off than our workers.' What also impressed these British workers about life in Germany was the absence of poverty and 'the lack of tramps and beggars' in all the German towns and cities they visited. Even the much derided German 'black bread', which the Liberals had constantly suggested they would 'not feed to a dog', was sampled by the Tariff Trippers and found to be 'tasty and nutritious'. In general, the British workers who visited Germany, in the summer of 1910, claimed the Liberal Party had been guilty of 'vicious fabrications' in its portrayal of social conditions in Germany.[53] The visit of the Tariff Trippers illustrates just how important it was for the electoral success of tariff reform to portray Germany as a prosperous and congenial place to live, with workers enjoying what they claimed was a much higher standard of living than in Britain. The motive behind much of this tariff reform propaganda was not designed to improve diplomatic relations between Britain and Germany but was an integral part of an electoral strategy designed to reassure potential working class Tory voters that their standard of living would not fall under protectionism. To support this case, life in Germany was used and abused by the Tariff Reform League and the Conservative Party for purely domestic political purposes.

The Imperial Maritime League, the most radical of these groups, was established on 27 January 1908 by a rebel group within the Navy League, led by Lionel Horton-Smith, a prominent barrister, and Harold Wyatt, a writer on naval affairs.[54] The Imperial Maritime League was a very small pressure group, positioned on the extreme right of the Conservative spectrum. It did not have an organisation or membership comparable to either the National Service League or the Tariff Reform League. The real importance of the Imperial Maritime League, for the purposes of this study, lies in the fact that it was supported by the most extreme and supposedly the most Germanophobic members of the so-called radical right. The two major factors behind the formation of the Imperial Maritime League were anger with the moderate Navy League leadership for refusing to criticise Sir John Fisher's decision to create a new Home Fleet in October 1906 by cutting back on battleship strength in the Atlantic, the English Channel and the Mediterranean, and dissatisfaction with the Navy League stance of refusing to protest against the decision of the Liberal Government to cut naval spending on battleships from £8.5 million to £6 million between 1906 and 1909. F.T. Jane, one of the leading rebels within the Navy League, commented, 'Every man – whatever he may call himself – who cuts down the Navy is to be regarded as a public enemy and should be treated as such'.[55] Maxse – who not surprisingly supported the Imperial Maritime League – described the struggle within the Navy League as one involving the 'deadheads' who supported the 'Fisher revolution', which, of course, included Balfour and those who were content to 'swallow whatever the Admiralty offers them', and the 'agitators' who realised that 'the strength of the navy would only be preserved by constantly emphasising the dangers Britain faced from the German fleet'.[56]

The leadership of the Navy League supported the principle of bi-partisanship in defence matters and wanted to keep the Navy a non-party issue. At the same rime, a rebel group within the Navy League wanted the Liberal cuts in naval expenditure to be vigorously attacked. In February 1907, the Navy League leadership tried to prevent dissidents from opening up a debate on the reductions in naval spending and emphasised that the Navy League would not engage in party political attacks on the naval policy of the Liberal Government.[57] The fierce debate between the moderate and rebellious sections of the Navy League became a leading topic of discussion in most of the popular Conservative newspapers. On 15 May 1907, at the Navy League annual general meeting, the split within the Navy League grew even wider. In a last ditch attempt to resolve the differences between the 'moderates' and the 'rebels', an extraordinary general meeting of the Navy League was held on 19 July 1907. At the meeting, Wyatt claimed that the Navy League had 'stifled public debate' over Liberal cuts in naval expenditure and rather than adopting the role of 'watchdog' of the navy it had become 'the spaniel of Whitehall'.[58] In response, the leadership of the Navy League branded the criticism of the rebels as party political.[59] The voting figures on an amendment, tabled by Wyatt and Horton Smith, at the extraordinary General Meeting, which called for the Navy League to adopt a critical stance against Liberal cuts in naval expenditure, show that 40 per cent of the branches of the Navy League actually supported the radical stance adopted by the rebels, even though the attempt to change of the policy of Navy League ended in failure.

In January 1908, the leaders of the rebellion, Horton-Smith and Wyatt, announced, in a blaze of publicity, that they were leaving the Navy League to set up a new naval pressure group grandly called The Imperial Maritime League. This group promised in a Cassandra-like tone to 'waken the nation from its sleep' and to take up 'the neglected or abandoned duties of the Navy League, by using propaganda to alert public opinion to the danger of reducing naval spending at a time when the German Navy was expanding'.[60] The Imperial Maritime League, dubbed sarcastically as the 'Sea Gallopers Society' and the 'Navier League' by the Liberal press set out to launch a propaganda campaign which aimed to protest against 'the Destructive Naval

Policy of the Present Government'[61] and to rouse the Conservative Party leadership to mount a 'vigorous opposition to cuts in the Navy' or else forfeit forever its claim to be termed 'the party of patriotism'.[62] From the very beginning, therefore, the Imperial Maritime League was determined to fight a jingoistic verbal battle with its Liberal opponents on the true meaning of patriotism. It was also a group that wanted to put pressure on the Conservative Party leadership to adopt a more independent line on naval policy. The leaders of the Imperial Maritime League claimed it was 'a patriotic duty' to denounce any Government which cut spending on the navy. But the impact of the Imperial Maritime League was severely hampered by the fact that the vast majority of members of the Navy League, the majority of whom were Conservative supporters who decided to remain loyal to the parent organisation, and the Conservative leadership blocked the progress of the organisation within the official party machinery and charged Horton Smith and Wyatt with 'dragging naval policy into party politics'.[63]

The openly rebellious and partisan language of the Imperial Maritime League positioned it firmly on the extreme right fringe of Conservatism. The membership was composed exclusively of right-wing members of the Conservative Party. It gained no support whatsoever from the Liberal Party, Irish Nationalists and the Socialist Left. Carlyon Bellairs, a Liberal MP, even greatly weakened the impact of the formation of the Imperial Maritime League by persuading 75 Liberal MPs to join the Navy League for the first time.[64] The highest ever membership figure recorded by the Imperial Maritime League was 1,460. By contrast, the moderate Navy League, which remained committed to the principles of bi-partisanship on defence matters saw its membership grow dramatically from 20,000 to 125,000 between 1908 and 1913. Geographically, the membership of the Imperial Maritime League was located almost exclusively in London and the south east, both areas of the strongest electoral support for the Conservative Party.

The very small number of Conservatives at Westminster who joined the Imperial Maritime League fall into three categories: first, those Conservative MPs and Peers who were most at odds with Balfour's restrained approach to Anglo-German relations at Westminster; second, Conservatives who opposed the bi-partisan approach to national defence; and third, extreme right wingers who were dissatisfied with Sir John Fisher's administration of the Admiralty. In numerical terms, the Imperial Maritime League gained open support from approximately 20 Conservative MPs between 1908 and 1910. Most of these were 'independently minded' backbench figures, including Arthur Bignold, Clive Bridgeman, Harvey Du Cros, Walter Faber, Claude Hay, H.S. Staveley-Hill, Edward Turnour and Rowland Hunt. The renegade Admiral Lord Charles Beresford also gave his support to the organisation. The most notable peers to give open support to the Imperial Maritime League were the Earl of Malmesbury, the Duke of Sutherland and Lord Willoughby De Broke.[65] The only Conservative front bench figure ever to appear on a very early membership list of the Imperial Maritime League was George Wyndham and the only well-known Conservative MP on the early membership list is F.E. Smith. Both quickly withdrew their support once it became abundantly clear that the party leadership greatly disapproved of the activities of the organisation. At Westminster, those few Conservatives who were sympathetic to the aims of the Imperial Maritime League formed a 'Joint Committee' which pledged to 'watch over naval questions in Parliament'.[66] Wyatt conceded that 'only the Conservative Party has the means, the organisation, the number of speakers and the prestige needed to arrest the attention of Britain and to penetrate the cloud of apathy and indifference towards the Navy'.[67] The Conservative Party leadership, however, regarded the Imperial Maritime League as an unwanted and somewhat embarrassing supporter.

The views of the Imperial Maritime League on Anglo-German relations can be regarded as coming from the most rebellious and extreme right-wing members of the Conservative Party. The Imperial Maritime League generally believed that the balance of power in Europe had been disturbed by the growth of Germany, and its members adopted a strongly pessimistic tone about the likely course of Anglo-German relations. 'The real secret of German hostility to Great Britain', argued Wyatt, 'is to be found in the birth rate, which accounts for Germany's desire for territorial expansion, and that is a fact that can scarcely be altered by diplomacy'.[68] The fear of a German invasion also looms large in the speeches and writings of leading activists of the Imperial Maritime League. As Beresford commented, 'There is no question that if there was a sudden surprise, without any warning, the Germans could land a large force ... as we have not the ships instantly ready'.[69] Rowland Hunt, a Conservative MP, who supported the Imperial Maritime League, was so little inclined to toe the party line at Westminster that the Conservative whip was withdrawn from him in 1907. 'Germany', he claimed 'by a grand coup, might throw an army into London, and once in possession of our capital could dictate here own terms of peace'.[70] In a similar manner, Wyatt argued that 'Germany might easily become the master of the Channel in 24 hours, with her large number of torpedo boats and her ever ready fleet'.[71] H.A. Gwynne, the editor of the *Standard*, who became a leading propagandist and activist within the Imperial Maritime League claimed that 'Germany was planning a raid in such numbers as to threaten our existence as a nation'.[72]

A major propaganda tactic employed by the Imperial Maritime League was to encourage its members to write letters and articles to newspapers and periodicals warning of a German invasion. Many of these contributions were often written by past and present admirals and naval officers.[73] Often such letters were written anonymously. A fairly typical example was offered by 'A Naval Officer' who argued that Germany, if achieving naval supremacy, 'could invade and conquer the United Kingdom without any serious difficulty and turn it into a mere province of the German empire'.[74] In a similar vein, 'An English Patriot' often claimed to have access to 'secret information' which indicated Germany was planning a naval assault on the British Isles.[75] The Imperial Maritime League was roundly attacked on all sides of the political mainstream for constantly raising the spectre of a German attack on Britain and for inflaming Anglo-German relations. Wyatt, speaking in 1908, gave the following explanation for his actions:

> There are a great many people who think it is wrong and mistaken, and even wicked, to allude to Germany in connection with the question of national defence, and their attitude, I must say, reminds me of that of children who are afraid to mention the word 'bogey man', lest the evil spirit should appear.[76]

The leadership of the Imperial Maritime League soon realised its own propaganda efforts could never hope to make a major political impact unless it could gain more converts from the Navy League or persuade the Conservative Party to rouse public opinion over the

German naval threat. Between 1908 and 1909, the Imperial Maritime League concentrated most of its time and energy in gaining official support from the Conservative Party. In May 1909, Wyatt asked Balfour if he would meet a deputation of the Imperial Maritime League in order to discuss 'the naval peril' which the country faced from Germany.[77] Balfour flatly refused this request and he never endorsed the Imperial Maritime League in any way either in private or in public.[78] In October 1910, Gwynne urged Balfour to place the state of the navy at the centre of the Conservative campaign for the second General Election in 1910, but the Conservative leader completely ignored this right-wing pressure.[79] Even without any official encouragement from Balfour or the official Conservative Party machine, the Imperial Maritime League went ahead and organised public meetings in Conservative constituencies during the two general elections of 1910. It also sent activists to campaign for the election of Conservative candidates in elections. In Ealing in October 1908, the Imperial Maritime League organised a major demonstration against Liberal cuts in the navy. However, the local Ealing Conservative Association, which initially gave cooperation to this effort, quickly withdrew it, following pressure from Conservative Central Office.[80] It also seems clear that pressure was placed on Conservative MPs and peers not to attend major demonstrations against Liberal naval cuts organised by the Imperial Maritime League. There were a few Conservatives who ignored these requests, but on many other occasions, a Conservative MP, who had promised to speak at an Imperial Maritime League meeting or demonstration, often mysteriously withdrew at the last minute, under pressure from Balfour, Central Office or the Conservative chief whips at Westminster.

By 1912, the leaders of the Imperial Maritime League were actually proposing a reconciliation with the Navy League. At the end of 1913, Lord Willoughby De Broke, the prominent 'Die Hard' Conservative peer was appointed president of the failing organisation. Not long afterwards, Wyatt and Horton-Smith both resigned their membership. In 1914, Imperial Maritime League propaganda was emphasising that 'neither party will take a strong line on the question of national defence'.[81] At the same time, the Imperial Maritime League announced that it would no longer advise members to support the Conservative Party, but would instead rouse public opinion in a 'non-partisan manner' in future. This important change of tactics was a clear admission by the Imperial Maritime League that its dual attempt to persuade the Conservative Party to abandon bi-partisanship on the navy and to weaken the Navy League had ended in complete failure. During the First World War, the Imperial Maritime League and the Navy League were back in harmony, and both organisations cooperated in the production of anti-German propaganda. Indeed, it was the Imperial Maritime League which, in true scaremongering style, produced the infamous poster in 1915 which depicted German soldiers eating babies on the Western Front.

It is clear that the three pressure groups examined in this chapter were deeply concerned with the 'German danger'. The National Service League highlighted, indeed exaggerated, the danger of a German invasion, but the solution it advocated to prevent invasion, namely, military training, was rejected by the leadership of the Conservative Party because of its supposed electoral unpopularity. The Tariff Reform League, which attracted widespread support within the Conservative Party, portrayed the German fiscal system and the social condition of the German people from 1905 to 1914 in positive, often glowing terms. However, supporters of the Tariff Reform League used the Anglo-German trade issue selectively in order to win the domestic battle over economic policy with the Liberal Party. Supporters of the Imperial Maritime League were extremely Germanophobic and presented German aims in openly hostile and negative terms. Many of its members thought Germans were already eating babies in Belgium before the war started. But the xenophobia of the Imperial Maritime League found very little support from within the official Conservative Party machinery. Overall, the activities of the Imperial Maritime League were castigated not just within the 'moderate' Navy League itself, an organisation dominated by Conservatives, and Liberal Imperialists, but from across the political spectrum. The two most persistent charges made by moderate Conservatives in the Navy League against the Imperial Maritime League was that it dragged the navy into party politics and soured Anglo-German relations.

It does seem that outright 'scaremongering' on the German threat was very much an extra-parliamentary activity, located primarily in the patriotic pressure groups. Indeed, the desperation, frustration, so evident in all the writings, speeches and private correspondence of the leading activists in the National Service League and the Imperial

Maritime League, with the perceived timidity of the Conservative Party at Westminster towards the German threat, indicates that the fomenting of Anglo-German antagonism was only practised in the public by those groups and individuals outside the mainstream of the Conservative Party and outside the official organisations of the Conservative party in the country. Open hostility towards Germany was, therefore, the preserve of those without any real influence over the Conservative leadership, without any political responsibility and was predominantly an extra-parliamentary phenomenon.

7
The Conservative Party and the Decision for War in 1914

In the summer of 1914, the Conservative Party was totally immersed with problems in Ireland. Each attempt to reach a deal between the Government and the Opposition over the Irish Home Rule question ended in deadlock. The obsession with Ireland in British politics, which had re-emerged after the two General Elections of 1910 had left the Liberal Government dependent on the votes of Irish Nationalist MPs to stay in power, ensured that problems of foreign policy had retreated into the background. This helps to explain why the assassination of Archduke Franz Ferdinand by Gavrilo Princip, a Bosnian terrorist, on 28 June 1914, did not instantaneously give rise to the prospect of British involvement in a European War.

Most Conservatives agreed with the initial view of the British press towards the assassination of Archduke Franz Ferdinand, which was to condemn the 'impossible Serbians' for inflaming relations with the Dual Monarchy.[1] The only newspaper editors who attempted to stress that the assassination at Sarejevo might be exploited by the German Government to further its own territorial aims in the Balkans were, not surprisingly, the leading 'scaremongers' Gwynne, then editor of the *Morning Post*, and Maxse still editor of the *National Review*. The one major Conservative figure who instantly grasped the wider European magnitude of the assassination of Archduke Franz Ferdinand was Balfour who was certain the destruction of Serbia by Austria-Hungary was part of a German plan to dominate Europe.[2]

At first, few members of the Conservative rank and file linked the complex Austro-Serb problem to the intricate European diplomatic balance of power. As a result, there was little early support within the

Conservative Party for British involvement in what seemed a localised Balkan war involving just Austria-Hungary and Serbia.[3] The majority of Conservatives were also strongly opposed to Britain becoming mixed up in the defence of Russian interests in the Balkan region.[4] The idea of supporting British participation in a war to save Russia alone was never seriously contemplated within the Conservative Party.

The Austrian and German ambassadors in London went on a charm offensive during July 1914 in order to influence the British press and leading figures in the two major political parties not to get involved in the Austro-Serb quarrel. On 13 July 1914, Count Mensdorff, the Austrian Ambassador, met with Lord Lansdowne, and he handed to him a batch of carefully selected press cuttings from the Serbian press which took a very sympathetic line towards the aims of the Serb terrorist group, which was thought responsible for the assassination of the Austrian Archduke. Lansdowne gave this information to Geoffrey Robinson, (later named Geoffrey Dawson) the editor of *The Times*. The leading editorial comment on the Austro-Serb squabble, which appeared in *The Times* on 16 July 1914 strongly denounced the anti-Austrian tone of the Serbian press but also urged the Austrian Government not to solve the quarrel by resort to force.[5] These views were very much in line with Lansdowne's own position towards the Austro-Serb quarrel, and it is pretty obvious he influenced the line Robinson adopted in his editorial.

During the last sunshine-filled days of July 1914, a European War, developing out of the Austro-Serb dispute started to became a real possibility after Austria-Hungary issued a stern and uncompromising ultimatum to Serbia, with the support of the German Government. It was now that discussions began not only within the British Cabinet, but also within the Conservative Party concerning what were Britain's exact obligations towards France under the terms of the Anglo-French Entente.[6] This ambiguity over the Entente had long been encouraged by Sir Edward Grey, the Foreign Secretary and supported by Lord Lansdowne, in effect, the shadow Foreign Secretary. Both had habitually stressed in speeches that the Anglo-French Entente was not a binding military alliance, but instead merely a voluntary and friendly 'colonial agreement' of a very restricted nature.[7] In private, Grey was convinced that Britain had to get involved on the side of France in the event of a German attack. What is more, Grey let it be known to his Cabinet colleagues during the July crisis of his readiness to resign as Foreign Secretary if France was not fully supported. It is also worth stressing that Grey encouraged Winston Churchill to engage in 'off the record talks' with leading figures in the Conservative 'inner circle' over the possible formation of a coalition Government in the event of a Cabinet split over supporting British intervention in a European war.[8]

The greatest problems which Grey faced in the days which preceded the outbreak of the First World War, therefore, were to win over a seemingly divided Liberal Cabinet and a sceptical and puzzled British public which asked why Britain, though not legally obligated to do so, should enter a European War, to save France and Russia. It quickly became apparent, at an emergency Cabinet meeting, held on 27 July 1914, that the majority of the Cabinet were not prepared to agree to go to war to defend France from a German attack in Western Europe.[9] At this stage, Herbert Asquith, the Prime Minister saw no reason why Britain 'should be more than spectators' in the event of the outbreak of a European War, growing out of the Austro-Serbian crisis.[10] In order to convince the divided Liberal Cabinet not to stand aside in the event of a Franco-German War, it was Grey who cleverly shifted his ground in the final days before war broke out away from supporting France under the vague terms on the entente to the closely connected issue of German forces violating Belgian neutrality, which Britain was pledged to defend under a 1839 Treaty.

Bonar Law informed Grey that the position of France or Belgium had to be endangered in order for the Conservative Party to support British intervention in a European War.[11] Bonar Law met with Grey on a number of occasions during July and at each meeting he assured the Foreign Secretary that the Opposition would offer him 'unqualified support' on the understanding that he remained determined to use the Anglo-French Entente to uphold the European balance of power.[12] It was, however, the decision of the Tsar Nicholas to declare Russian mobilisation on Thursday, 30 July 1914, which fixed the attention of the Conservative 'inner circle' on the growing European crisis more fully than ever before. The very same day, the Russian army mobilised, in preparation for war, Bonar Law had a meeting with Asquith in his room in the House of Commons. They both immediately agreed to postpone the second reading of the amending bill on Irish Home Rule in the interests of maintaining national unity between the two parties during the impending European crisis.[13] Bonar Law's meeting with Asquith appears to have reassured him that the outbreak of a European war was not in the offing, because on Friday, 31 July 1914, the Opposition leader decided to go ahead with a pre-existing arrangement to spend the bank holiday weekend at Wargrave Manor, the country home of Sir Edward Goulding, MP, in the company of F.E. Smith, Sir Edward Carson and Max Aitken. The original aim of this weekend get-together was to discuss Conservative policy towards the Irish Home Rule question. But it was the growing European crisis which became the main topic of conversation. On arrival at Wargrave Manor, F.E. Smith informed Bonar Law that Churchill had told him how bitterly divided the Cabinet was over the question of going to war in support of France.[14] It seems Lansdowne was also unconvinced that war was imminent that weekend as he also left London on 31 July 1914 to relax in the English countryside. The only leading Conservative figure who remained in London that particular weekend was Balfour, who had already decided to cancel a proposed holiday to Austria. On Thursday, 30 July 1914, Balfour had breakfasted with George Lloyd, the Conservative MP, who later recalled how quickly the ex-Prime Minister grasped the significance of the Russian decision to mobilise, and he put forward the firm view that Britain had to go to war in defence of France.[15] In Balfour's view, the logic of Britain's commitment to France, built up over the years since the signing of the Entente, was clear and unambiguous: 'We have chosen our side, and must bide by the result'.[16]

On Saturday, 1 August 1914, the European crisis reached a higher level of intensity when Germany suddenly declared war on Russia. This dramatic news led to a frantic day of activity among the Conservative 'inner circle' and among leading activists on the extra-parliamentary 'radical right'. In the morning, reports had appeared in the popular Tory press, claiming that the Conservative Party leadership was 'dithering' over whether to offer support to France at all. Balfour became so alarmed by these reports that he quickly sent off letters, without consulting Bonar Law or Lansdowne, to the French and the Russian ambassadors in London informing them that the press reports were completely without foundation.[17] At the same time, a number of leading 'radical-right' activists, including Maxse, Beresford, Gwynne, Amery and Sir Henry Wilson held a meeting that same morning to discuss the European crisis at which they agreed that Bonar Law was taking a very unhurried approach to the unfolding European crisis and he should be persuaded to return to London as soon as possible.[18]

On the beautiful sunny afternoon of Saturday, 1 August 1914, two completely unconnected attempts were made to convince the Conservative leader to come back to London. Balfour, a dependable and influential member of the Conservative 'inner circle', instigated the first attempt. He sent separate telegrams to Law and Lansdowne, appraising them of the growing gravity of the European situation and urged them to come back immediately to the capital.[19] The second attempt to persuade Bonar Law to return to London was made by two representatives of the 'radical right': Charles Beresford and George Lloyd, who journeyed by car to Wargrave Manor. They arrived, late in the afternoon, to find Bonar Law playing a gentle game of tennis with a friend. Apparently, Beresford, observing this scene, walked straight up to the Opposition leader while he was preparing to serve in his tennis match and told him bluntly he should be 'ashamed of himself', for ignoring the seriousness of the international crisis and engaging in such a trivial pursuit.[20] Whether this took place is unclear. Max Aitken, who was at Wargrave Manor on the same day, does not refer to this altercation between Beresford and Law, but there seems no reason to doubt that it probably occurred, given what we know of Beresford's temperament.[21] In any case, Law had already received Balfour's telegram before Beresford and Lloyd had arrived, and the Conservative leader had already decided to return to London and had made the necessary travel arrangements. He was in no way persuaded to return by the unsolicited intervention of members of the radical right. This view is re-enforced by the fact that Lord Lansdowne, who also received Balfour's telegram alerting him to the gravity of the situation, had also decided to return to London that same afternoon. There was quite obviously further telegraphic or telephone contact between Law and Lansdowne during that same afternoon, because a meeting of leading members of the Conservative 'inner circle' was arranged to take place at Lansdowne House, the London home of the ex-Foreign Secretary, later the same evening.

Shortly after arriving back in London, in the early evening, Bonar Law was invited to dine with Grey and Churchill. It is important to note that the Opposition leader declined this invitation, believing that Grey was likely to suggest Conservative participation in a coalition

Government in the event of the Cabinet failing to endorse British intervention in a European War. At this time, Bonar Law appears to have been disinclined to engage in unofficial negotiations with Grey on the possibility of a coalition, before he had the opportunity of discussing the international situation with his close Shadow Cabinet colleagues.[22]

The Conservative 'inner circle' met for 90 minutes at Lansdowne House very late in the evening of 1 August 1914 to talk about the Conservative stance towards the European crisis. Those present at this important meeting were Bonar Law, Lord Lansdowne, Balfour, Sir Henry Wilson, Law's military adviser, and the Conservative Chief Whips in the Commons (Lord Edmond Talbot) and the Lords (the Duke of Devonshire). Austen Chamberlain, the Shadow Chancellor of the Exchequer, was also urged by George Lloyd to attend this meeting, but he did not arrive back in London in time to do so. The only backbench MP present was Lloyd, a close friend of Bonar Law, who subsequently gave two contradictory accounts of the attitude of Lansdowne and Law at this meeting, which must cast some doubt on his dependability as a reliable witness. Lloyd told Austen Chamberlain that Lansdowne and Law 'did not seem to grasp the gravity of the situation' during the course of the crisis meeting at Lansdowne House.[23] But in a subsequent account of the meeting, later given in an interview with Ian Colvin, Lloyd claimed that Lansdowne was fully aware of the gravity of situation and he tried to make contact with Asquith by telephone during the meeting to request a meeting between the Prime Minister and the Opposition leaders to discuss the European crisis.[24] The account given by Lloyd to Colvin does appear more trustworthy, when compared to the evidence of others who attended the meeting. There is no difference of opinion about the major outcome of the meeting at Lansdowne House. It was agreed by the Conservative 'inner circle' that Lord Lansdowne should immediately send a letter to the Prime Minister informing him that the Conservative leadership would be willing to meet him at any time to appraise him of their views towards the crisis. However, the letter, which was sent to Asquith that evening, did not actually outline the Conservative position towards the crisis.

On the morning of Sunday, 2 August 1914, the German Government sent an ultimatum to the 'poor defenceless' Belgian Government, requesting authorisation to allow the German army safe passage across its territory. The Cabinet was due to meet later the same morning in emergency session to discuss its response to this new and extremely disturbing development. Meanwhile, Law, with Lansdowne and Balfour in attendance, awaited Asquith's reply to their letter of the previous evening at Pembroke Lodge, Bonar Law's London home. Austen Chamberlain, who arrived at Pembroke Lodge, shortly after breakfast, suggested a second letter should be sent to the Prime Minister, which clearly outlined the position of the Opposition towards the crisis. There was some discussion between Law, Lansdowne and Balfour on Austen Chamberlain's proposal. It was finally decided by Law, seemingly on the spur of the moment, to write to the Prime Minister outlining the views of the Opposition towards the European crisis. It seems that Lansdowne was uneasy about the wisdom of stating the position of the Opposition too explicitly in the letter in case it highlighted differences between the Government and the Opposition over foreign policy and thereby breached the principles of bi-partisanship.[25] The letter which Bonar Law sent to Asquith, is significant, because it puts on record the position taken by the Conservative leadership towards the European crisis and agreed upon the night before at Lansdowne House. The views expressed in the letter were already well known to Grey and Asquith as Bonar Law, during the last week of July 1914, had gone 'daily to Grey's room at the House of Commons to be briefed on diplomatic developments',[26] In the letter to the Prime Minister, dated 2 August 1914, Bonar Law wrote:

> Dear Mr. Asquith,
> Lord Lansdowne and I feel it is our duty to inform you
> that in our opinion, as well as in that of all the colleagues
> with whom we have been able to consult, it would be
> fatal to the honour and security of the United Kingdom
> to hesitate in supporting France and Russia at the
> present moment; and we offer our unhesitating support
> to the Government in any measures they may consider
> necessary to that object[27]

There are two important points to make about the views expressed by Bonar Law in this letter. First, the letter makes very clear the unanimity of the Opposition 'inner circle' towards supporting France and Russia during the crisis. Second, the letter does not even mention the question of Belgian neutrality, which was the issue being constantly highlighted by Grey to his Cabinet colleagues as the chief reason why Britain should go to war. In reply, Asquith, who was chiefly concerned with maintaining Cabinet unity over the question of Belgian neutrality, rather than focusing on Britain's obligations towards France, informed Bonar Law that Britain was under 'no obligation' to France or Russia. The Prime Minister even questioned whether British obligations towards Belgium made British participation in a European war inevitable. Asquith also pointed out to the Opposition leader that Britain's decision to go to war would be determined by three issues: treaty obligations to Belgium, a determination to uphold naval supremacy and a concern that France should not be crushed as a great power. In a more conciliatory passage, Asquith did promise to meet with Law and Lansdowne at 10 Downing Street on Monday, 3 August 1914 to discuss the crisis with them in person. In the reply to Bonar Law, Asquith had acknowledged the position of the Opposition towards the crisis, but had skilfully distanced himself and the Cabinet from the course of action which Bonar Law had proposed even though it was a course of action he knew Grey fully supported. According to Austen Chamberlain, the Conservative 'inner circle' expressed some concern about Asquith's reply but took some comfort in the fact that Asquith did mention in one passage in the letter that the Government could not stand by and see France 'crushed'.[28]

The Prime Minister at the first emergency Cabinet meeting on 2 August 1914 read out Bonar Law's letter.[29] Asquith later claimed the letter had no influence on the deliberations of the Cabinet at all. The same view is put forward in the memoirs of Sir Edward Grey.[30] However, the accounts of other Cabinet ministers, particularly those who opposed intervention, recall that Bonar Law's letter was used negatively by Asquith and Grey, and their Liberal Imperialist colleagues, to increase the mounting pressure on the 'waverers' in the Cabinet to 'stand together' during the crisis rather than lead the way to an inevitable Conservative–Liberal Imperialist coalition Government.[31] In fact, Grey was openly telling his Cabinet colleagues that he would definitely resign if Britain did not intervene. Moreover, Churchill claimed that during the break between the first and second emergency Cabinet meetings on 2 August 1914, he actually discussed with Balfour the possibility of the Conservatives joining a coalition with the Liberal Imperialists, if the Cabinet failed to agree about intervention.[32] During the second emergency Cabinet meeting on 2 August 1914, however, the Cabinet did agree, with only two exceptions, to support British intervention, if Belgian neutrality was violated.[33] It does seem that fear of the consequences of a Conservative-dominated coalition taking power if the Cabinet had split apart was certainly an important influence on the decision of 'waverers' in the Cabinet to support British intervention.

On Monday, 3 August 1914, Bonar Law, accompanied by Lord Lansdowne met Asquith at 10 Downing Street at 10.30 in the morning. They both urged the Prime Minister to intervene in the European conflict.[34] According to Asquith's account of this meeting, Bonar Law and Lansdowne both cited the violation of Belgian neutrality as the chief reason for their support of British intervention and did not even mention Britain's obligations towards France. It seems the emphasis which Bonar Law and Lansdowne placed on Belgian neutrality at this meeting was a premeditated decision which aimed to restore bi-partisan harmony between both party leaders at a time of great national emergency.[35] The Shadow Cabinet, which had played no part whatsoever in defining the Opposition attitude towards the European Crisis, met at Lansdowne House, an hour later, and quickly agreed that the policy of the Opposition towards the European crisis was to offer the 'unconditional support' for the policy of the Liberal Government.

On the afternoon of 3 August 1914, Sir Edward Grey, in a very restrained speech, told the House of Commons that the Anglo-French Entente did not legally bind Britain to enter the war on behalf of the French Empire. He stressed that the British Government was free to decide between peace and war. When Grey explained that Germany's violation of Belgian neutrality placed Britain under more of a legal obligation to enter the war, he received loud cheers from both sides of the House. Grey also stressed in his speech that if the German fleet attacked France then Britain's 'national interests' would be threatened, and he warned MPs that if Britain backed away from supporting France there would be 'a severe loss of respect and honour'.[36] Speaking on behalf of the Opposition, Bonar Law praised the Foreign Secretary for attempting to maintain peace in the face of insurmountable odds. He also gave a firm assurance that the Government 'could rely on the unhesitating support of the Opposition' in 'whatever steps they think it necessary to take for the honour and security of this country'.[37] The bi-partisan consensus once more stood firm in the public forum of the House of Commons. However, some Liberal radicals, supported by several Labour MPs demanded an adjournment debate to discuss whether Britain should intervene on behalf of Belgium. This debate took place on the evening of 3 August 1914. The Prime Minister, the Foreign Secretary and the Opposition leader did not attend it. One Liberal MP claimed that the reason why Britain was contemplating intervention in a European war was a direct consequence of the 'war fever against Germany' which had been waged for many years by the Conservative Party and 'their supporters in the press'.[38] After listening to several more speeches from the Liberals and socialists opposed to war, Balfour suddenly stood up and appealed to the speaker to curtail the debate which he thought was 'not adding to our dignity, and which, I venture to think, will possibly be misunderstood in the country and will be certainly misunderstood abroad'.[39] Only minutes later, the speaker ended the debate.

On 4 August 1914, Bonar Law asked the Prime Minister in the House of Commons, 'if he has any information to give us to-day?' Asquith replied, 'Our Ambassador at Berlin received his passports at seven o'clock, last evening, and since eleven o'clock last night a state of war has existed between Germany and ourselves'.[40] At this time, the news that Germany had invaded Belgium was already known. By the end of 4 August 1914, therefore, Britain was already at war with Germany, ostensibly in defence of Belgium's independence.

The German violation of Belgian neutrality was vital in uniting the wavering and uncertain Liberal Cabinet and convincing British public opinion of the need to enter 'The Great War'. However, it was the prevention of the destruction of France by Germany, which determined the decision of the Conservative Party leadership to strongly support British intervention. There was a very strong and united interventionist spirit within the Conservative Party during the latter stages of the July crisis. As one Liberal MP observed, 'The overwhelming mass of the Tory Party seem to suggest war is inevitable and some seem eager to take the best chance of smashing Germany'.[41] Winston Churchill later recalled that he only received 'one or two letters' from Conservatives who opposed British intervention.[42] Throughout the July crisis, backbench opinion in the Conservative Party had played no part in the discussions of the Conservative 'inner circle', nor did rank and file opinion in anyway influence the decisions which were taken by the Conservative leadership.

If the Liberal Cabinet had split apart, which was a real possibility, there was the equally real prospect of a coalition composed of Conservatives and the Liberal–Imperialists. The very fact that Grey was putting out informal feelers to the Conservative Party in July 1914 for a coalition reinforces the view that the Foreign Secretary was determined to ensure Britain did intervene, no matter what that meant for the unity of the Liberal Party. The arrival of the Conservatives in Government would have meant the decision to go to war with Germany would have been taken anyway. Therefore, it was the 'balance of forces' in favour of intervention in both of the major political parties which ensured that Britain was certain to go to war once Germany had mounted a military attack in western Europe. The Conservative Party, therefore, provided Grey with an additional reserve group of parliamentary supporters for the policy of intervention, which would almost certainly have been used, if the Cabinet fell apart. In the end, Grey persuaded the Liberal radicals in the Cabinet that it made sense to 'stick with nurse for fear of something worse'.

Conclusion

The most important aim of this study was to critically examine whether the conventional depiction of Conservative Party from 1905 to 1914 as consisting primarily of 'anti-German' scaremongers who reacted to Anglo-German relations whether in connection with trade rivalry, the naval arms race, foreign policy and conscription in a hostile fashion which contributed to the growth of Anglo-German estrangement was valid.[1] It can now be seen this is one myth about the British road to the First World War which must now be seriously discussed and re-evaluated by scholars. It can now be convincingly argued that the Conservative Party in the Edwardian years did not consist of anti-German scaremongers who openly fomented Anglo-German antagonism. On the contrary, the public attitudes of Conservatives towards the key aspects of Anglo-German relations showed a high level of public restraint and a marked absence of open hostility. Scaremongering against Germany in public is shown in this study to have been the preserve of ultra right-wing 'outcasts' on the 'radical right' of the party, without any real influence over the Conservative leadership. Indeed, the so-called radical right was more a 'loony right' who had a very limited impact in persuading the Conservative leadership to adopt a more strident Germanophobic approach.

What really emerges from this study is a complex picture of the Conservative response to Anglo-German relations from 1905 to 1914. The Conservative Party consistently supported the principles of bi-partisanship on matters foreign and defence policy.[2] The control of Opposition foreign and defence policy was kept in the hands of the Conservative leader and a very small and exclusive 'inner circle' of advisers. This allowed the two Conservative leaders in this period, Balfour and Bonar Law, to enjoy a unique measure of independence in the presentation of the Opposition attitude towards the key aspects of Anglo-German relations. Zara Steiner's view that foreign policy formulation within the British Government was made by 'a few men who are easily identifiable' can be equally applied, as this study has shown, to the conduct and presentation of foreign and defence affairs by the Opposition.[3]

Given the importance of the party leader over foreign and defence policy, the views of Balfour and Bonar Law required detailed analysis. It has been shown that Balfour's attitude towards Germany was dramatically transformed between 1905 and 1914 in a much more significant manner than has been emphasised by his biographers. In 1905, Balfour claimed that he was 'the last person to believe in the German threat', but during the July crisis he was the most energetic and influential supporter of a swift British declaration of war against Germany in order to 'prevent France being crushed'.[4] The single most profound cause of this shift in Balfour's attitude towards Germany between 1905 and 1914 was not commercial rivalry, but the growth of a German navy, deployed in the North Sea, which he believed represented a clear challenge to Britain's national and imperial interests. Balfour's approach to Anglo-German relations as Opposition leader is best described as realistic statesmanship which avoided making hostile comments on Germany and helped to bolster Grey's foreign policy in the interests of bi-partisanship.

It has now become commonplace for historians to emphasise sharp differences in leadership style and policy between the apparently diffident Balfour and the seemingly strident Bonar Law.[5] But what this study has revealed is that there were many important elements of similarity and continuity in how these two Conservative leaders dealt with Anglo-German relations. In fact, Bonar Law emerges in this study as more open minded on Anglo-German relations than Balfour. The bi-partisanship approach to foreign affairs was continued and enthusiastically supported by Bonar Law. At the same time, Bonar Law's speeches on Anglo-German relations were full of friendly, constructive and extremely positive comments. He concentrated his arguments in support of tariff reform, not on the economic threat from Germany but on the intransigence of supporters of free trade within the Liberal Party. But Law's outwardly restrained approach towards Anglo-German relations was also underpinned by underlying and realistic fears about the growth of German economic, naval and military power. Yet Bonar Law, like Balfour, was not prepared to adopt or support policies to meet the German threat which breached the bi-partisan consensus or were electorally unpopular. He flatly refused to adopt the 'fighting independent policy' on naval and army issues which was energetically demanded by many of his 'die hard' right-wing supporters. On the issue of conscription, Bonar Law was a political realist who was unwilling to commit the Conservative Party to a deeply unpopular policy, even though he strongly believed conscription was necessary to deal with the German military threat, in the event of a European war. In fact, as this study has shown, Bonar Law showed admirable political skill in handling the conscription issue. He put forward a restrained posture on the conscription issue in public but worked behind the scenes in the hope of hammering out a cross-party agreement on the proposal. These backstage discussions impressed many of the politicians who would become his partners in the wartime coalition Government. What is perhaps most startling about the new material presented here on Bonar Law's approach to the foreign, defence and economic aspects of Anglo-German relations is that the often bitter confrontational style he adopted in domestic politics, particularly over Lloyd George's People's Budget, the House of Lords crisis and the Irish Home Rule affair was not carried over into how he handled foreign and defence matters. As this study has shown, Bonar Law, greatly influenced by Lord Lansdowne showed a quite remarkable level of restraint when discussing Anglo-German relations. Pragmatic realism is the best way to describe Law's overall response to Anglo-German relations as leader of the Opposition.

Most Conservatives in the Westminster sphere of political activity followed the restrained attitude of the party leadership towards Anglo-German relations. This is not to suggest there was not significant private anxiety about the 'German peril', among Conservatives at Westminster, especially, in relation to the naval arms race. A great many Conservatives believed a war with Germany was a distinct possibility. The comment of George Wyndham that 'the Germans mean to have war: not necessarily in the immediate future, but some day, and pretty soon', was a fairly typical private Conservative view.[6] Yet these pessimistic Conservative views on the likely course of Anglo-German relations were hardly ever uttered in parliamentary debate. In fact, a quite remarkable level of caution was maintained whenever Conservatives discussed Anglo-German relations in parliament. In general, a few provocative statements or moral judgements about the German desire for 'a place in the sun' marked the Conservative response to Anglo-German naval rivalry. Conservative speeches in support of tariff reform certainly included discussions of German social and economic conditions but support for tariff reform was an integral part of the domestic political struggle with the Liberals over economic policy rather than being intimately linked to foreign policy.[7] Conservative tariff reformers more often saw Germany as a model rather than a threat. There was also a general consensus among Conservatives at Westminster that conscription was a deeply unpopular policy which could only be implemented within a bi-partisan framework.

It is only when the focus of analysis moves away from Westminster politics to examine key public sphere of political activity outside Westminster that a much more complex picture emerges. As explained in Chapter 5, the most sustained period of Conservative electoral activity on the German threat was confined to the period immediately prior to the general election of January 1910. At that election, the naval and economic threat posed by Germany did play a very important role in the electioneering and the propaganda tactics of the Conservative Party. But there is no real evidence of an orchestrated plan by the Conservative Party to create a systematic form of 'xenophobic propaganda' against Germany on the naval arms race and trade rivalry at the two elections of 1910.[8] In fact, Balfour never believed Germanophobia was likely to be 'the electoral cannonball' which many right-wing press editors thought it would. An examination of the content of Conservative electoral propaganda reinforces this view more clearly. It cannot be argued with any conviction that 'anti-Germanism' was the chief characteristic of the language of Conservative propaganda on tariff reform.[9] On the contrary, the dominant feature of official Conservative Party propaganda on tariff reform was the projection of the German fiscal system as a model and the portrayal of the German way of life in positive terms. Conservative propaganda on the navy focused on those so-called unpatriotic Liberals who wanted to reduce naval expenditure and was not focused on attacking the aims of German naval policy. At the two elections of 1910, the Conservative Party did not project a single consistent view on Germany. Potential voters were offered very confusing images of Germany as a threat and a model. Underlying this ambiguous presentation of Germany in Conservative propaganda were deep organisational problems within the party structure. Balfour's mastery of the Westminster sphere of political activity was not transferred to the organisation of the party in the country, especially at election time. Attempting to 'keep the party on message' proved impossible, and canvassing at the local level was often chaotic with many of the competing types of propaganda being offered to voters as if they represented the view of the party leader. Those historians who have argued that the Conservative Party, under the leadership of Balfour, lacked a streamlined and professional organisation outside parliament have found much to support that view in the examination of the electoral and propaganda tactics of the party in the two general elections of 1910 which forms part of this study.

What has also been revealed in this study is that 'scaremongering' on the German threat was predominantly an extra-parliamentary phenomenon which had very little support from those in positions of responsibility at the top of the Conservative Party. As revealed in Chapter 6, there was a strong feeling of paranoid desperation, isolation and alienation among the leading 'radical-right' activists in Conservative pressure groups, concerning their complete lack of influence over the Conservative leadership. But, the 'scaremongers' never contemplated either forming or supporting a party that was not 'Conservative'. Lord Charles Beresford, one of the leading right-wing agitators in the Imperial Maritime League claimed that in his attempt to warn the public of the dangers of the German naval threat, Balfour 'was the greatest enemy I had'.[10] He also admitted that Bonar Law 'did not take the slightest note' of his requests for the Conservative Party to engage in a strong agitation over the German threat between 1911 and 1914.

In the final chapter, it was shown, in a very revealing and rare micro-study of Opposition foreign policy, how the Conservative 'inner circle' reacted to the unfolding European crisis which led to the outbreak of the First World War. If Chapter 1, explained the nature of the 'inner circle', who controlled Opposition foreign and defence policy and who had the greatest influence, Chapter 7 showed how policy operated in practice. It was the Conservative leader and his 'inner circle' that decided the Opposition position towards the

European crisis in 1914, with scant reference to the Shadow Cabinet and complete indifference to the views of the party rank and file. The roles of Bonar Law and Lord Lansdowne, supported by the influential Balfour were dominant in the construction of Opposition foreign policy towards the July crisis. The prevention of the destruction of France by Germany was the major reason why the Conservative Party leadership supported British intervention, not the German violation of Belgian neutrality, which was the vital issue that united the Liberal Cabinet and convinced British public opinion of the need to go to war. The 'balance of forces' in favour of British intervention in both the major political parties ensured that Britain was certain to go to war against Germany in August 1914 even if the Liberal Cabinet had fallen apart.

The motives behind the high level of restraint and marked absence of open hostility towards Germany displayed by the Conservative Party from 1905 to 1914 can now be more fully understood. In the arena of domestic politics, the depiction of Germany as a role model in the debate over tariff reform is shown in this study as a calculated tactical device designed to win the domestic struggle with the Liberals over economic policy. In the arena of foreign policy, Conservative restraint on Germany was designed to give support to the foreign policy, followed by Sir Edward Grey. Lord Lansdowne constantly urged the Conservative Party to offer unqualified support for Grey. The leadership of the Conservative Party gave wholehearted support to Grey not on the basis they supported everything he did, but on the understanding that Grey would use the Anglo-French Entente to uphold the balance of power in Europe. Grey used Conservative support for his foreign policy negatively during the European crisis in 1914 in order to convince 'waverers' in the Liberal Cabinet to back his policy or face a Conservative–Liberal Imperialist coalition. In a very real sense, Conservative support for Grey during the July crisis was the important fear factor which kept a disunited Liberal Cabinet together. However, the decision to go to war against Germany helped to make a coalition with the Conservative Party of Bonar Law, which the Liberals only narrowly avoided in 1914, a more likely possibility because as Ivor Jennings quite rightly puts it, 'War is always good for the Conservative Party, not because its members are "bloody minded", but because their imperialism makes them single minded'.[11]

The Key Characters

Arthur James Balfour, first Earl of Balfour, (1848–1930) was a major Conservative politician between 1886 and 1930, and Prime Minister between 1902 and 1905. He was educated at Eton and Trinity College, Cambridge. In 1874, he was elected MP for Hertford, and he rose in the Conservative Party, many contemporaries claimed, because he was pushed forward by his 'Uncle Bob' – that giant late Victorian Prime Minister, Lord Salisbury. In 1878, he accompanied his uncle to the Congress of Berlin and gained his first experience of international relations, an interest he retained for the rest of his political life. In 1878, he wrote a book entitled *In Defence of Philosophic Doubt*, which established him as an intellectual politician. He held many notable Cabinet posts in the late Victorian age, including, Secretary of State for Ireland, First Lord of the Treasury and Foreign Secretary. After 1892, he acted as Conservative leader in the House of Commons. A popular joke in the late Victorian age suggested anything was possible if 'Bob's your uncle', but in spite of the charge of nepotism, Balfour became highly respected and produced logical and convincing speeches in the House of Commons. In July 1902, he became Prime Minister, but his leadership of the Conservative Party was dogged by internal party disputes, most notably over tariff reform. One notable achievement was the establishment of the Committee of Imperial Defence (CID) which helped to plan and coordinate British defence policy. In December 1905, Balfour resigned, and the Conservative party suffered a major election defeat in 1906. After two more election defeats in 1910, Balfour's position as leader was greatly weakened, and in 1911, he resigned. He remained an important figure in the Conservative party and British politics. In May 1915, he was appointed First Lord of the Admiralty, due to his great expertise on naval affairs, in Asquith's coalition government. He also became Foreign Secretary in Lloyd George's coalition. In 1917, he issued what became known as 'The Balfour Declaration' which promised a homeland for Jewish people. He resigned as Foreign Secretary after the Versailles Conference, but remained in the Cabinet as Lord President of the Council until he resigned in 1922, with most of the Conservative leadership, following the revolt that swept Lloyd George from office. In 1925, Baldwin persuaded him to join his government as Lord President of the Council. He died in 1930 and was praised for his major contribution to political life, foreign affairs and national defence.

Charles William Beresford, first Baron Beresford (1846–1919), was known as Lord Charles Beresford in the Edwardian era. He became a Conservative MP in

1875 but continued to serve in the Royal Navy. He constantly pushed for greater expenditure on the navy. He was in command of the Mediterranean fleet from 1905 to 1907. He had a long-running battle during the Edwardian era with John Fisher over his modernising naval reforms. Beresford returned to parliament as MP for the naval town of Portsmouth. He retired from the navy in 1911 and was a leading backbench critic of Balfour.

Sir Joseph Austen Chamberlain (1863–1937) was a leading Conservative figure who won the Nobel Peace Prize. He was the son of Joseph Chamberlain and was educated at Rugby Public School and Trinity College, Cambridge. He visited Germany and took classes at the University of Berlin, His time in Germany led him to believe German nationalism was a potential danger to the peace of Europe. He was first elected to parliament as a member of his father's Liberal Unionist Party in 1892. From 1895 to 1900, he was appointed Civil Lord of the Admiralty. In 1903, he was appointed Chancellor of the Exchequer. After 1906, Chamberlain became the leading Opposition spokesman on economic matters and the standard bearer of the tariff reform wing of the party. In 1911, he was a leading contender to succeed Balfour as Conservative leader, but he lost out to Bonar Law. In 1915, he joined the wartime coalition as Secretary of State for India but resigned in 1917 after the failure of British forces in Mesopotamia. In 1918, he was appointed as Chancellor of the Exchequer again. In 1921, he became leader of the Conservative Party. In 1922, Chamberlain resigned as leader after the backbench revolt that brought Bonar Law to power. He was one of the very few Conservative leaders who never became Prime Minister. From 1924 to 1929 he was Foreign Secretary and helped to negotiate the Locarno treaty, under whose terms the German government accepted the western borders decided upon at the Paris Peace settlement of 1919. For his efforts, he was awarded the Nobel Prize for Peace. He returned to office in 1931 as First Lord of the Admiralty in the National Government, but he resigned after being forced to deal with the Invergordon Mutiny. He was very critical, from 1933 until his death, of the National Government's policy of appeasing Nazi Germany.

Joseph Chamberlain (1836–1914) was one of the most influential British political figures of the period 1886–1914. In his early life, he was a successful businessman and a radical Liberal. He was the father of two leading Conservative figures: Neville Chamberlain and Austen Chamberlain. He went to University College School, but never attended university. At eighteen, he joined the family screw-making company in Birmingham, and it is with that city that he is most identified. In 1873, he became Lord Mayor of Birmingham, and as a Liberal reformer he introduced a series of reforms in housing, education, and public and utility services dubbed as 'gas and water socialism'. In 1876, he became Liberal MP for Birmingham and was then a critic of Disraeli's jingoistic imperialist policies. In 1880, he was appointed President of the Board of Trade in Gladstone's Liberal government. In March 1886, he split from the Liberal Party over Gladstone's plans for Home Rule for

Ireland and joined the Liberal Unionist Association which soon aligned with the Conservative Party to form the Conservative and Unionist Party, often called 'The Unionist Party'. Most Liberals saw Chamberlain as a traitor. In 1895, he was appointed Colonial Secretary and became involved in the expansionist plans of Cecil Rhodes in southern Africa. In 1895, he supported a bungled attack on the Transvaal ('The Jameson Raid') which ended in humiliating failure. He also soured relations with the Transvaal and the Orange Free State. Britain's relations with the Boer Republics – as these two countries were known – deteriorated between 1895 and the outbreak of the Second Boer War (1899–1902). Joseph Chamberlain made a number of efforts to improve Anglo-German relations as Colonial Secretary. In March 1898, he opened talks with the German government about the possibility of an Anglo-German understanding on colonial issues, but von Bulow, the German Chancellor rejected this offer suggesting Britain was not a 'reliable' potential ally. Later that year, Britain cooperated with Germany over the partition of the Portuguese empire. This agreement prompted Chamberlain to press again for an Anglo-German agreement. In 1899, Britain, Germany and the USA again cooperated over the future of Samoa. In a speech at Windsor Castle in November 1899, with Kaiser Wilhem II in attendance, Chamberlain said he desired an 'understanding' between Britain and Germany. The Kaiser responded by saying that although he wanted friendly Anglo-German relations, he did not want to antagonise Russia by openly allying with Britain. When von Bulow heard of this, he said the best way for Britain to have friendly relations was to ensure Germany was spoken of in positive terms by leading politicians and the British press. On 30 November 1899, Chamberlain said in a speech at Leicester that a Triple alliance involving Britain, Germany and the USA would 'become a potent influence on the future of the world'. But von Bulow poured cold water on such an idea and claimed Britain was a 'jealous' and declining power. Even so, Chamberlain continued to press for an Anglo-German agreement. In January 1901, he told the German ambassador that he supported Britain joining the Triple Alliance. During the autumn of 1901, the German government invited Britain to join the Triple alliance, but Lord Salisbury rejected the offer. With the dream of an Anglo-German alliance over, Chamberlain began to look at the prospect of closer Anglo-French relations more favourably. In September 1903, Chamberlain resigned from the Balfour Cabinet and started a campaign for Tariff Reform, which divided the Conservative party, united the Liberals and contributed to three Conservative election defeats in the Edwardian period. After the 1906 defeat, the tariff reform debate dominated the party. In July 1906, Chamberlain suffered a severe stroke, which paralysed his right side and led to difficulties in speaking and writing. Henceforth, his political career was over at a time when the Tariff reform crusade was at its height. On 2 July 1914, his wife Mary read him details of the assassination of Franz Ferdinand, and later that very same day he had a severe heart attack and died.

Andrew Bonar Law (1858–1923) was a leading Conservative politician and Prime Minister. He was born in Rexton in New Brunswick, Canada. In 1860, his mother died, and he later moved to live with his mother's family in Glasgow. The family were rich merchant bankers, and after attending Glasgow High School, he joined the family business. In 1891, he married Annie Robley in 1891, and they had seven children. His financial independence, gained from the family business, allowed him to pursue a career in politics. He became Conservative MP for Glasgow Blackfriars in 1900 and soon became a supporter of tariff reform. He was made parliamentary secretary at the Board of Trade in 1902. After 1906, Law was considered, along with Austen Chamberlain, as one of the most passionate supporters of tariff reform in the Conservative opposition. Law developed a reputation as a blunt and fearless debater and was known for his honesty. He lost his seat in 1906 election but returned to represent Dulwich in a by-election later that year. In 1911, he was elected as Conservative leader, and he focused his attention on tariff reform and fought a bitter opposition to Liberal plans for Home Rule in Ireland. He entered the coalition government as Colonial Secretary in 1915 and served in Lloyd George's War Cabinet as Chancellor of the Exchequer and Leader of the House of Commons. His two eldest sons were killed in action during the First World War, which added to the sadness he already endured after the death of his beloved wife several years earlier. At the 1918 election, he was elected MP for Glasgow Central. In 1921, ill health forced him to resign as Conservative leader, and he was replaced by Austen Chamberlain. He returned to office as Prime Minister in October 1922 when Conservative MPs forced Lloyd George out of office. In May 1923, he resigned after being diagnosed with throat cancer and was replaced by Stanley Baldwin. He became known as the 'unknown Prime Minister' and was the shortest serving Prime Minister of the twentieth century, but he was an extremely important political figure in the early twentieth century.

William St John Fremantle Brodrick, first Earl of Midleton, commonly known as St John Brodrick, (1856–1942) was the Conservative spokesman for army affairs in the House of Lords from 1905 to 1914. He was educated at Eton and Balliol College, Oxford. He entered parliament as MP for Surrey West in 1880. He held several ministerial posts related to imperial and foreign affairs and national defence, most notably, Secretary of State for War and Secretary of State for India.

Lord Cawdor, Frederich Archibald Vaughan Campbell, third Earl of Cawdor (1847–1911), was educated at Eton and Christ Church College, Oxford. He married Edith Turnor in 1868, and they had ten children. He served as First Lord of the Admiralty briefly in the 1902–1905 Balfour Government. He was the leading Conservative naval spokesman in the House of Lords from 1905 until his death in 1911.

George Nathaniel Curzon, first Marquess Curzon of Kedleston (1859–1925), was a leading Conservative politician in the early twentieth century. Educated at Eton and Balliol College, Oxford where he was a brilliant student and inspired a poem which contained the lines, 'My name is George Nathaniel Curzon, I am a most superior person'. He entered parliament in 1886 as

Conservative member for Southport. He was Under-Secretary of State for India (1891–1892) and Foreign Affairs (1895–1898). In 1899, he was appointed Viceroy of India and henceforth was deeply antagonistic towards Russia. He instituted a number of reforms as Viceroy involving administration, education and reform of the police force. In 1904, he decided to partition Bengal which roused bitter opposition and was later revoked in 1912. In 1905, he resigned as Viceroy and returned to England. He spoke on imperial affairs for the Conservatives in the House of Lords from 1905 to 1914. He also took an active part in opposition to the Liberal government's plans to remove the veto power of the House of Lords. From December 1916, he served in Lloyd George's War Cabinet as leader of the House of Lords. After the First World War, he became Foreign Secretary, and when Bonar Law retired in May 1923, Curzon was a leading contender to become leader of the Conservative party, but he was beaten in the leadership contest by Stanley Baldwin largely because it was felt it would be an unpopular move to make a rich aristocrat leader of the Conservative Party during an age of mass democracy. When Baldwin became Prime Minister in November 1924, he did not continue with Curzon as Foreign Secretary and made him Lord President of the Council, a post he held until his death in March 1924. It was widely felt that Curzon never fulfilled his brilliant early promise and that he failed in most of the major posts he held in government.

Lord Esher, Reginald Baliol Brett, second Viscount Esher (1852–1930), was a leading defence expert in the Edwardian era. In 1901, he became deputy governor of Windsor Castle, and he remained on close terms with the Royal family for the rest of his life. He edited Queen Victoria's papers and published a book called *The Correspondence of Queen Victoria* in 1907. He was a Liberal and a fervent supporter of the Anglo-French Entente and a close adviser to Balfour between 1905 and 1914.

John Arbuthnot 'Jackie' Fisher, first Baron Fisher (1841–1920), is the second most well-known naval figures in history, after Lord Nelson, and he was the leading figure in the Edwardian naval administration. He was born in Ceylon (now Sri Lanka) to an English family. He joined the navy on 1854 and studied at Excellent, the naval gunnery school. From 1876 to 1883, he was the captain of five different Royal naval vessels. He was part of the British fleet that bombarded Alexandria in the Egyptian War of 1882. In October 1905, he was appointed First Sea Lord. In December 1905, he became Admiral of the fleet. Fisher was known as a 'moderniser' and reformer, and he was appointed to reform the navy in order to reduce its budget. He sold off 90 obsolete battleships and a further 64 reserve vessels. Fisher believed the Dreadnought, the high-speed big-gun battleship, supported by new high-speed battle cruisers, would allow the Royal Navy to continue to 'rule the waves' and keep Britain safe from overseas invasion. He also encouraged the introduction of submarines. He was severely criticised by right-wing sections of the Conservative Party for suggesting Germany had no chance of invading Britain, and he was also opposed to conscription. Not only did Fisher advise the Liberal government, but he was also a key adviser to A.J. Balfour, as leader of the Opposition. He died of cancer in 1920.

Sir Edward Grey, first Viscount Grey of Fallodon (1862–1933), was British Foreign Secretary in the Edwardian period. He was educated in Winchester and Balliol College, Oxford. He was elected Liberal MP in 1885. He was parliamentary under-secretary for foreign affairs between 1892 and 1895. He was a strong supporter of the British Empire and was dubbed a 'Liberal-Imperialist'. In 1905, Grey was appointed as Foreign Secretary: a post he held until 1916 and the longest holder of that office in the twentieth century. Grey's policy was to ensure that if war came Britain would be allied against Germany, a power he thought was intent on dominating the continent. He signed the Anglo-Russian convention in 1907, and he maintained his support for a bi-partisan or non-partisan approach to foreign affairs with the Conservatives, something he was criticised for by radicals on the left of the Liberal Party. In 1914, Grey played a key role in the events which led to the outbreak of war. He was determined to support France, but in public he used the neutrality of Belgium as the pretext for Britain entering the war, something that did not deter Germany. He is best remembered for a remark he made on hearing of the outbreak of the First World War: 'The lamps are going out all over Europe: we shall not see them lit again in our lifetime'. After the war, he wrote his memoirs and was a highly regarded elder statesman.

Lord Lansdowne, Henry Charles Keith Petty-FitzMaurice, fifth Marquess of Lansdowne (1845–1927), was a very wealthy Irish peer, who was Foreign Secretary between 1900 and 1905 and the leading Conservative spokesman on foreign affairs between 1905 and 1914. He went to Eton and Oxford. He entered the House of Lords as a Liberal in 1866, and served as Lord of the Treasury in Gladstone's government from 1869 to 1872 and as Under-Secretary for war between 1872 and 1874. He was Governor-General of Canada between 1883 and 1888, and Viceroy of India from 1888 to 1894. On his return to England, he aligned as a Liberal Unionist with the Conservative Party and was appointed Secretary of State of War in June 1895. As Foreign Secretary, he negotiated the 1904 Anglo-French Entente, and in 1906, he became Conservative leader in the House of Lords. In 1915, he joined the wartime coalition of Herbert Asquith as minister without portfolio, but he was not given a post in Lloyd George's coalition government formed in 1916, and he never held high office again.

Arthur Hamilton Lee, first Viscount Lee of Fareham, (1868–1947) was the leading Conservative spokesman for naval affairs in the House of Commons from 1905 to 1914. He came from humble origins and did not attend university. His wife Ruth was the daughter of a wealthy New York banker, and the couple were prominent in New England society. He was Conservative MP for Fareham in Hampshire between 1900 and 1918. He founded the Courtauld Institute of Art, and he owned the Buckinghamshire estate Chequers which was left in his will to be used as the official retreat of British prime ministers.

Walter Hume Long, first Viscount Long, (1854–1924) was a leading Conservative politician in the Edwardian era. He was educated at Harrow and Christ Church College, Oxford. He served as a Conservative MP from 1880 to 1921. Long held a number of Cabinet posts, most notably, as President of the Board of Agriculture, as Chief Secretary of Ireland during 1905 and First Lord of the Admiralty from 1919 to 1921. Long's wife and mother had Irish connections, and he was a strong supporter of Irish Unionism throughout his political career. In 1907, he helped to establish the Ulster Unionist Defence League. He sat as an MP for a Dublin constituency from 1905 to 1910. He was one of the few Conservatives who remained sympathetic to free trade in Opposition, and he is best known as a leading candidate to succeed Balfour in 1911, but he lost out to Bonar Law. He played a leading role in the Government of Ireland Act and the establishment of the Irish Free State. He retired from politics in 1921 and died just three years later.

Leopold James Maxse (1864–1932) was a noted right-wing journalist and editor of the *National Review* from 1893 to 1932. He attended Cambridge University and was made President of the Cambridge Union Society in 1886. Maxse was famous for being pro-French and anti-German during the Edwardian period, and he even wrote a book called *'Germany on the Brain'* in 1916. He continued to be anti-German after the war and thought the Versailles Treaty was too lenient on Germany. He was also a strong opponent of the League of Nations. At the general election of 1918, he supported the extreme right-wing National Party.

Alfred Milner, first Viscount Milner (1854–1925), was a controversial British imperialist statesman. He was born in Giessen, Hesse-Darmstadt in Germany. He was educated in Germany and then became a scholar at Balliol College, Oxford. He was awarded a first in classics in 1877. He spoke with the trace of a German accent for most of his life, which was a great irony, as he often described himself as a 'British race patriot', and he dreamed of an expanded British Empire with its own global imperial parliament. In 1897, Joseph Chamberlain appointed him as High Commissioner of South Africa and Governor of Cape Colony. He was a controversial appointent, having little government experience. He told a friend before his departure that while in South Africa he was determined to 'teach those bloody Boers a lesson'. He was a leading figure in causing the outbreak of the Anglo-Boer War (1899–1902). In February 1901, he took over the administration of the Boer states, and it was Milner who was responsible for the concentration camps which housed 27,000 Boer women and children in appalling conditions that produced widespread controversy. After the war he was appointed Governor of the Transvaal and the Orange free state. Suffering from ill health, he resigned in April 1905 and returned to Britain. He became a passionate advocate of tariff reform, the unity of the empire and a strong national defence to meet the German threat during the Edwardian age. In 1910, he founded 'The Round Table', which promoted ideas of imperial unity and acted as a policy think-tank on imperial and defence matters. He also became chairman of Rio Tinto

Zinc and was a strong opponent of attempts to curb the veto powers of the House of Lords. In 1918, Milner was appointed as Secretary of State for War and then Colonial Secretary. He attended the Paris Peace Conference and was one of the signatories of the Treaty of Versailles. He died of sleeping sickness after a visit to South Africa in 1925.

Ernest Pretyman (1860–1931) was a leading Conservative spokesman on naval affairs from 1908 to 1914. He was educated at Eton and The Royal Military Academy at Woolwich. In 1894, he married Lady Beatrice Adine Bridgeman, the daughter of the fourth Earl of Bradford. He was a Conservative MP for Suffolk (1895–1906) and Chelmsford (1908–1923). He was Civil Lord of the Admiralty from 1900 to 1903 and Financial Secretary to the Admiralty between 1903 and 1906.

Field Marshal Frederich Sleigh Roberts, first Earl Roberts (1832–1914), was one of the most famous soldiers of the Victorian era and the President of the National Service League. He was born in Cawnpore, India on 20 September 1832 and educated at Eton and Sandhurst. He had the nickname 'Bobs' and played a significant role in several important military campaigns, including the Indian Mutiny of 1857 and the Second Boer War (1899–1902). He died of pneumonia in 1914 while visiting Indian troops fighting at St. Mar in France in the First World War. Such was his reputation that he was allowed to lie in state at Westminster Hall, an honour only bestowed on one other non-Royal in the twentieth century: Sir Winston Churchill in 1965. He was buried in St. Paul's Cathedral in London.

Lord Selborne, William Waldegrave Palmer, second Earl of Selborne (1859–1942) was a leading Conservative figure on Naval affairs during the Edwardian era. He was educated at Winchester and University College, Oxford and gained a first class degree in history. In 1883, he married Lady Maud Cecil, elder daughter of Robert Cecil (Lord Salisbury), who later became Prime Minister. He started his political life as the Liberal MP for East Hampshire, but he became a 'Liberal Unionist' in 1886 outraged with Gladstone's proposal for Irish Home Rule. From 1895 to 1900, he was Under Secretary of State for the Colonies under Joseph Chamberlain. From 1900 to 1905, he was First Lord of the Admiralty and supported the introduction of the new Dreadnought class of battleships. From 1905 to 1910 he was High Commisioner for South Africa and Governor of the Transvaal. He returned to England in 1910 and became a leading supporter of Tariff Reform and Colonial preference and spoke on naval affairs at Westminster.

Frederick Edwin Smith, first Earl of Birkenhead (1872–1930), was a rising star of the Conservative Party during the Edwardian years. He was born in Birkenhead in Cheshire and was educated at Birkenhead School and Wadham College, Oxford. He married Margaret Eleanor Furneaux in April 1901, and they had three children. In 1906, he was elected Conservative MP for the Liverpool constituency of Walton, which was then a Conservative stronghold. He was known as 'F.E. Smith' and made his name as skilled lawyer. He was a hard-drinking, witty character and a brilliant orator. At the outbreak of the First World War, he was put in charge of the Governments Press Bureau. In 1915, he was made Solicitor General, and he then became Attorney General. In 1919, he became Lord Chancellor in Lloyd George's coalition government. Between 1924 and 1928, he was Secretary of State for India. After retiring from politics, he became Director of Tate and Lyle. Margot Asquith once said, 'F.E. Smith is very clever, but sometimes his brains go to his head'.

George Wyndham (1863–1913) was the leading Conservative Spokesman on army questions in the House of Commons from 1905 and 1913. In 1887, he married Sibell, Countess Grosvenor (née Lumley), after the death of her first husband, who was the son of the first Duke of Westminster. He was a prolific writer and scholar, noted for his elegance and charm. He was Chief Secretary for Ireland from 1900 to 1905, and he took a keen interest in army questions until his death in 1913.

Notes

Introduction

1. See S. Hoggart, 'Hard wired to be beastly to the Germans', *Guardian*, 17 May 2002.
2. *Daily Mirror*, 24 June 1996.
3. The most important examples of studies focused on the 'Official Mind' of British Foreign policy are: F. Hinsley (ed.), *The Foreign Policy of Sir Edward Grey*, Cambridge, Cambridge University Press, 1977; C. Lowe and M. Dockrill, *The Mirage of Power*, vol. 1, *British Foreign Policy 1902–1914*, London, Routledge, 1972; K. Robbins, *Sir Edward Grey*, London, Cassell, 1971; Z. Steiner, *The Foreign Office and Foreign Policy 1898–1914*, Cambridge, Cambridge University Press, 1968; Z. Steiner, *Britain and The Origins of the First World War*, London, Macmillan, 1977; K. Wilson, *The Policy of The Entente: Essays on the Determinants of British Foreign Policy 1904–1914*, Cambridge, Cambridge University Press, 1985. For the role of key figures in the military–naval establishment see: J. Gooch, *The Plans of War: The General Staff and British Military Strategy 1900–1916*, London, Routledge, 1974; P.M. Kennedy (ed.), *The War Plans of the Great Powers*, London, Allen and Unwin, 1980; P.M. Kennedy, The Rise and Fall of British Naval Mastery, London, Allen Lane, 1976; A.J. Marder, From Dreadnought to Scapa Flow, vol. 1, *The Road to War 1900–1914*, Oxford, Oxford University Press, 1961.
4. Wilson, *Entente*, pp.1–2.
5. See F. Fischer, *Germany's Aims in the First World War*, London, Macmillan, 1967.
6. See A. Mayer, 'Internal Causes and Purposes of War in Europe 1870–1956, A Research Assignment', *Journal of Modern History*, vol. 41 (1969), p. 291.
7. See J.A. Moses, *The Politics of Illusion, the Fischer Controversy in German historiography*, London, 1975.
8. Steiner, *Origins*, pp. 1–2.
9. The most notable biographies, include: P. Fraser, *Joseph Chamberlain: Radicalism and Empire, 1868–1914*, London, Cassell, 1966; H.S. Zebel, *Balfour*, Cambridge, Cambridge University Press, London, 1973.
10. The most noteworthy monographs are G. Phillips, *The Die Hards: Aristocratic Society and Politics in Edwardian Britain*, Cambridge, MA, Harvard University Press, 1979; J. Ramsden, *The Age of Balfour and Baldwin*

1902–1940, London, Longman, 1978; A. Sykes, *Tariff Reform in British Politics 1903–1913*, Oxford, Clarendon Press, 1979.

11. See F. Coetzee, *For Party or Country: Nationalism and the Dilemmas of Popular Conservatism in Edwardian England*, Oxford, Oxford University Press, 1990; G.R. Searle, 'The "Revolt from the Right" in Edwardian Britain', in P.M. Kennedy and A.J. Nicholls (eds), *Nationalist and Racialist Movements in Britain and Germany in Britain and Germany before 1914*, London, Macmillan, 1981, pp. 21–39.

12. P. Kennedy, 'The Pre War Right' in P.M. Kennedy and A.J. Nicholls, *Nationalist and Racialist Movements*, p. 2.

13. See F. Coetzee, 'Pressure Groups, Tory Businessmen and the Aura of Political Corruption before the First World War', *Historical Journal*, vol. 29 (1988), pp. 833–852; E.H. Green, 'Radical Conservativism and the Electoral Genesis of Tariff Reform' *Historical Journal*, vol. 28, (1985), pp. 667–692. For a stimulating comparative survey of right wing groups in Britain and Europe see: M. Blinkhorn (ed.), *Fascists and Conservatives. The radical right and the establishment in twentieth century Europe*, London, Allen and Unwin, 1990.

14. D. Dutton, *'His Majesty's Loyal Opposition': The Unionist Party in Opposition 1905–1915*, Liverpool, Liverpool University Press, 1992, pp. 293–300.

15. Kennedy, 'The Pre-War Right', p. 1.

16. Blinkhorn, *Conservatives*, p. 2.

17. Lord Winterton, *Pre-War*, London, Macmillan, 1932, p. 20.

18. E. Hobsbawm, *Industry and Empire*, London, 1968, p. 163.

19. P.M. Kennedy, *The Rise of the Anglo-German Antagonism 1860–1914*, London, Allen and Unwin, 1980, p. 435.

20. Kennedy, 'Pre-War Right', p. 2.

21. The leading contributions include: R.J. Hoffman, *Great Britain and the German Trade rivalry 1875–1914*, London, 1933; W.R. Louis, *Great Britain and Germany's Lost Colonies 1914–1919*, Cambridge, Cambridge University Press, 1967; R.J. Sontag, *Germany and England, Background to Conflict 1848–1894*, London, 1969.

22. Kennedy, *Antagonism*, p. 470.

23. Ibid., p. 486.

24. See P. Cain, 'The Political Economy in Edwardian England: The Tariff Reform Controversy, in A. O'Day (ed.), *The Edwardian Age*, London, Macmillan, 1979, p. 51; W. Fest, 'Jingoism and Xenophobia in the Electioneering Strategies of British Ruling Elites before 1914', in P.M. Kennedy and A.J. Nicholls, Nationalist and Racialist Movements, pp. 171–189.

25. Paul Kennedy has claimed what is needed to complement the various studies of the 'radical right' pressure group in the Edwardian period is a study of how the Conservative Party as a whole responded to the growth of German power. See Kennedy, 'The Pre-War Right', pp. 1–20.

Chapter 1 The Nature and Organisation of Conservative Foreign and Defence Questions at Westminster

1. A. Ponsonby, *Democracy and Diplomacy*, London, Methuen, 1915, p. 49.
2. T. Coates, *Lord Rosebery, His Life and Speeches*, vol. 2, London, Hutchinson, 1900, pp. 542–543.
3. *The Times*, 18 November 1910.
4. *The Times*, 7 November 1905.
5. Conservative Party Archive, 'The Benefits of Conservative Rule', Conservative Election Leaflet, 1905.
6. *National Review*, February 1911.
7. *The Outlook*, 5 January 1907.
8. *Hansard*, 16 February 1909, col. 23.
9. K.M. Wilson, 'The Opposition and the Crisis of the Liberal Cabinet over Foreign Policy in November 1911, *International History Review*, vol. 3(1981), p. 403.
10. S. Low, *The Governance of England*, London, Fisher, 1904, p. 252.
11. F.A. Johnson, *Defence by Committee: The Committee of Imperial Defence 1885–1959*, Oxford, Oxford University Press, 1960, p. 75.
12. Ibid., p. 55.
13. Gwynne Papers, 3/dep. 16, Beresford to Gwynne, 24 May 1912.
14. *Hansard*, 21 March 1902, cols. 322–368.
15. *The Times*, 18 May 1904.
16. Low, *Governance*, p. 251.
17. J. Spender, *Public Life*, London, Longman, 1925, p. 40.
18. Low, *Governance*, p. 166.
19. M. Egremont, *Balfour*, London, Collins, 1980, pp. 109–121.
20. Law Papers, 18/2/16, Arnold-Foster to Law, 24 April 1906.
21. Balfour Papers, 49777, fols. 82–89, Memorandum to Balfour, by Walter Long, October 1911.
22. R. Blake, *The Unknown Prime Minister: The Life and Times of Andrew Bonar Law 1858–1923*, London, Eyre and Spottiswoode, 1955, p. 103.
23. A. Clark (ed.), *'A Good Innings': The Private Papers of Viscount Lee of Fareham*, London, John Murray, 1974, p. 120.
24. B. Dugdale, *Arthur James Balfour*, vol. 2, London, Hutchinson, 1936, p. 68.
25. Ibid.
26. Ibid.
27. A. Chamberlain, *Politics From the Inside: An Epistolary Chronicle, 1906–1914*, London, Cassell, 1936, p. 350.
28. J. Vincent (ed.), *The Crawford Papers: The Journals of David Lindsay, twenty seventh Earl of Crawford and tenth Earl of Balcarres 1871–1940 during the years 1892–1940*, Manchester, Manchester University Press, 1984, p. 192.
29. Sandars Papers, c.764, fols. 157–172, a note on Mr. Balfour's Resignation, 8 November 1911.
30. Sandars Papers, c.751, fols. 114–115, Balfour to Sandars, 25 January 1906.

31. Sandars Papers, c.764, fol. 47, Balfour to Stamfordham, 18 September 1911.
32. Sandars Papers, c.756, fol. 83. Lansdowne to Sandars, 3 February 1908.
33. Sandars Papers, c.757, fols. 193–195,Cawdor to Sandars, 2 December 1908.
34. Sandars Papers, c.758, fol. 134, Lansdowne to Sandars, 21 March 1909.
35. Selborne Papers, 3/fol. 81, St. John Brodrick to Selborne, 3 October 1908.
36. Chamberlain, *Politics*, p. 471.
37. Lord Newton, *Lord Lansdowne: A Biography*, London, Macmillan, 1929, pp. 371–372.
38. Sandars Papers, c.757, fols. 207–210, Note by Walter Long on Naval Policy, November 1908.
39. Balfour Papers, 49777, fols. 33–36, Long to Balfour, 15 January 1909.
40. Cawdor Papers, Box 290, Fisher to Cawdor, 11 July 1907.
41. Sandars Papers, c.751, fols. 127–128, Lansdowne to Sandars, 3 March 1906.
42. Selborne Papers, 79/fols. 20–21, Lansdowne to Selborne, 4 April 1907.
43. Cawdor Papers, Box 290, 'The Organisation of the Admiralty and the State of the Navy', (1904).
44. Chamberlain, *Politics*, p.170.
45. Selborne Papers, 3/fol. 1, Selborne to St. John Brodrick, 14 January 1908.
46. Selborne Papers, 79/fols. 80–93, 'Notes on navy', July 1912.
47. Sandars Papers, c.764, fols. 113–116, Long to Balfour, 29 September 1911.
48. R. Williams, *Defending the Empire: The Conservative Party and British Defence Policy 1899–1915*, New Haven, Yale University Press, 1991, p. 192.
49. Ibid., p. 131.
50. Clark, Lee Papers, p. 107.
51. Ibid.
52. Ibid., p. 92.
53. Ibid., p. 91.
54. Selborne Papers, 71/fols. 171–184, Selborne to Pretyman. 13 January 1909.
55. Law Papers, 31/2/68, Beresford to Vesey, 29 January 1914.
56. Sandars Papers, c.757, fols. 207–10, Balfour to Long, 9 November 1908.
57. Chamberlain, *Politics*, p.159.
58. Selborne Papers, 71/fols. 171–184, Selborne to Pretyman, 13 January 1909.
59. Maxse Papers, 458/649, A. Chamberlain to Maxse, 5 February 1908.
60. Bonar Law Papers, 31/3/13, Lee to Law, 6 February 1914.
61. *The Times*, 23 January 1913.
62. Sandars Papers, c.751, fol. 139, Sandars Memorandum, 1906.
63. Bonar Law Papers, 25/1/46, Lee to Law, 21 January 1912.
64. Williams, *Defending the Empire*, pp. 145–146.
65. Vincent, *Crawford Papers*, p. 137, p. 217, p. 276.
66. Sandars Papers, c.754, fol. 274, Midleton to Balfour, 16 December 1907.
67. D. James, *Lord Roberts*, London, 1954, p. 438.
68. Ibid., p. 182.
69. Chamberlain, *Politics*, pp. 255–256.
70. *Annual Register*, London, 1902, p. 62.
71. *Hansard*, 5 March 1912, col. 209.
72. *The Times*, 30 April 1909.

73. P. Williamson (ed.), *The Modernisation of Conservative Politics: The Diaries and Letters of William Bridgeman 1904–1935*, Manchester, Manchester University Press, 1988, p. 30.
74. *Morning Post*, 30 January 1907.
75. Balfour Papers, 49764, fol. 210, Balfour to Bridgeman, 4 August 1906.
76. Gwynne Papers, 3/dep. 16, Gwynne to Beresford, 28 May 1907.
77. *National Review*, September 1906, pp. 38–50.
78. *Hansard*, vol. 162. cols. 77–80.
79. Gwynne Papers, 3/dep. 16, Beresford to Gwynne, 24 May 1912.
80. Gwynne Papers, 3/dep.16, Beresford to Gwynne, 16 August 1912.
81. Bonar Law Papers, 31/2/68, Vesey to Beresford, 29 January 1914.
82. Gwynne Papers, 3/dep.16, Beresford to Gwynne, 16 August 1912.
83. Sandars Papers, c.761, fol. 67, Page-Croft to Sandars, 12 September 1910.
84. Sandars Papers, c.764, fol. 56, Balfour to Imbert-Terry, 21 September 1911.
85. Sandars Papers, c.764, fol. 56, Balfour to Sandars, 21 September 1911.
86. A.J.A. Morris, *Radicalism Against War 1906–1914: The Advocacy of Peace and Retrenchment*, London, Longman 1972.
87. *Hansard*, 27 November 1911, col. 74.
88. Ibid.
89. House of Lords Debates, 28 November 1911, col. 389.
90. Ponsonby, *Democracy and Diplomacy*, pp. 48–49, pp. 121–123.

Chapter 2   Leadership: (1) A.J. Balfour and Anglo-German Relations

1. Balfour held this post from 1887 to 1891.
2. Many studies of the Conservative Party in Opposition during the period 1905 to 1914 pay no attention at all to foreign, naval or defence matters. For example, see D. Dutton, *'His Majesty's Loyal Opposition': The Unionist Party in Opposition, 1905–1914*, Liverpool, Liverpool University Press, 1992.
3. B. Dugdale, *Arthur James Balfour*, London, Hutchinson, 1936; M. Egremont, *Balfour*, London, Collins, 1980; R. Mackay, *Balfour: Intellectual Statesman*, Oxford, Oxford University Press, 1985; K. Young, *Arthur James Balfour: The Happy Life of the Politician, Prime Minister, Statesman and Philosopher, 1848–1930*, London, Bell, 1963; S.H. Zebel, *Balfour*, Cambridge, Cambridge University Press, 1973.
4. B. Webb, *Our Partnership*, London, 1926, p. 248.
5. A. Marder, *Fear God and Dread Nought: the Correspondence of Admiral of the Fleet Lord Fisher of Kilverstone*, vol. 2, Oxford, Oxford University Press, 1961, p. 114.
6. *The Times*, 11 January 1900.
7. Viscount D'Abernon, *Portraits and Appreciations*, London, Hodder and Stoughton, 1931, p. 43.

8. Balfour Papers, 49747, fols. 175–176, Balfour to M. D'Estounelles de Constant, 8 May 1905.
9. Young, *Balfour*, p. 228.
10. P.M. Kennedy, *The Rise of the Anglo-German Antagonism, 1860–1914*, London, Allen and Unwin, 1981, p. 270.
11. *Hansard*, 11 May 1905, col. 78.
12. Balfour Papers, 49779, fol. 47, Balfour to Hewins, 17 June 1908.
13. Balfour Papers, 49727, fols. 172–173, Balfour to Landsowne, 12 December 1901.
14. Egremont, *Balfour*, p. 163.
15. *Documents Diplomatic Francais, 1871–1914*, Paris, Ministere des Affaires Etrangers, 1929–1959, vol. 11, no. 33.
16. National Archives, CAB 31/1/A 'Draft report on the possibility of serious invasion', 11 November 1903.
17. The Anglo-French Entente was signed in April 1904.
18. National Archives, CAB 41/30, Balfour to King Edward VII, 8 June 1905.
19. Cawdor Papers, Box 291, 'Draft of A.J. Balfour's evidence to CID invasion sub-committee', 29 May 1908.
20. Viscountess Milner, *My Picture Gallery*, London, Murray, 1951, p. 233.
21. National Archives, CAB 41/30, Balfour to King Edward VII, 22 June 1905.
22. Young, *Balfour*, p. 182.
23. G.W. Monger, *The End of Isolation*, London, Nelson, 1963, p. 20.
24. Balfour Papers, 49727, fols. 26–27, Balfour to Lansdowne, 12 December 1901.
25. This is not to suggest that Balfour admired German militarism or the style of German diplomacy. In 1905, for example, Balfour stressed that their 'ill mannered behaviour' during the Morocco crisis revealed what 'poor diplomats Germans are'.
26. *National Review*, March 1903.
27. MacKay, *Balfour*, p. 31.
28. Young, *Balfour*, p. 228.
29. Balfour Papers, 49711, fols. 65–69, 'British Intervention in the event of France being suddenly attacked', a paper by A.J. Balfour, June 1904.
30. Young, *Balfour*, p. 248.
31. Balfour Papers, 49747, fols. 155–162, Balfour to Lascalles, 2 January 1905.
32. Ibid.
33. Selborne Papers, 3/fols. 5–6, Balfour to Selborne, 5 April 1902.
34. Balfour Papers, 49747, fols. 155–162, Balfour to Lascalles, 2 January 1905.
35. *Die Grosse Politik der Europaischen Kabinette 1871–1914*, Berlin, *Deutsche Verlagsgesellschaft fur Politik and Geschichte, 1922–1927*, vol. 21, no. 7206 and vol. 24, no. 8215.
36. Lascalles Papers, FO 800/12, fols. 198–202 'File on Anglo-German Union Club'.
37. *Hansard*, 11 May 1905, cols. 74–77.
38. J. Mackail and G. Wyndham, *The Life and Letters of George Wyndham*, vol. 2, London, Hutchinson, 1925, pp. 546–566.

39. *Hansard*, 2 August 1904, col. 620.
40. National Archives, CAB 3/1/34A, 'The Possibility of a raid by a hostile force on the British coast', memorandum by A.J. Balfour, 12 December 1902.
41. R. Williams, *Defending the Empire, The Conservative Party and British Defence Policy,1899–1915*, New Haven, Yale University Press, p. 33.
42. *The Times*, 11 November 1907.
43. Sydenhan Papers, 50836, 4/fols. 14–15, 'Note on the Distribution of our naval forces', by Sir George Clark, 1907.
44. *National Review*, June 1906.
45. Balfour Papers, 49703, fol. 27, Clarke to Balfour, 14 September 1906.
46. N. Hiley, 'The Failure of Espionage towards Germany, 1907–1914', *Historical Journal*, vol. 26 (1983), p. 867.
47. Sandars Papers, c.754, fols. 274–279, Midleton to Balfour, 16 December 1907.
48. Repington Papers, Repington to Roberts, 11 November 1907.
49. National Archives, CAB 3/2/42A, 'Note by George Clark on Invasion', July 1907.
50. Williams, *Defence*, p. 131.
51. M. Brett (ed.), *The Journals and Letters of Reginald Viscount Esher*, vol. 1, London, Nicholson and Watson, 1934.
52. Selborne Papers, 3/fols. 16–18, Selborne to St. John Brodrick, 27 February 1908.
53. Balfour Papers, 49712, Fisher to Balfour, 29 November 1907.
54. Sandars Papers, c.765, fols. 2–4, Balfour to Fisher, 1 January 1908.
55. National Archives, CAB 43, 'A Statement by Mr. A.J. Balfour before the sub-committee on Invasion', 29 May 1908.
56. Sandars Papers, c.756, fols. 151–152, Lord Esher to King Edward VII, 1 January 1909.
57. National Archives, CAB 16/3, 'A Report and Proceedings of the sub-committee, appointed by the Prime Minister, to reconsider the question of overseas attack', 22 November 1908.
58. Balfour told the German Ambassador[Metternich] in 1908 that the Anglo-German naval race was the primary reason for the deterioration of Anglo-German relations. See *Grosse Politik*, vol. 24, no. 8215.
59. Selborne Papers, 3/fol. 12, Lady Selborne to Lord Selborne, 16 September 1908.
60. F. Coetzee, *For Party or Country: Nationalism and the Dilemmas of Popular Conservatism in Edwardian England*, Oxford, Oxford University Press, 1990, p. 108.
61. J. Vincent (ed.), *The Crawford Papers: The Journals of David Lindsay, twenty seventh Earl of Crawford and tenth Earl of Balcarres 1871–1940*, Manchester, Manchester University Press, 1984, p. 122.
62. The Conservative agitation was summed up by George Wyndham's popular slogan: 'We want eight and we won't wait'.
63. *The Times*, 17 March 1909.

64. Williams, *Defence*, pp. 164–165. In private, Asquith, a committed Liberal Imperialist, supported the building of the eight battleships straight away. He came up with the 'four now and four later' in the hope of pacifying the Liberal rank and file, most of whom opposed excessive spending on the navy.

65. The motion of censure stated 'That in the view of this House the declared policy of His Majesty's Government respecting the immediate provision of battleships of the newest types does not sufficiently secure the safety of the Empire.'

66. *Hansard*, 22 March 1909, col. 65.

67. *The Times*, 23 March 1909.

68. Sandars Papers, c.758, fols. 178–185, Balfour to Esher, 16 April 1909.

69. *Hansard*, 29 July 1909, cols. 1396–1397.

70. Selborne Papers, 1/fols. 144–146, Balfour to Selborne, 7 January 1914.

71. The memorandum was sent by Balfour to a number of senior Shadow Cabinet figures in the weeks leading up to the General Election of December 1910.

72. Vincent, *Crawford Papers*, pp. 255–257.

73. Sandars Papers, c.764, fols. 57–58a, Balfour to Sandars, 21 September 1911.

74. Balfour Papers, 49862, fol. 169, Balfour to Spender, 30 May 1912.

75. Balfour Papers, 49747, fol. 218, Balfour to Mensdorf, 1 May 1913. Balfour and Lansdowne were frequently briefed 'off the record' by William Tyrell, Grey's private secretary, who constantly stressed the German 'menace' in conversation with them.

76. Balfour Papers, 49731, fol. 1, Grey to Balfour, 1 June 1912.

77. A.J. Balfour, 'Anglo-German Relations', *Nord and Sud*, July 1912, pp. 22–34.

78. Balfour Papers, 49747, fol. 213 'Anglo-German Relations', notes and comments on *Nord and Sud* article.

79. 'Episodes of the Month', *National Review*, July 1912.

80. *Hansard*, 22 July 1912, cols. 860–868.

81. Balfour insisted on this clause because he was not prepared for Britain to be 'dragged at her heels into a war for the recovery of Alsace Lorraine'.

82. Bonar Law Papers, 39/D/7, 'Memorandum on Anglo-French relations by Mr. A.J. Balfour sent by request to Sir Edward Grey', November 1912.

83. Bonar Law Papers, 29/4/49, Balfour to Bonar Law, 12 November 1912.

84. A. Chamberlain, *Politics from the Inside*, vol. 1, London, Cassel, 1936, p. 413.

85. Bonar Law Papers, 29/4/49, Balfour to Bonar Law, November 1912.

86. J. Rohl (ed.), *1914: Delusion or Design*, London, Elek, 1973, p. 108.

87. Egremont, *Balfour*, pp. 260–262.

88. National Archives, CAB 3/2/5/62 A, 'Report of Standing sub-Committee of the Committee of Imperial Defence on attack on the British Isles from overseas', April 1914.

89. Balfour Papers, 49731, fols. 17–19, Balfour to Grey, 16 December 1913.

Chapter 3 Leadership: (2) Andrew Bonar Law and Anglo-German Relations

1. H.A. Taylor, *The Strange Case of Andrew Bonar Law*, London, Stanley Paul, 1938; R. Blake, *The Unknown Prime Minister*, London, Eyre and Spottiswoode, 1955.
2. Taylor, *Law*, p. 279.
3. Blake, *Unknown Prime Minister*, p. 533.
4. The Kidston brothers later became partners in the Clydesdale Bank.
5. The school can also boast Sir Henry Campbell-Bannerman, the Liberal Prime Minister, as another former pupil.
6. Blake, *Unknown Prime Minister*, p. 43.
7. The marriage produced seven children. The untimely death of Bonar Law's wife in 1909, following a routine gall stone operation, was a shattering blow to Law, because his marriage had provided him with a vital support system from the daily grind of politics.
8. Bonar Law lost his seat in the 1906, but soon gained a seat, following a by-election victory at Dulwich later the same year. Law was defeated in Manchester North West in December 1910, but he won a by-election in Bootle in 1911.
9. Blake, *Unknown Prime Minister*, p. 42.
10. Taylor, *Law*, p. 206.
11. Ibid., p. 21.
12. *Hansard*, 27 November 1911, col. 68.
13. Law Papers, 29/1/30, 'Letter concerning Anglo-German hospital at Dalston', 27 July 1913.
14. Taylor, *Law*, p. 207.
15. *Hansard*, 30 March 1909, col. 287.
16. Ibid., col. 287.
17. *Monthly Notes on Tariff Reform*, August 1908, vol. 8, p. 249.
18. *Monthly Notes on Tariff Reform*, January 1908, vol. 8, p. 71.
19. Taylor, *Law*, p. 125.
20. *Monthly Notes on Tariff Reform*, December 1908, vol. 8, p. 396.
21. *Monthly Notes on Tariff Reform*, January 1908, vol. 8, pp. 20–22.
22. *Monthly Notes on Tariff Reform*, December 1908, vol. 8, pp. 392–397.
23. *Monthly Notes on Tariff Reform*, August 1908, vol. 8, pp. 243–244.
24. J. Vincent (ed.), *The Crawford Papers: The Journal of David Lindsay, twenty seventh Earl of Crawford and tenth Earl of Balcarres 1871–1940*, Manchester, Manchester University Press, 1984, pp. 247–248.
25. *Hansard*, 27 November 1911, col. 68.
26. *Hansard*, 14 January 1912, col. 21.
27. Ibid., col. 23.
28. Ibid., col. 22.
29. *Hansard*, 27 November 1911, col. 67.
30. *Hansard*, 14 February 1912, col. 33.
31. Vincent, *Crawford Papers*, p. 253.

32. 'Episodes of the Month', *National Review*, November 1905.
33. J. Barnes and D. Nicholson (eds), *The Leo Amery Diaries*, vol. 1, London, Hutchinson, p.116.
34. House of Lords Debates, 28 November 1911, cols. 388–399.
35. A. Chamberlain, *Politics From the Inside: An Epistolary Chronicle 1906–1914*, London, Cassell, 1937, p. 471.
36. Ibid.
37. P. Adelson, *Mark Sykes: Portrait of an Amateur*, London, 1975, p. 110.
38. Law Papers, 38/D/5, 'Our Parliamentary Attitude to Foreign Affairs', memorandum by Lord Balcarres, 20 May 1912.
39. *Hansard*, 27 November 1911, col. 67.
40. *The Times*, 7 November 1905.
41. Law Papers, 24/3/72, 'Briefing Notes for Bonar Law for Agadir Debate', prepared by Lord Lansdowne, 22 November 1911.
42. Law Papers, 24/3/63, Gwynne to Law, 20 November 1911.
43. Gwynne Papers, 3/dep. 20, Law to Gwynne, 29 June 1912.
44. *Hansard*, 27 November 1911, col. 69.
45. *Hansard*, 27 November 1911, col. 69.
46. Gwynne Papers, 3/dep. 16, Gwynne to Beresford, 3 June 1907.
47. *Daily News*, 19 March 1909.
48. Selborne Papers, 79/fols. 99–103, Selborne to Austen Chamberlain, 19 August 1912.
49. Selborne Papers, 79/fols. 107–110, Austen Chamberlain to Selborne, 20 August 1912.
50. Selborne Papers, 79/fols. 114–120, Selborne to Lansdowne, 29 August 1912.
51. Selborne Papers, 79/fols. 117–118, Lansdowe to Selborne, 4 September 1912.
52. Selborne Papers, 79/fol. 113, Law to Selborne, 2 September 1912.
53. Law Papers, 31/2/68, Beresford to Vasey, 29 January 1914.
54. Law Papers, 25/3/15, 'Conversations with Herr von Riepenhausen, Councillor of Legation, and Commander Widenmann, German Naval Attaché concerning the German Naval Programme', memorandum by George Armstrong, 26 February 1912.
55. Law Papers, 25/3/14, Armstrong to Law, 7 March 1912.
56. *Hansard*, 20 December 1912, col. 1901.
57. Law Papers, 18/8/10, Law to Fabian Ware, 8 September 1908.
58. Wilson Papers, DS. MISC./ 80/HHW21, Wilson's Diary, 26 October 1912.
59. Selborne Papers, 79/fols. 78–79, Roberts to Selborne, 15 May 1912.
60. Law Papers 26/5/5, Lee to Law, 3 July 1912.
61. Law Papers 26/5/11, Landowne to Law, 6 July 1912.
62. This recommendation seems to have been included at Midleton's insistence, because Lee and Wyndham, in a brief minority report, rejected the idea of the Opposition declaring 'hypothetical' spending estimates.
63. Bonar Law Papers, 29/1/14, 'Report on the Sub-Committee on Land Forces', 4 February 1913.
64. Blake, *Unknown Prime Minister*, pp. 93–94; Taylor, Law, pp. 164–175.

Chapter 4 The Views of the Conservative Party at Westminster towards Anglo-German Relations, 1905–1914

1. J. Mackail and G. Wyndham, *The Life and Letters of George Wyndham*, vol. 2, London, Hutchinson, 1951, pp. 564–66.
2. H. Page-Croft, *My Life of Strife*, London, Hutchinson, 1949, p. 47.
3. Maxse Papers, 458/698, A. Chamberlain to Maxse, 2 June 1908.
4. R. Williams, *Defending the Empire: The Conservative Party and National Defence 1899–1915*, New Haven, Yale University Press, 1991, p. 89.
5. A. Clark (ed.), *'A Good Innings': The Private Papers of Viscount Lee of Fareham*, London, John Murray, 1974, p. 89, p. 130, p. 120.
6. J. Amery, *The Life of Joseph Chamberlain*, vol. 4, London, Macmillan, 1951, p. 197.
7. Selborne Papers, 3/fols. 16–18, Selborne to Midleton, 27 February 1908.
8. Selborne Papers, 97/fols. 97–98, 21 August 1905.
9. P.M. Kennedy, *The Rise and Fall of the Anglo-German Antagonism 1860–1914*, London, Allen and Unwin, 1980, p. 256.
10. Kennedy, *Antagonism* ,p. 316.
11. Ibid.
12. The *Conservative*, January 1905, p. 10.
13. *Morning Post*, 12 July 1912.
14. Kennedy, *Antagonism*, p. 420.
15. House of Lords Debates, 24 November 1908, cols. 25–33.
16. *Hansard*, 5 March 1912, col. 213.
17. *Hansard*, 14 December 1911, cols. 2555–2558.
18. *Hansard*, 29 March 1909, cols. 725–729.
19. Ibid., cols. 39–52.
20. House of Lords Debates, 24 November 1908, cols. 10–61.
21. Ibid., col. 1696.
22. *Hansard*, 29 March 1909, cols. 70–73.
23. Ibid., cols. 107–109.
24. Ibid., cols. 112–115.
25. House of Lords Debates, 24 November 1908, cols. 25–33.
26. *Hansard*, 29 March 1909, cols. 39–52.
27. Ibid., cols. 107–109.
28. *Hansard*, 15 March 1912, col. 213.
29. *Hansard*, 14 December 1911, col. 2645.
30. *Hansard*, 29 March 1909, cols. 725–729.
31. House of Lords Debates, 23 November 1908, cols. 39–52.
32. *Hansard*, 14 December 1911, cols. 74–78.
33. Ibid., cols. 112–115.
34. *Nineteenth Century and After*, April 1909, p. 507.
35. Report of the Departmental Committee on the Importation of Foreign Prison Made Goods, Public Record Office, Cmnd No. 7902.
36. E. Williams, *Made in Germany*, London, 1886, pp. 1–2.
37. *Nineteenth Century and After*, vol. 41, 1897, p. 993.

38. *Daily News*, 26 August 1896.
39. *National Review*, June 1899.
40. F. Coetzee, *For Party or Country: Nationalism and the Dilemmas of Popular Conservatism in Edwardian England*, Oxford, Oxford University Press, 1990, p. 95.
41. P. Cain, 'Political Economy in Edwardian England: The Tariff Reform Controversy', in A. O'Day (ed.), *The Edwardian Age*, London, Macmillan, 1979, p. 51.
42. *Monthly Notes on Tariff Reform*, January 1908, vol. 8, p. 18.
43. *Monthly Notes on Tariff Reform*, December 1907, vol. 7, p. 389.
44. *Hansard*, 29 March 1908, cols. 107–109.
45. *Monthly Notes on Tariff Reform*, December 1908, vol. 8, pp. 392–397.
46. *Hansard*, 29 March 1909, cols. 112–115.
47. *The Times*, 17 December 1909.
48. *Monthly Notes on Tariff Reform*, July 1907, vol. 7, p. 69.
49. *Monthly Notes on Tariff Reform*, July 1908, vol. 8, p. 18.
50. *Monthly Notes on Tariff Reform*, December 1908, vol. 8, p. 386.
51. *Monthly Notes on Tariff Reform*, March 1908, p. 65.
52. *Monthly Notes on Tariff Reform*, December 1907, p. 386.
53. *Hansard*, 14 April 1908, col. 1014.
54. *Hansard*, 30 March 1909, cols. 285–286.
55. Ibid., col. 260.
56. *Hansard*, 13 June 1906, col. 1035.
57. Coetzee, *For Party or Country*, p. 42.
58. A.J.A. Morris, *The Scaremongers: The Advocacy of War and Rearmament 1896–1914*, London, Routledge, 1984, p. 246.
59. Law Papers, 27/4/49, Balfour to Law, July 1912.
60. Earl Percy, 'The British Army in a Future War', *National Review*, July 1910.
61. Lord Roberts, 'Imperial and National Safety', *Nineteenth Century and After*, July 1913, p. 457.
62. House of Lords Debates, 23 November 1908, cols. 1738–1741.
63. Law Papers, 25/46, Lee to Law, 21 January 1912.
64. House of Lords Debates, 23 November, 1908, cols. 1707–1714.
65. House of Lords Debates, 10 July 1906, cols. 682–689.
66. Ibid., cols. 656–667.
67. H.B. Jeffreys, 'Invasion and National Safety', *Nineteenth Century and After*, March 1913, p. 478.
68. Jeffreys, 'Invasion and National Safety', p. 478.
69. Maxse Papers, 458–746, Roberts to Maxse, 2 September 1908.
70. House of Lords Debates, 27 November 1908, col. 1685.
71. Ibid., col. 1685.
72. M. Brett, *Journals and Letters of Reginald Brett, Viscount Esher*, vol. 1, London, Nicolson and Watson, 1934, p. 361.
73. D. James, *Lord Roberts*, London, 1954, p. 438.
74. Ibid.
75. Earl Percy, 'Our Military Weakness', *National Review*, July 1913.
76. Earl Percy, 'The True Doctrine of National Defence', *National Review*, April 1914.

Chapter 5   The Role of the German Threat in the Propaganda and Electioneering Tactics of the Conservative Party at the Two General Elections of 1910

1. P.M. Kennedy, *The Rise and Fall of the Anglo-German Antagonism, 1860–1914*, London, Allen and Unwin, 1980, pp. 343–345.
2. Walter Long Papers, 947/444/9, Lawrence to Long, 22 December 1910.
3. J. Ramsden, *The Making of Conservative Policy*, London, Longman, 1980, p. 15.
4. N. Blewett, *The Peers, The Parties and the People: The General Elections of 1910*, London, Macmillan, p. 270.
5. Conservative Party Archive, 'Memorandum on Origin of Lobby Press Services' by Mr Burchett, October 1927.
6. Kennedy, *Antagonism*, p. 369.
7. Blewett, *Elections*, p. 307.
8. Gwynne Papers, dep. 16, Gwynne to Beresford, 25 May 1907.
9. Balfour Papers, 49795, fols. 3–9, 'Memorandum on Campaign Literature', by J.L. Garvin, 1909.
10. Sandars Papers, c. 759, fols. 64–70, Garvin to Northcliffe, 4 August 1909.
11. F. Coetzee, *For Party or Country: Nationalism and the Dilemmas of Popular Conservatism in Edwardian England*, Oxford, Oxford University Press, 1990, pp. 109–111.
12. A.J.A. Morris, *The Scaremongers. The Advocacy of War and Rearmament, 1896–1914*, London, Routledge, 1984, pp. 201–204.
13. Sandars Papers, c.759, fols. 64–70,Garvin to Northcliffe, 4 August 1909.
14. Gwynne Papers, dep. 27, 'A Note on General Election', Percival Hughes, January 1910.
15. Blewett, *Elections*, p. 317.
16. Conservative Party Archives, 'Are The Unionists Scaremongers?', National Union pamphlet, no. 1333, 1910.
17. *How To Canvass For the Unionist Party*, London, National Union, 1910. This version was used extensively at the January election in 1910.
18. *The Campaign Guide; A Handbook for Unionist Speakers*, London, National Union,1909, pp. 117–120, pp. 133–153, pp. 425–435, pp. 454–456. This version was used extensively for both elections during 1910.
19. *Campaign Guide*, pp. 20–27.
20. 'Britons Beware'. National Union, pamphlets and leaflets, no. 780, 1909.
21. 'Can we trust the radical government to guarantee naval supremacy?' National Union, pamphlets and leaflets, no. 1416, 1909.
22. 'Under which Flag?', National Union leaflet, no. 859, 1909.
23. 'The Radicals and Foreign Affairs', National Union leaflet, no. 1173.
24. 'Britain Betrayed: A Deadly Danger and a National Shame', National Union, pamphlets and leaflets, no. 851, 1909.
25. National Union pamphlets and leaflets, no. 851, 1909.
26. *Campaign Guide*, 1909, p. 22.

27. 'Radicals and Foreign Affairs', National Union pamphlets and leaflets, no. 1173.
28. National Union pamphlets and leaflets, no. 1063, 1909.
29. Coetzee, *Party or Country*, p. 94.
30. *How to Canvass*, London, National Union, 1910.
31. 'Ourselves versus Germany', National Union leaflet, no. 1443, 1910.
32. *Facts About Food Taxes*, London, National Union, 1910, pp. 12–18.
33. *Facts About Food Taxes*, pp. 12–19.
34. Sandars Papers, c.760, fol. 26, Garvin to Percival Hughes, 4 January 1910. 'What Price the Radical Loaf', National Union poster, no. 759, 1909.
35. The issue was highlighted by 64 per cent of Liberal candidates and 80 per cent of Labour candidates. See Blewett, *Elections*, p. 321.
36. Kennedy, *Antagonism*, p. 345.
37. There were an enormous number of pamphlets and leaflets produced for the two elections on this theme, including, 'The Employment Question', National Union leaflet, no. 779, 1909; 'Give Home Industry a Chance', National Union leaflet, no. 766, 1909; 'Free Imports Starve British Workmen', National Union leaflet, no. 998, 1909; 'Free Imports Mean Idle Mills', National Union leaflet, no. 1001, 1909; 'Fiscal Reform Means more Employment', National Union leaflet, no. 756, 1909.
38. Blewett, *Elections*, p. 321.
39. 'No Hops', Tariff Reform League poster, 1909.
40. 'Facts for the Hop Grower', Tariff Reform leaflet, 1909.
41. 'A Note to the Working Man', National Union leaflet, no. 739, 1909.
42. 'Tariff Reform', National Union leaflet, no. 1204, 1909.
43. 'Foreigners Tax us. Let us Tax Them', National Union poster, no. 998, 1909.
44. National Union leaflet, no. 1195, 1910.
45. Coetzee, *Party or Country*, p. 95.
46. L.S. Amery, *My Political Life*, vol. 1, London, Hutchinson, 1953, p. 236.
47. G.A. Lebzelter, 'Anti Semitism – A Focal Point for the British Right' in P.M. Kennedy and A.J. Nicholls (eds), *Nationalist and Racialist Movements*, pp. 88–105.
48. Ibid., p. 97.
49. Blewett, *Elections*, p. 311.
50. The series of articles on the 'German threat' by Blatchford appeared in the *Daily Mail* from 13 to 24 December 1909.
51. *The Times*, 5 January 1910.
52. The seat in question was Everton, Liverpool, which was one of the strongest 'Orange' constituencies in the country.
53. Blewett, *Elections*, p. 403.
54. R. Williams, *Defending the Empire: The Conservative Party and Defence Policy, 1899–1915*, New Haven, Yale University Press, 1991, p. 176.
55. *Westminster Gazette*, 14 December 1909.
56. W. Fest, 'Jingoism and Xenophobia in the Electioneering Strategies of British Ruling Elites Before 1914', in P.M. Kennedy and A.J. Nicholls (eds),

Nationalist and Racialist Movements in Britain and Germany before 1914, London, Macmillan, 1981, p. 181.

57. Austen Chamberlain Papers, 8/5/1, Austen Chamberlain to Balfour, 29 January 1910.
58. Sandars Papers, c.760, fol. 102, 'Report of sub-committee on organisation, Yorkshire Division', National Union, 29 April 1910.
59. Sandars Papers, c.760, fol. 157, Short to Sandars, 13 May 1910.
60. Conservative Party Archive, 'Minutes of Executive Council of National Union', 8 March 1910, p. 8.
61. The Tariff Reform trips to Germany will be dealt with in more detail in Chapter 6.
62. *How to Canvass for the Unionist Party*, London, National Union, 1910. This version was used for the second general election in December 1910.
63. Sandars Papers, c.760, fol. 199, Garvin to Balfour 17 October 1910.
64. Balfour Papers, 49796, Garvin to Sandars, 14 November 1910.
65. Blewett, *Elections*, p. 326.
66. H. Taylor, *The Strange Case of Andrew Bonar Law*, London, Stanley Paul, 1938, p. 137.
67. Blewett, *Elections*, p. 388.
68. Coetzee, *Party or Country*, p. 135.
69. Sandars Papers, c.762, fols. 190–193, St John Brodrick to Steel Maitland, 22 December 1910.
70. Sandars Papers, c.763, fol. 16, 'Petition of 1900 Group', January 1911.
71. D. Dutton, *'His Majesty's Loyal Opposition': The Unionist Party in Opposition 1905–1915*, Liverpool, Liverpool University Press, 1992, p. 134.
72. Ibid., p. 137.
73. Coetzee, *Party or Country*, p. 147.
74. This interpretation casts doubt on the view put forward by Fest. See Fest, 'Xenophobia', p. 181.
75. Coetzee, *Party or Country*, p. 95.

Chapter 6 Extra Parliamentary Pressure Groups and Germany

1. The following studies examine patriotic pressure groups in the Edwardian period: F. Coetzee, *For Party or Country: Nationalism and the Dilemmas of Popular Conservatism in Edwardian England*, Oxford, Oxford University Press, 1990; F. Coetzee, 'Pressure Groups, Tory Businessmen and the aura of Political Corruption before the First World War', *Historical Journal*, vol. 29, 1986, pp. 833–852; A. Summers, 'Militarism in Britain before the First World War', *History Workshop Journal*, vol. 2, 1976; A. Sykes, 'The Radical Right and the Crisis of Conservatism'. *Historical Journal*, vol. 26, 1983, pp. 661–676.
2. H. Taylor, *Jix: Viscount Brentford*, London, Stanley Paul, 1933, p. 89.
3. *National Service League Journal*, March 1904, p. 101.
4. *Nation in Arms*, January 1911, p. 3.

5. Ibid.
6. Ibid.
7. R. Williams, *Defending the Empire: The Conservative Party and British Defence Policy 1899–1915*, New Haven, Yale University Press, 1991, p. 184.
8. P.M. Kennedy, *The Rise of the Anglo-German Antagonism, 1860–1914*, London, Allen and Unwin, p. 371.
9. *Nation in Arms*, August 1911, p. 405.
10. Coetzee, *Party or Country*, p. 41.
11. *Nation in Arms*, February 1911, p. 99.
12. *Nation in Arms*, Midsummer 1913, p. 47.
13. *Nation in Arms*, Christmas, 1913, p. 467.
14. *Nation in Arms*, Midsummer, 1913, p. 381.
15. G.R. Searle, 'The "Revolt from the Right" in Edwardian Britain', in P.M. Kennedy and A. Nichols (eds), *Nationalist and Racialist Movements in Britain and Germany before 1914*, London, Macmillan, 1981, p. 24.
16. *National Review*, February 1908.
17. *National Review*, May 1905.
18. *National Review*, January 1908.
19. *National Review*, October 1908.
20. L.J. Maxse, *Germany on the Brain*, London, Hodder and Stoughton, 1915, p. 7.
21. *National Review*, May 1912.
22. *The Times*, 7 November 1905.
23. Gwynne Papers, 3/dep. 14, Amery to Gwynne, 3 January 1913.
24. Searle, 'Revolt From the Right', p. 27.
25. Bonar Law Papers, 18/4/53, Gwynne to Law, 11 February 1908.
26. Maxse Papers, 458/699, Spring-Rice to Maxse, 3 June 1908.
27. *Nation in Arms*, Midsummer 1914, pp. 614–615.
28. Coetzee, *Party or Country*, p. 115.
29. *Nation in Arms*, Christmas 1913, p. 498.
30. Ibid., p. 484.
31. *Nation in Arms*, Midsummer, no. 2, 1912, pp. 95–96.
32. Ibid., p. 67.
33. H.S. Cheetham, 'German Thoroughness' in *Nation in Arms*, October 1911, pp. 561–562.
34. *Titbits*, 13 March 1909.
35. B.S. Townroe, *A Nation in Arms: A Play in Four Acts*, London, National Service League, 1910.
36. National Archives, 'Report of C.I.D. Sub-Committee on Invasion, 1908', CAB 16/3A.
37. Roberts Papers, R62/19, Repington to Roberts, 12 November 1907.
38. Bonar Law Papers, 18/4/53, B.K. Murray to Law, 11 February 1908.
39. *Nation in Arms*, Spring 1912, p. 93.
40. Coetzee, *Party or Country*, p. 97.
41. See A. Sykes, *Tariff Reform in British Politics 1903–1913*, Oxford, Oxford University Press, 1979.

42. R. Jay, *Joseph Chamberlain: A Political Study*, Oxford, Oxford University Press, 1981, p. 277.
43. B. Semmel, *Imperialism and Social Reform: English Imperial Thought 1895–1914*, Cambridge, Harvard University Press, 1960, pp. 102–105.
44. Coetzee, *Party or Country*, p. 95.
45. *Monthly Notes on Tariff Reform*, December 1908, p. 395.
46. 'Taxing the Poor', Tariff Reform leaflet, no. 197.
47. 'Railway Workers and Tariff Reform', Tariff Reform leaflet, no. 190.
48. 'The Foreigner and The Glass Trade', Tariff Reform leaflet, no. 124.
49. 'An Injured Industry; The Granite Trade', Tariff Reform leaflet, no. 125.
50. 'Look at Germany', Tariff Reform leaflet, no. 184.
51. *Daily News*, 21 April 1910.
52. *The Times*, 13 January 1913.
53. The Conservative and Unionist, July 1910, p. 120.
54. *The Times*, 28 January 1908.
55. Ibid.
56. *National Review*, 20 July 1907.
57. *Standard*, 13 November 1907.
58. *Standard*, 20 July 1907.
59. Coetzee, *For Party or Country*, p. 133.
60. *Standard*, 9 November 1907.
61. *Standard*, 2 December 1908.
62. *Standard*, 6 May 1908.
63. *Standard*, 29 November 1906.
64. *Standard*, 21 May 1908.
65. *The Times*, 28 January 1908.
66. *Morning Post*, 3 November 1908.
67. *Daily Express*, 7 August 1908.
68. *Morning Post*, 20 November 1907.
69. Gwynne Papers, 3/dep. 16, Beresford to Gwynne, 22 November 1907.
70. *Morning Post*, 17 July 1907. See also a letter from Rowland Hunt entitled 'Danger of a Successful Invasion', published in *Standard*, 12 June 1908.
71. *Standard*, 29 November 1906.
72. Law Papers, 18/4/53, Gwynne to Law, 11 February 1908. Gwynne worked closely with Charles Beresford to further the cause of the Imperial Maritime League. As Gwynne commented to Beresford about Wyatt's constant stress on the danger of a German invasion, 'Mr Wyatt, who is absolutely on our way of thinking' is 'fighting the fight on our lines'. See Gwynne Papers, 3/dep. 16, Gwynne to Beresford, 25 May 1907.
73. *Daily Express*, 26 January 1909.
74. A. Pollock, 'A Bolt from the Blue', *National Review*, August 1908.
75. 'An English Patriot', *Standard*, 7 August 1907.
76. *Standard*, 19 November 1908.
77. Sandars Papers, c.758, fol. 228, Wyatt to Balfour, 22 May 1909.
78. Sandars Papers, c.758, fol. 229, Balfour to Wyatt, 23 May 1909.

79. Gwynne Papers, 3/dep. 15, Gwynne to Balfour, 28 October 1910.
80. *Ealing Gazette*, 31 October 1908.
81. Coetzee, *For Party or Country*, p. 142.

Chapter 7   The Conservative Party and the Decision for War in 1914

1. Z. Steiner, *Britain and the Origins of the First World War*, London, Longman, 1977, p. 220.
2. Balfour Papers, 49832, fol. 21, Balfour to Alice Balfour, 8 August 1914.
3. Bonar Law Papers, 24/3/72, 'Briefing Notes for Andrew Bonar Law for Agadir Debate' by Lord Lansdowne, 22 November 1911.
4. House of Lords Debates, 27 November 1911, col. 58
5. D.C. Watt, 'British Reactions to the Assassination at Sarejevo', *European Studies Review*, vol. 1, 1971, p. 242.
6. J. Barnes and J. Nicholson, *The Leo Amery Diaries 1896–1929*, London, Hutchinson, 1980, p. 116.
7. House of Lords Debates, 28 November 1908, cols. 388–389.
8. The offer to form a coalition was made by Churchill to F.E. Smith on 30 July 1914 and was discussed with Law on 31 July 1914. Law told Smith that he would only discuss the question of a coalition with Asquith – not with any intermediaries. See Lord Beaverbrook, *Politicians and the War*, London, Hutchinson, 1916, p. 18.
9. Steiner, *Origins*, p. 223.
10. M. Brock and E. Brock (eds), *H.H. Asquith: Letters to Venetia Stanley*, Oxford, Oxford University Press, 1982, p. 123.
11. Viscount Grey, *Twenty Five Years 1892–1916*, vol.1, London, Hodder and Stoughton, 1925, p. 337
12. W. Churchill, *The World Crisis 1911–1914*, London 1923, p. 216.
13. See *Hansard*, 15 September 1914, col. 896.
14. R. Blake, *The Unknown Prime Minister*, London, Eyre and Spottiswoode, 1955, p. 220.
15. Maxse Papers, 475/335, Beresford to Maxse, 22 September 1918.
16. Balfour Papers, 49748, fols. 3–4, Balfour to Nicolson, 2 August 1914.
17. B. Dugdale, *Arthur James Balfour*, vol. 2, London, Hutchinson, 1936, pp. 82–86.
18. *National Review*, August 1918.
19. Balfour Papers, 49836, fols. 197–198, 'Notes of a Conversation between Mrs. Dugdale and A.J. Balfour', 8 November 1928.
20. Maxse Papers, 475/332, Beresford to Maxse, 8 September 1918.
21. Beaverbrook, *Politicians and the War*, pp. 19–20.
22. R. Blake, *The Unknown Prime Minister: The Life and Times of Andrew Bonar Law, 1858–1923*, London, Eyre and Spottiswoode, 1955, p. 221.
23. A. Chamberlain, *Down the Years*, London, Cassell, pp. 93–95. For details of the reaction of Conservative politicians in the period from 31 July to 4 August 1914, see Austen Chamberlain Papers, Birmingham University Library, 14/2/2.

24. I. Colvin, *The Life of Lord Carson*, vol. 3, London, 1932, pp. 16–19. See also C. Adam, *Life of Lord Lloyd*, London, 1960, pp. 59–61, for Lloyd's account.
25. Blake, *Unknown Prime Minister*, p. 222.
26. R. Williams, *Defending the Empire. The Conservative Party and British Defence Policy 1899–1915*, New Haven, Yale University Press, p. 227.
27. Bonar Law Papers, 37/4/1, Law to Asquith, 2 August 1914.
28. Chamberlain, *Down The Years*, pp. 101–102.
29. Bonar Law Papers, 34/3/2, Asquith to Law, 2 August 1914.
30. Blake, *Unknown Prime Minister*, p. 223.
31. K.M. Wilson, 'The British Cabinet's Decision for War', *British Journal of International Studies*, vol. 1, 1975, pp. 151–157.
32. Churchill, *World Crisis*, p. 218.
33. P.M. Kennedy, *The Rise of the Anglo-German Antagonism, 1860–1914*, London, Allen and Unwin, 1980, p. 461. Only two Cabinet members – Morley and Burns disagreed with the policy of intervention.
34. Chamberlain, *Down the Years*, p. 102.
35. H. Asquith, *Memories and Reflections, 1852–1927*, vol. 2, London, Hutchinson, 1928, p. 20.
36. *Hansard*, 3 August 1914, cols. 1809–1827.
37. Ibid., cols. 1827–1828.
38. Ibid., cols. 1835–1836.
39. Ibid., col. 1883.
40. *Hansard*, 4 August 1914, col. 1963.
41. C. Hazelhurst, *Politicians at War, July 1914 to May 1915: A Prologue to the Triumph of Lloyd George*, London, 1971, p. 42.
42. Churchill, *World Crisis*, pp. 214–215.

Conclusion

1. The 'anti-German' nature of the Conservative Party is emphasised in a number of studies. See P. Cain, 'The Political Economy in Edwardian England: The Tariff Reform Controversy, in A. O'Day (ed.), *The Edwardian Age*, London, Macmillan, 1979, p. 51; F. Coetzee, *For Party or Country: Nationalism and the Dilemmas of Popular Conservatism in Edwardian England*, Oxford, Oxford University Press, 1990, p. 95; W. Fest, 'Jingoism and Xenophobia in the Electioneering Strategies of British Ruling Elites before 1914', in P.M. Kennedy and A.J. Nicholls (eds), *Nationalist and Racialist Movements in Britain and Germany before 1914*, Oxford, Macmillan, 1981, pp. 171–189.
2. This interpretation takes issue with the views of those historians who claim that the Conservative Party used foreign and defence policy for party political gain. See R. Williams, *Defending the Empire, The Conservative Party and British Defence Policy 1899–1915*, New Haven, Yale University Press, 1990, p. 155, p. 202, p. 224; Fest, 'Xenophobia', pp. 171–189.
3. Z. Steiner, *Britain and the Origins of the First World War*, London, Macmillan, 1977, p. 3.

4. Balfour Papers 49731, fols. 17–19, Balfour to Grey, 16 December 1913.
5. R. Blake, *The Unknown Prime Minister*, London, Eyre and Spottiswoode, 1955, pp. 93–94.
6. J. Mackail and G. Wyndham, *The Life and Letters of George Wyndham*, vol. 2, p. 614.
7. Coetzee, *For Party or Country*, p. 163.
8. This interpretation casts doubt on the view put forward by Fest, 'Xenophobia', p. 181.
9. Coetzee, *For Party or Country*, p. 95.
10. Gwynne Papers, 3/dep.16, Beresford to Gwynne, 24 May 1912.
11. I. Jennings, *Party Politics: vol 1: The Growth of Parties*, Cambridge, Cambridge University Press, p. 205.

Bibliography

Sources

Private Papers

Balliol College, Oxford
C.P. Scott Papers

Bodleian Library, Oxford
H.H. Asquith Papers

Conservative Party Archive
H.A. Gwynne Papers
Lord Milner Papers
J.S.Sandars Papers
Lord Selborne (2nd Earl) Papers

British Library, London
Lord Avebury Papers
H.O. Arnold Foster Papers
A.J. Balfour Papers
Robert Cecil Papers
Lord Sydenham (Sir George Clarke) Papers

Churchill College, Cambridge
Henry Page-Croft Papers
Lord Fisher Papers
A. Lyttleton Papers, A. MSS
C. Spring-Rice Papers

Dorset County Record Office, Dorchester
R. Williams Papers

Durham Record Office
H. Chaplin Papers

Dyfed Record Office Carmarthen
Earl Cawdor Papers

Hastings Public Museum
Arthur Du Cross Papers

House of Lords Record Office
Max Aitken (Beaverbrook) Papers
A. Bonar Law Papers
Patrick Hannon Papers
D. Lloyd George Papers
Lord Willoughby De Broke Papers

Hull University, Library
Mark Sykes Papers

Imperial War Museum, London
Lord Curzon Papers

Liverpool Record Office
Lord Derby (17th Earl) Papers

National Army Museum, London
Lord Roberts Papers

National Archives, London
Lord Beresford Papers
F. Bertie Papers
E. Grey Papers
F. Lascalles Papers
Lord Midleton Papers

Scottish Record Office, Edinburgh
A. Steel-Maitland Papers

Somerset Record Office, Taunton
A. Acland-Hood Papers

Times Archives, London
V. Chirol Papers
C. Repington Papers

University of Birmingham Library
J. Chamberlain Papers
A. Chamberlain Papers

University of Liverpool, Special Collections Department
J. Brunner Papers

University of Sheffield Library
W. Hewins Papers

University of Southampton, Hartley Library
Lord Mount Temple Papers
West Sussex Record Office, Chichester
Lord Bessborough (9th Earl)
L. Maxse Papers

Wiltshire Record Office, Trowbridge
Walter Long Papers

Official Papers

Parliament
Hansard Parliamentary Debates, 4th and 5th Series, 1905–1914
House of Lords Debates, 1905–1914

National Archives, London
Cabinet Papers, 1905–1914
Committee of Imperial Defence, 1905–1914
Invasion Sub Committees, 1903–1914
Files on Germany, 1905–1914

Works of Reference

Annual Register
Burke's Peerage
Dictionary of National Biography
G. Block, *A Source Book of Conservatism*, London, 1964
D. Butler and J. Freeman (eds), *British Political Facts*, London, 1984
F. Craig, *British Parliamentary Election Results, 1885–1918*, London, 1974
F. Craig, *British General Election Manifestos*, 1900–1974, London, 1975

Newspapers

National Newspapers
Daily Chronicle
Daily Express
Daily Graphic
Daily Mail
Daily Mirror
Daily News

Daily Telegraph
Morning Leader
Morning Post
Sunday (National)
Observer
Sunday Times

Local Newspapers

Ealing Times
Standard
Liverpool Courier
Manchester Guardian
Yorkshire Post
The Scotsman
Irish Times

Periodicals

Anglo-German Courier
The Conservative
The Conservative Agents Journal
Monthly Notes on Tariff Reform
Edinburgh Review
National Service League Journal
Our Flag
Spectator
Punch
Nation
Nation in Arms
Navy League Journal
Blackwood's Magazine
National Review
Nineteenth Century and After
Quarterly Review
Westminster Review
Review of Reviews
Jane's Fighting Ships
The Army and Navy Gazette

Select Bibliography

Contemporary Printed Works

N. Angell, *The Great Illusion*, Heinemann, 1910

N. Angell, *The Policy Behind Armaments*, London, Heinemann, 1911

H.O. Arnold-Foster, *Military Needs and Military Policy*, London, Edward Arnold, 1910

A.J. Balfour, *A Defence of Philosophic Doubt*, London, Macmillan, 1879

C. Beresford, *The Betrayal*, London, Methuen, 1912

R. Blatchford, *Germany and England*, London, Associate Newspapers, 1909

T. Brex, *Scaremongerings from the Daily Mail, 1896–1914*, London, Constable, 1914

H. Cecil, *Conservatism*, London, Williams and Norgate, 1912

J.A. Cramb, *Germany and England*, London, Booth, 1914

J.A. Farrer, *Invasion and Conscription: Some Letters from a Mere Civilian to a Famous General*, London, Fisher Unwin, 1909

K. Feiling, *Toryism: A Political Dialogue*, London, Bell, 1913

I. Hamilton, *Compulsory Service: A Study of the Question in the Light of Experience*, London, Lane, 1910

F.W. Hirst, *The Six Panics and Other Essays*, London, Methuen, 1913

J.A. Hobson, *The German Panic*, London, Cobden Club, 1913

H. Lucy, *The Balfour Parliament, 1900–1905*, London, Hodder and Stoughton, 1906

J. Malmesbury (ed.), *The New Order: Studies in Unionist Policy*, London, Francis Griffiths, 1908

L.J. Maxse, *'Germany on the Brain' or the Obsession of a 'Crank': Gleanings from the National Review, 1899–1914*, London, National Review, 1915

T.J. Macnamara, *Tariff Reform and the Working Man*, London, Hodder and Stoughton, 1910

H. Peel, *The Tariff Reformers*, London, Methuen, 1915

A. Ponsonby, *Democracy and Diplomacy*, London, Constable, 1906

Lord Roberts, *A Nation in Arms*, London, John Murray, 1907

Lord Roberts, *Fallacies and Facts*, London, John Murray, 1911

Lord Roberts, *Defence of the Empire*, London, John Murray, 1905

F.E. Smith, *Unionist Policy and Other Essays*, London, Williams and Norgate, 1913

Lord Willoughby De Broke (ed.), *National Revival*, London, Herbert Jenkins, 1913

H. Wilson and A. White, *When War Breaks Out*, London, Swan, 1898

Diaries, Memoirs, Speeches and Printed Papers

H. Asquith, *Fifty Years of Parliament*, London, Hutchinson, 1926

H. Asquith, *The Genesis of the War*, London, Hutchinson, 1923

H. Asquith, *Memories and Reflections*, London, Hutchinson, 1920

L. Amery, *My Political Life*, 3 vols, London, Hutchinson, 1953–1955

M. Arnold-Foster, *The Right Honourable Hugh Oakeley Arnold-Foster: A Memoir by his Wife*, London, Edward Arnold, 1910

J. Barnes and D. Nicholson (eds), *The Leo Amery Diaries*, vol. 1, London, Hutchinson, 1980

C. Beresford, *Memoirs of Admiral Lord Beresford*, 2 vols, London, Methuen, 1914

Earl Birkenhead, *Contemporary Personalities*, London, Hutchinson, 1924

R. Blumenfield, *The Press in my Time*, London, Heinemann, 1933

R. Blumenfield, *R.D.B.'s Diary, 1887–1914*, London, Heinemann, 1930

W.S. Blunt, *My Diaries: Being a Personal Narrative of Events, 1884–1914*, 2 vols, London, Seller, 1931

D.G. Boyce (ed.), *The Crisis of British Unionism: The Domestic Political Papers of the Second Earl of Selborne 1885–1922*, London, Historians' Press, 1987

C. Callwell, *Sir Henry Wilson: His Life and Diaries*, London, Cassell, 1927

R. Cecil, *Great Experiment, An Autobiography*, Oxford, Cape, 1941

A. Chamberlain, *Down the Years*, London, Cassell, 1935

A. Chamberlain, *Politics from the Inside: An Epistolary Chronicle, 1906–1914*, London, Cassell, 1937

A. Clark (ed.), *'A Good Innings': The Private Papers of Viscount Lee of Fareham*, London, John Murray, 1974

Documents Diplomatic Francais, 1871–1914, Paris, Ministres des Affaires Etrangers, 1929–1959

E. Grey (first Viscount Fallodon), *Twenty Five Years, 1892–1916*, London, Hodder and Stoughton, 1925

S. Gwynne (ed.), *The Anvil of War: Letters between F. S. Oliver and His Brother, 1914–1918*, London, Constable, 1936

S. Gwynne (ed.), *The Letters and Friendships of Cecil Spring-Rice*, 2 vols, London, Constable, 1929

W.A.S. Hewins, *The Apologia of an Imperialist: Forty Years of Empire Policy*, 2 vols, London, Constable, 1929

S. Leslie, *Sir Mark Sykes: His Life and Letters*, London, Constable, 1923

W. Long, *Memories*, London, Hutchinson, 1922

J. Mackail and G. Wyndham (eds), *The Life and Letters of George Wyndham*, 2 vols, London, Hutchinson, 1925

Lord Midleton, *Records and Reactions, 1856–1939*, London, John Murray, 1939

H. Page-Croft, *My Life of Strife*, London, Hutchinson, 1949

J. Ramsden (ed.), *Real Old Tory Politics: The Political Diaries of Sir Robert Sanders: Lord Bayford, 1910–1935*, Manchester, Manchester University Press, 1984

J. Ridley and C. Percy (eds), *The Letters of Arthur Balfour and Lady Elcho, 1885–1917*, London, Hamish Hamilton, 1992

N. Rose (ed.), *The Diaries of Blanche Dugdale 1936–1947*, London, Vallentine Mitchell, 1973

Lord Ullswater, *A Speaker's Commentaries*, London, Hodder and Stoughton, 1925

J. Vincent (ed.), *The Crawford Papers: The Journals of David Lindsay, Twenty Seventh Earl of Crawford and Tenth Earl of Balcarres, 1871–1940, during the Years 1892–1940*, Manchester, Manchester University Press, 1984

P. Williamson (ed.), *The Modernisation of Conservative Politics: The Diaries and Letters of William Bridgeman 1904–1935*, Manchester, Manchester University Press, 1988

Lord Willoughby De Broke, *The Passing Years*, London, Constable, 1924

E. Winterton, *Orders of the Day*, London, Macmillan, 1952

Biographies

B. Ash, *The Lost Dictator: A Biography of Field Marshal Sir Henry Wilson*, London, Cassell, 1968

G. Bennet, *Charlie B: A Biography of Admiral Lord Charles Lord Beresford*, London, Macmillan, 1968

R. Blake, *The Unknown Prime Minister: The Life and Times of Andrew Bonar Law, 1858–1923*, London, Eyre and Spottiswoode, 1955

J. Campbell, *F.E. Smith, First Earl of Birkenhead*, London, Cape, 1983

E. Crankshaw, *The Forsaken Idea: A Study of Viscount Milner*, London, Putnam, 1952

B. Dugdale, *Arthur James Balfour*, 2 vols, London, Hutchinson, 1936

D.J. Dutton, *Austen Chamberlain: Gentleman in Politics*, Bolton, Ross Anderson, 1985

M. Egremont, *Balfour: A Life of Arthur James Balfour*, London, Collins, 1980

J.L. Garvin and H.J. Amery, *The Life of Joseph Chamberlain*, 6 vols, London, Macmillan, 1932–1969

A.M. Gollin, *Lord Milner: Proconsul in Politics*, London, Anthony Blond, 1964

P. Fraser, *Joseph Chamberlain: Radicalism and Empire, 1868–1914*, London, Cassell, 1966

P. Fraser, *Lord Esher: A Political Biography*, London, Cassell, 1973

H. Hutchinson, *Life of Sir John Lubbock, Lord Averbury*, 2 vols, London, Macmillan, 1914

D. James, *Lord Roberts*, London, John Murray, 1954

R. Jay, *Joseph Chamberlain: A Political Study*, Oxford, Oxford University Press, 1981

R.F. MacKay, *Fisher of Kilverstone*, Oxford, Oxford University Press, 1973

Lord Newton, *Lord Landsdowne: A Biography*, London, Macmillan, 1929

E. Spiers, *Haldane: An Army Reformer*, Edinburgh, Edinburgh University Press, 1981

J. Wrench, *Alfred Lord Milner: The Man of no Illusions*, Hutchinson, 1958

K. Young, *Arthur James Balfour: The Happy Life of the Politician, Prime Minister, Statesman and Philosopher, 1848–1930*, London, Bell, 1963

H. Zebel, *Balfour*, Cambridge, Cambridge University Press, 1973

Selected Secondary Works

R.J.Q. Adams and P. Poirer, *The Conscription Controversy in Great Britain, 1900–1918*, London, Macmillan, 1987

S. Ball and A. Seldon, *Recovering Power: The Conservatives in Opposition since 1867*, London, Palgrave Macmillan, 2005

I. Beckett and J. Gooch (eds), *Politicians and Defence*, Manchester, Manchester University Press, 1981

N. Blewett, *The Peers, The Parties and The People: The Two General Elections of 1910*, London, Macmillan, 1972

M. Blinkhorn (ed.), *Fascists and Conservatives*, London, Unwin Hyman, 1990

P.A. Bromhead, *The House of Lords and Contemporary Politics, 1911–1957*, London, Routledge, 1972

P.F. Clarke, *Voices Prophesying War, 1763–1945*, Oxford, Oxford University Press, 1970

F. Coetzee, *For Party or Country: Nationalism and the Dilemmas of Popular Conservatism in Edwardian England*, Oxford, Oxford University Press, 1990

B. Coleman, *Conservatives and the Conservative Party in the 19th Century*, London, Edward Arnold, 1988

R. Colls and P. Dodd (eds), *Englishness: Politics and Culture, 1880–1920*, London, Croom Helm, 1986

H. Cunningham, *The Volunteer Force: A Social and Political History 1859–1908*, London, Croom Helm, 1975

R. Eccleshall, *English Conservatism since the Restoration*, London, Unwin Hyman, 1990

J. Ehrman, *Cabinet Government and War 1890–1940*, Cambridge, Cambridge University Press, 1958

M. Fforde, *Conservatism and Collectivism 1860–1914*, Edinburgh, Edinburgh University Press, 1990

F.R. Flourney, *Parliament and War: The relation of the British Parliament to the Administration of Foreign Policy in Connection with the Initiation of War*, Oxford, Oxford University Press, 1927

A.M. Gollin, *Mr. Balfour's Burden: Arthur Balfour and Imperial Preference*, London, Arthur Blond, 1965

A.M. Gollin, *The Observer and J.L. Garvin*, London, Arthur Blond, 1960

J. Gooch, *The Plans of War, The General Staff and British Military Strategy 1900–1916*, London, Routledge, 1974

J.H. Granger, *Patriotisms: Britain, 1900–1939*, London, Routledge, 1985

E.H.H. Green, *The Crisis of Conservatism: The Politics, Economics and Ideology of The Conservative Party, 1880–1914*, London, Routledge, 1996

W.L. Guttsman, *The British Political Elite*, New York, Basic Books, 1963

O.J. Hale, *Germany and the Diplomatic Revolution: A Study in Diplomacy and the Press*, Princeton, NJ, Princeton University Press, 1931

E. Halevy, *The Rule of Democracy: 1905–1914*, London, Ernest Benn, 1934

C. Hazelhurst, *Politicians at War, July 1914 to May 1915*, London, Cape, 1971

R. Henig, *The Origins of The First World War*, second edition, London, Routledge, 1989

F.H. Hinsley (ed.), *The Foreign Policy of Edward Grey*, Cambridge, Cambridge University Press, 1977

J.A. Hutchinson, *Leopold Maxse and the National Review 1893–1914: Right Wing Politics and Journalism in the Edwardian Era*, New York, Garland, 1989

F.A. Johnson, *Defence by Committee: The British Committee of Imperial Defence 1885–1959*, Oxford, Oxford University Press, 1960

P.M. Kennedy, *The Rise and Fall of British Naval Mastery*, London, Allen and Unwin, 1976

P.M. Kennedy, *The Rise of the Anglo-German Antagonism, 1860–1914*, London, Allen and Unwin, 1980

P.M. Kennedy (ed.), *The War Plans of the Great Powers*, London, Allen and Unwin, 1977

P.M. Kennedy and A.J. Nicholls (eds), *Nationalist and Racialist Movements in Britain and Germany before 1914*, London, Macmillan, 1981

C.J. Lowe and M.L. Dockrill, *The Mirage of Power: Vol. I: British Foreign Policy 1902–1914*, London, Routledge, 1972

J.M. MacKenzie (ed.), *Imperialism and Popular Culture*, Manchester, Manchester University Press, 1986

J.M. MacKenzie, *Propaganda and Empire*, Manchester, Manchester University Press, 1984

J. Mander, *Our German Cousins: Anglo-German Relations in the 19th and 20th Centuries*, London, John Murray, 1974

A.J. Marder, *From the Dreadnought to Scapa Flow: Vol. I: The Road to War, 1904–1914*, Oxford, Oxford University Press, 1961

A.J. Mayer, *The Persistence of The Old Regime: Europe to the Great War*, London, Croom Helm, 1981

R.T. McKenzie, *British Political Parties: The Distribution of Power Within the Conservative and Labour Parties*, London, Heinemann, 1963

G.W. Monger, *The End of Isolation*, London, Nelson, 1963

A.J.A. Morris, *The Scaremongers: The Advocacy of War and Re-armament 1896–1914*, London, Routledge, 1985

A. O'Day (ed.), *The Edwardian Age: Conflict and Stability 1900–1914*, London, Macmillan, 1979

A. Offer, *The First World War: An Agrarian Interpretation*, Oxford, Clarendon Press, 1989

P. Padfield, *The Great Naval Race*, London, Hart, Davies and MacGibbon, 1974

P. Padfield, *Rule Britannia: The Victorian and Edwardian Navy*, London, Routledge, 1981

C. Petrie, *The Power Behind Prime Ministers*, London, Eyre and Spottiswoode, 1959

G. Phillips, *The Die Hards: Aristocratic Society and Politics in Edwardian England*, Cambridge, MA, Harvard University Press, 1979

R.M. Punnet, *Front Bench Opposition*, London, Heinemann, 1973

P.G. Richards, *Parliament and Foreign Affairs*, London, Allen and Unwin, 1967

J. Ramsden, *The Age of Balfour and Baldwin 1902–1940*, London, Longman, 1978

J. Ramsden, *Don't Mention the War: The British and the Germans since 1890* London, Little Brown, 2006

R.A. Rempel, *Unionist Divided: Arthur James Balfour, Joseph Chamberlain and the Unionist Free Traders*, Newton Abbot, David and Charles, 1972

K. Robbins, *Sir Edward Grey*, London, Cassell, 1971

P. Rollo, *Entente Cordiale: The Origins and Negotiations of the Anglo-French Agreements of 8 April 1904*, London, Macmillan, 1969

P. Rowland, *The Last Liberal Governments*, 2 vols, London, Barrie and Rockcliff, 1968–1971

R.J. Scally, *The Origins of the Lloyd George Coalition: The Politics of Social Imperialism, 1900–1918*, Princeton, NJ, Princeton University Press, 1975

G.R. Searle, *Corruption in Britain Politics 1895–1930*, Oxford, Clarendon Press, 1987

G.R. Searle, *Eugenics and Politics in Britain, 1900–1914*, Oxford, Clarendon Press, 1976

G.R. Searle, *The Quest for National Efficiency: A Study in British Politics and British Political Thought, 1899–1914*, Oxford, Basil Blackwell, 1971

A. Sharp and G. Stone (eds), *Anglo-French Relations in the Twentieth Century: Rivalry and Cooperation*, London, Routledge, 2000

D. Southgate (ed.), *The Conservative Leadership 1832–1932*, London, Macmillan, 1974

P. Stanworth and A. Giddens (eds), *Elites and Power in British Society*, Cambridge, Cambridge University Press, 1974

Z. Steiner, *Britain and the Origins of the First World War*, London, Macmillan, 1977

Z. Steiner, *The Foreign Office and Foreign Policy 1898–1914*, Cambridge, Cambridge University Press, 1968

A. Sykes, *Tariff Reform in British Politics 1903–1913*, Oxford, Clarendon Press, 1979

A.J.P. Taylor, *Rumours of War*, London, Hamilton, 1952

A.J.P. Taylor, *The Struggle for Mastery in Europe 1848–1918*, Oxford, Clarendon Press, 1954

A.J.P. Taylor, *The Troublemakers: Dissent Over Foreign Policy 1792–1914*, London, Hamilton, 1969

A.J.P. Taylor, *War by Time-Table: How the First World War Began*, London, MacDonald, 1969

J. Thomas, *The House of Commons, 1906–1911: An Analysis of its Economic and Social Character*, Cardiff, University of Wales Press, 1958

J.A. Thompson and A. Meiji (eds), *Studies in Edwardian Conservatism: Five Studies in Adaptation*, Oxford, Oxford University Press, 1988

J. Tomes, *Balfour and Foreign Policy: The International Thought of a Conservative Statesman*, Cambridge, Cambridge University Press, 1997

G. Weber, *The Ideology of the British Right 1918–39*, London, Croom Helm, 1986

R. Williams, *Defending the Empire: The Conservative Party and British Defence Policy 1899–1915*, New Haven, Yale University Press, 1991

K. Wilson, *The Policy of the Entente: Essays on the Determinants of British Foreign Policy 1904–1914*, Cambridge, Cambridge University Press, 1985

Articles and Papers

N. Blewett, 'Free Fooders, Balfourites, Whole Hoggers: Factionalism Within the Unionist Party, 1906–10', *Historical Journal*, vol. 11 (1968), pp. 95–124

M.G. Brock, 'Britain Enters the War', in R. Evans and H. Pogg von Strandmann (eds), *The Coming of the First World War*, Oxford, Oxford University Press, 1988, pp. 145–178

F. Coetzee, 'Pressure Groups, Tory Businessmen and the Aura of Political Corruption Before the First World War', *Historical Journal*, vol. 29 (1986), pp. 833–852

F. Coetzee and M. Coetzee, 'Rethinking the Radical Right in Germany and Britain Before 1914', *Journal of Contemporary History*, vol. 21 (1986), pp. 515–537

H. Cunningham, 'The Conservative Party and Patriotism', in R. Colls and P. Dodd (eds), *Englishness: Politics and Culture, 1880–1920*, London, Croom Helm, 1986, pp. 283–307

D.J. Dutton, 'Life Beyond the Political Grave: Joseph Chamberlain, 1906–1914', *History Today*, vol. 34 (1984), pp. 23–28

R. Eccleshall, 'English Conservatism as Ideology', *Political Studies*, vol. 25 (1977), pp. 62–83

M. Ekstein, 'Sir Edward Grey and Imperial Germany in 1914', *Journal of Contemporary History*, vol. 6 (1971), pp. 121–131

M. Ekstein, 'Some Notes on Sir Edward's Grey's Policy in July 1914', *Historical Journal*, vol. 15 (1972), pp. 321–324

W. Fest, 'Jingoism and Xenophobia in the Electioneering Strategies of British Ruling Elites Before 1914', in P.M. Kennedy and A.J. Nicholls (eds), *Nationalist and Racialist Movements in Britain and Germany before 1914*, London, Macmillan, 1981, pp. 171–189

P. Fraser, 'The Unionist Debacle of 1911 and Balfour's Retirement', *Journal of Modern History*, vol. 15 (1963), pp. 149–166

D. French, 'The Edwardian Crisis and the Origins of the First World War', *International History Review*, vol. 4 (1982), pp. 207–221

D. French, 'Spy Fever in Britain 1906–1915', *Historical Journal*, vol. 21 (1978), pp. 355–370

J. Gooch, 'Sir George Clarke's Career at the Committee of Imperial Defence, 1904–1907', *Historical Journal*, vol. 18 (1975), pp. 555–569

M. Gordon, 'Domestic Conflict and the Origins of the First World War: The British and German Cases', *Journal of Modern History*, vol. 46 (1974), pp. 191–226

E.H. Green, 'Radical Conservativism and the Electoral Genesis of Tariff Reform', *Historical Journal*, vol. 28 (1985), pp. 667–692

J.E. Helmreich, 'Belgium Concern over Neutrality and British Intentions, 1906–1914', *Journal of Modern History*, vol. 36 (1964), pp. 416–427

C. Howard, 'The Policy of Isolation', *History*, vol. 10 (1962), pp. 32–41

R.B. Jones, 'Balfour's Reform of Party Organisation', *Bulletin of the Institute of Historical Research*, vol. 38 (1965), pp. 94–101

D. Kaiser, 'Germany and the Origins of the First World War', *Journal of Modern History*, vol. 55 (1983), pp. 442–474

H. Koch, 'The Anglo-German Alliance Negotiations: Missed Opportunity or Myth?', *History*, vol. 54 (1969), pp. 378–379

R. Langthorne, 'The Naval Question in Anglo-German Relations, 1912–1914', *Historical Journal*, vol. 14 (1971), pp. 359–370

K. Mackensie, 'Some British Reactions to German Colonial Methods, 1885–1907', *Historical Journal*, vol. 17 (1974), pp. 165–175

S. Mahajan, 'The Defence of India and the End of Isolation: A Study in the Foreign Policy of the Conservative Government, 1900–1905', *Journal of Imperial and Commonwealth History*, vol. 10 (1982), pp. 168–193

G. Marcus, 'The Croydon By-Election and the Naval Scare of 1909', *Journal of the Royal United Services Institution*, vol. 103 (1958), pp. 500–504

A.J.A. Morris, 'The English Radicals and the Second Hague Conference 1907', *Journal of Modern History*, vol. 43 (1971), pp. 367–393

A.J.A. Morris, 'Haldane's Army Reforms, 1906–1908: The Deception of the Radicals', *History*, vol. 56 (1971), pp. 17–34

A.J.A. Morris, 'A Not So Silent Service: The Final Stages of the Fisher-Beresford Quarrel and the Part Played by the Press', *Moirae*, vol. 6 (1981), pp. 42–81

A. Offer, 'Empire and Social Reform: British Overseas Investment and Domestic Politics, 1908–1914', *Historical Journal*, vol. 26 (1983), pp. 119–138

G. Phillips, 'The Die Hards and the Myth of the Backwoodsmen', *Journal of British Studies*, vol. 17 (1977), pp. 105–120

G. Phillips, 'Lord Willoughby de Broke and the Politics of Radical Toryism 1909–1914', *Journal of British Studies*, vol. 20 (1980), pp. 205–224

J. Remak, '1914: The Third Balkan War: Origins Reconsidered', *Journal of Modern History*, vol. 43 (1971), pp. 353–366

J. Ridley, 'The Unionist Social Reform Committee 1911–1914: Wets Before the Deluge', *Historical Journal*, vol. 30 (1987), pp. 391–413

W.D. Rubinstein, 'Henry Page Croft and the National Party, 1917–1922', *Journal of Contemporary History*, vol. 9 (1974), pp. 129–148

P. Schroeder, 'World War 1 as a Galloping Gertie: A Reply to Joachim Remak', *Journal of Modern History*, vol. 44 (1972), pp. 319–345

A. Sharp, 'Britain and the Channel Tunnel', *Australian Journal of Politics and History*, vol. 25 (1979), pp. 210–215

A. Sharp, 'The Foreign Office in Eclipse, 1919–1922', *History*, vol. 61 (1976) pp. 198–218

J. Steinberg, 'The Copenhagen complex', *Journal of Contemporary History*, vol. 1 (1966), pp. 23–46

Z. Steiner, 'The Last Years of the Old Foreign Office 1898–1905', *Historical Journal*, vol. 6 (1963), pp. 59–90

E. Stokes, 'Milnerism', *Historical Journal*, vol. 6 (1962), pp. 47–60

A. Summers, 'Militarism in Britain Before the Great War', *History Workshop Journal*, vol. 2 (1976), pp. 104–123

A. Sykes, 'The Confederacy and the Purge of the Unionist Free Traders, 1906–1910', *Historical Journal*, vol. 18 (1975), pp. 349–366

A. Sykes, 'The Radical Right and the Crisis of Conservatism Before the First World War', *Historical Journal*, vol. 26 (1983), pp. 661–676

A.J.P. Taylor, 'British Policy in Morocco 1886–1908', *English Historical Review*, vol. 66 (1951), pp. 342–374

C. Trebilcock, 'Legends of the British Armaments Industry', *Journal of Contemporary History*, vol. 5 (1970), pp. 2–19

A. Tucker, 'The Issue of Army Reform in the Unionist Government, 1903–1905', *Historical Journal*, vol. 9 (1966), pp. 90–100

D.C. Watt, 'British Reactions to the Assassination at Sarejevo', *European Studies Quarterly*, vol. 1 (1971), pp. 233–247

H. Weinroth, 'The British Radicals and the Balance of Power, 1902–1914', *Historical Journal*, vol. 13 (1970), pp. 653–682

H. Weinroth, 'Left Wing Opposition to Naval Armaments in Britain Before 1914', *Journal of Contemporary History*, vol. 6 (1971), pp. 93–120

H. Weinroth, 'Norman Angell and the Great Illusion', *Historical Journal*, vol. 17 (1974), pp. 551–574

B. Williams, 'The Strategic Background to the Anglo-Russian Entente', *Historical Journal*, vol. 9 (1966), pp. 360–373

K. Wilson, 'The Agadir Crisis: The Mansion House Speech and the Double-Edgedness of Agreements', *Historical Journal*, vol. 15 (1972), pp. 513–532

K. Wilson, 'The Opposition and the Crisis in the Liberal Cabinet Over Foreign Policy in November 1911', *International History Review*, vol. 3 (1981), pp. 319–413

Unpublished Theses

M. Allison, 'The National Service Issue, 1899–1914', Ph.D., University of London (1975)

G. Jones, 'National and Local Issues in Politics: A Study of National and Local Issues and the Lancashire Spinning Towns, 1906–1910', D.Phil., University of Sussex (1965)

R. Jones, 'The Conservative Party, 1906–1911', B.Litt., Oxford University (1960)

R. Murphy, 'Walter Long and the Conservative Party 1905–1921', Ph.D., University of Bristol (1985)

J. McEwen, 'Conservative and Unionist MPs 1914–1939', D.Phil., University of London (1959)

J. Ramsden, 'The Organisation of the Conservative and Unionist Party in Britain, 1910–1930', D.Phil., Oxford University (1974)

J. Ridley, 'Leadership and Management in the Conservative Party in Parliament, 1906–1914', D.Phil., Oxford University (1985)

D. Swallow, 'The Transition in British Editorial Germanophobia, 1899–1914: A Case Study of J.L. Garvin, L.J. Maxse, and St. Leo Strachey', Ph.D., MC Master University, Canada (1980)

Index